2,3,5,6

Examp 3   1 ─most.

W9-CEB-776

Proposal ideas
Pg 93- Gen+Spec. attributes)

Implicit Psychology

→ Implicit Psychology ≠♭

An Introduction to
Social Cognition

⌐ Daniel M. Wegner ⌐

TRINITY UNIVERSITY

Robin R. Vallacher

ILLINOIS INSTITUTE OF TECHNOLOGY

ELMHURST COLLEGE LIBRARY

MAY 2 3 1979

New York

OXFORD UNIVERSITY PRESS

1977

301.11
W412i

Library of Congress Cataloging in Publication Data

Wegner, Daniel M.   1948–
   Implicit psychology.

   Bibliography: p.
   Includes index.
   1. Social perception. 2. Cognition.
I. Vallacher, Robin R., 1946–   joint author.
II. Title.
HM132.W365   301.1   76-57484
ISBN 0-19-502228-9
ISBN 0-19-502229-7 pbk.

Copyright © 1977 by Oxford University Press, Inc.

Printed in the United States of America

contents

Preface   vii

ONE   **Introduction to Implicit Psychology:**
Social Cognition   1
Cognitive Structure   4
Implicit Theory   16

THE IMPLICIT PSYCHOLOGIST   28
The Development of the Implicit Psychologist   29
Differences Among Implicit Psychologists   32

TWO   **Implicit Motivation Theory:** Attribution   39
Internal and External Causes   43
Causes of Success and Failure   53
Divergent Perspectives: Actor and Observer   59
Divergent Perspectives: Layman and Psychologist   68

THE IMPLICIT PSYCHOLOGIST   77
Developmental Changes   78
Individual Differences   80

THREE   **Implicit Personality Theory:**
Impression Formation   89
Selecting Information   90
Generating Information   98
Organizing Information   108
Combining Information   120

THE IMPLICIT PSYCHOLOGIST   128
Developmental Changes   129
Individual Differences   133

FOUR   **Implicit Abnormal Psychology:**
Evaluation   139
Good and Bad   140
Judging Good and Bad: Sources of Evaluative Information   148
Implicit Abnormal Psychology and Clinical Psychology   167

THE IMPLICIT PSYCHOLOGIST   177
Developmental Changes   177
Individual Differences   181

FIVE   Implicit Social Relations Theory:
Balance and Group Organization   189

Social Relations   190
Belonging Schemas   196
Liking Schemas   203
Dominance Schemas   217

THE IMPLICIT PSYCHOLOGIST   223
Developmental Changes   224
Individual Differences   226

SIX   Implicit Self-Theory: Self-Perception   231

Selecting Information   233
Generating Information   243
Organizing Information   249
Combining Information   260
The Relevance of Self-Theory   266

THE IMPLICIT PSYCHOLOGIST   272
Developmental Changes   273
Individual Differences   276

SEVEN   Overview of Implicit Psychology   283

Principles of Implicit Psychology   284
The Accuracy of Implicit Psychology   293
New Directions   301

References   306

Index   319

preface When the two of us were graduate students in social psychology at Michigan State University, we shared an office, a coffee pot, a fondness for frisbees, and a desire to impart wisdom to mankind. During one of our daily discussions on the meaning of life, this book was launched. It started with the comment, "You know, most people know what other people are like without ever taking a course in psychology."

As it turned out, we soon found that we were not alone in considering this idea. A number of influential psychologists and philosophers had been talking about "commonsense theories of psychology" long before either of us could talk about anything at all. The social psychologist Fritz Heider, for instance, studied what he called the "naive psychological theories" held by individuals. The personality theorist George Kelly wrote of the person as a "scientist" building theories abtut the social world. Sociologist Alfred Schutz based his theories on the parallel between the social scientist and the individual. Even the developmental psychologist Jean Piaget considered the manner in which the individual conceptualizes his or her social environment. Each of these theorists argued that the person behaves toward people on the basis of his or her conceptions of them. The study of such conceptions, therefore, is a natural and important part of psychology.

One aim of this book is to acquaint you with your own implicit psychological theories. We expect you will find much about your own view of people in these pages, and you may even be surprised. After all, although you may spend a great deal of time thinking about people, about yourself, and about the social situations you encounter, it is probably only seldom that you reflect on the nature of your thought processes. Your theories of psychology are assumed rather than examined, and are therefore implicit rather than explicit. Another aim of this book is to introduce you to the field of cognitive social psychology. Psychologists studying *social cognition*—how people think about people—have conducted research and developed formal theories about the individual's implicit theories. We hope that this book will be useful to students, particularly undergraduates, as an introduction to this rapidly expanding area of psychology. *Implicit Psychology* may be used as a supplementary text in courses in social psychology, and is appropriate for courses in personality and cognitive psychology as well.

Contemporary psychology includes many topics relevant to social cognition. Terms such as "person perception," "attribution," "impression formation," "cognitive balance," and "self-concept" appear frequently throughout texts in social and personality psychology. This book represents an attempt to organize these and other topic areas in terms of the common theme of implicit psychology. Chapter One introduces the idea that an individual's understanding of reality is similar to a scientist's theory, and that his or her understanding of social reality is like an implicit psychological theory. Chapter Two extends these ideas by showing that the individual makes attributions of causality for behavior using an "implicit motivation theory." Chapter Three illustrates the person's use of an "implicit personality theory" in forming impressions of others. Chapter Four is devoted to evaluation, the behavioral component of social cognition; the individual makes use of "implicit theories of abnormal psychology" in determining whether persons or groups are good or bad. In Chapter Five, the implicit psychology approach is expanded to include "implicit social relations theory"; attention is given to cognitive balance and the manner in which the individual conceptualizes relationships among people. Chapter Six focuses on the central figure in everyone's social reality—the self. In discussing "implicit self theory," we show that many of the principles relevant to the perception of others also apply to self-perception. In Chapter Seven we close the book with a summary and overview of implicit psychology. As part of this discussion, we address the important topic of the accuracy of implicit psychology and, in addition, we consider the implications of this approach for the field of psychology as a whole. The implicit theories outlined in each chapter portray the processes of social cognition shared by all adults. But since people differ somewhat in the structure and content of their theories, each chapter closes with a section entitled "The Implicit Psychologist," in which developmental changes and individual differences in implicit theories are explored. Each chapter, therefore, views a particular area of social thought not only from a social psychological perspective, but from developmental and personality perspectives as well.

A few features of this book deserve some comment. First of all, in our concern with providing a thorough introduction to the cognitive perspective in social psychology, we have paid little attention to other theoretical orientations. The serious student of social psychology would do well to explore these alternative perspectives; social learning theory, for example, provides compelling insights into many of the phenomena described in this book. A second feature of this book is its emphasis on behavior. Historically, a concern with behavior has been absent in cognitive theories. As part of our commitment to show that the cognitive approach is applicable to a wide range of social phenomena, we have discussed the relationships among cognition, evaluation, and behavior in some depth. A final feature of this book should be noted. We have taken the liberty of injecting humor into our narrative; a little levity now and then keeps the writer and reader alike from falling asleep.

Certain acknowledgments are in order. Although *Implicit Psychology* is a product of our collaboration, it is doubtful that this project would have been completed had we not been inspired by various mentors, colleagues, and friends. William D. Crano, Lawrence A. Messé, James L. Phillips, and Henry Clay Smith instructed us in psychology; many of their ideas and interests became ours and are presented here. Philip Brickman, David H. Brooks, Christopher Gilbert, Ellen Harwicke-

Vallacher, Seymour Rosenberg, Mary Beth Rosson, Henry Clay Smith, and Robert Wicklund read and commented upon portions of the manuscript; we are grateful for their help. We also wish to thank our editor, William C. Halpin, for his encouragement and advice during all stages of this project. Part of the success of this venture is attributable to each of the people mentioned above, and to many others who have not been mentioned; any shortcomings, of course, are a reflection on my co-author.

D.M.W.   August, 1977
San Antonio, Texas

R.R.V.
Chicago, Illinois

chapter one

The stereoscope was a common item to be found in a sitting room a hundred years ago. The viewer would look through the eyepieces of this hand-held gadget at a picture—actually a pair of identical pictures, one for each eye—and see a three-dimensional image. Special cameras that took such double pictures were sold; souvenir postcards of vacation spots often were in the form of stereograms designed for viewing through the device; even three-dimensional photos of scarlet women were available from discreet sources. And while the popularity of the stereoscope in sitting rooms has waned with the years, its popularity in psychological laboratories has grown.

In 1957, for instance, Hadley Cantril conducted an intriguing demonstration with a stereoscope in his lab. He prepared a stereogram with two *different* pictures. Each was a photo of a statue in the Louvre, but one was a Madonna with Child and the other a lovely young nude. Thus, someone viewing the pictures would see one statue with his left eye and the other with his right. Cantril coaxed a pair of his psychologist friends into the lab and asked each to look into the stereoscope. The first psychologist immediately reported that it was a picture of the Madonna and Child. As he stared a while longer, however, he exclaimed, "But my God, she's undressing!" He first reported that the baby was gone and that the robe had dropped to her shoulders, and then that the robe had disappeared completely and he was seeing the young nude. The other psychologist saw the nude first and then became more and more disenchanted as he watched her acquire first a robe and then a baby.

In a second experiment Cantril

introduction to implicit psychology

Social Cognition

described, people were asked to look at faces. Stereograms were prepared with facial photos of two different Princeton football players. Through the stereoscope, the two were seen as a single person with some of the features of each. When the viewer was asked to close one eye and then the other so he could recognize the illusion, he was likely to comment that the new fellow was better-looking than either of the originals, and seemed more like the kind of person he would like to meet and have as a friend. In yet another experiment, Cantril found that people do not always see the best or most attractive person possible. When Zulu tribesmen in South Africa viewed stereograms made up of a Zulu and an Indian, a European and an Indian, and so on, they were likely to see the Indian in every pair. Zulus at that time were highly prejudiced against Indians and the two groups were often in conflict, so it seems that the Zulus were seeing the more threatening part of the image as the entire image.

The stereoscope demonstrations of the process of perception, while somewhat unusual and amusing, are not just clever parlor games psychologists play. The experiments suggest some important things about the nature of human beings. Consider the "faces" experiment—the one in which the viewer saw a new figure, a combination of the figures presented to each eye. The viewer was seeing and describing the face of a person, a face that did not correspond completely with either of the faces that were actually being shown to him, and a face that only he could see. In effect, he was *constructing* what he was seeing. He was not just passively experiencing reality, but rather was actively building it. This idea seems to conflict with many of our usual ideas about perception. We usually assume not only that there is a perfect correspondence between our perceptions and reality, but also that there is a reality "out there" that we need only sit back and observe. These experiments require that our philosophy of how we acquire knowledge of the world be somewhat more complex.

Why did one psychologist see the Madonna and the other the nude? They both were presented the same "reality"—the two superimposed pictures—but each reported seeing a different image at first and different image changes later. Obviously these two psychologists could argue all day about what was really there, and each would have a solid basis for his argument—his own perceptions. This conflict over different accounts of reality is repeated every moment every day as people interact with one another: father and son arguing over who should get the family car; teacher and student in conflict over the fairness of a test question; President and Congress battling over national issues. To explain these many cases, psychologists have found it necessary to view people as active and constructive perceivers of reality, to conclude that each person puts the puzzle of reality together in his own way.

Why did the Zulu tribesmen see only Indians? It is unlikely that an American college student would always see Indians in the stereograms. Something about the common experiences of the Zulu must have contributed to their common perceptions. This insight has prompted psychologists to suggest that the way in which the individual constructs his own reality is shaped by his past experiences. Very simply, the person uses what he has seen and known to help him understand what is occurring and to help him predict what will occur. The Zulu had experienced uncomfortable interactions with Indians in the past. These experiences led them to anticipate more difficult confrontations in the future, and therefore to be wary of Indians even in stereoscope images. In short, experiences guide our constructions of reality.

Each of the three experiments described by Cantril illustrates a basic point. The "faces" experiment shows us that each person constructs his own reality; the "Madonna" experiment shows us that different people construct different realities; and the "Zulu" experiment shows us that each person's construction of reality is guided by his experiences.

Cognitive Structure   To talk about the construction of reality, we must distinguish between each person's perceived reality and "general" reality, the existence of which we all have come to acknowledge. Philosophers and psychologists call the person's perceived reality—the constellation of thoughts, perceptions, and feelings that are real for him—his *phenomenal field*. Theories of psychology that make use of this notion are called phenomenological theories. These perspectives hold in common the idea that a person behaves not on the basis of what the world is like, but rather on the basis of his perception of what it is like. So, for example, if the movie heroine tied to the railroad track is being approached by a speeding locomotive, she will not thrash or struggle unless the reality of the situation impinges on her phenomenal field. Once she perceives her position on the track and the oncoming train, her notions of what trains are like—their size, weight, and potential for damage—determine her actions. She screams and the hero saves her.

Psychologists have also noted that each person's phenomenal field is highly organized. It is not simply a conglomerate of disconnected thoughts and perceptions but instead is an orderly and structured system. Observing once more the heroine on the railroad tracks, recall that her perception of the train invokes a variety of thoughts about trains and that these thoughts move her to action. Clearly, an unorganized phenomenal field could lead her to thoughts of hot cheese, drunken sailors, and grocery carts—or to any other randomly occurring ideas. The organization of the phenomenal field, frequently called the individual's *cognitive structure,* is the system of interrelations among thoughts that allows the individual to respond appropriately to incoming sensations from the environment. Although the exploration of this structure is interesting in its own right, we will reserve further discussion until we have reflected on the process by which the structure is generated—the individual's construction of reality.

The Construction of Reality

Jean Piaget, the Swiss psychologist, has built an influential theory about cognitive development (the construction of reality) on the basis of many observations of children. One observation that is particularly germane to our discussion involves the developing cognitive structure of the six-month-old infant. Imagine, if you will, that the infant is playing with a stuffed animal and that you enter the room and take the toy away. If the child can still see it, he will inevitably start fussing until you return it. But if you place it behind your back, he will not fuss and instead will probably return to looking around the room or playing with his toes. What has happened? Doesn't the child realize the toy is behind your back? Apparently not, because if you produce it once more and fail to hand it to him, he will fuss again. For Piaget, these observations suggest that the child cannot conceptualize an object that exists outside his perceptual field. When the perception of the toy is not experienced—when the child cannot see the toy—it is gone.

If you were to experiment with the child a few months later, trying again to play tricks on a baby, you would find the child much harder to fool. He would fuss when the toy was gone, whether he could see it or not. To explain this, it is necessary to propose that some important change has taken place in the child's perception of reality that has enabled him to respond to the environment in a more reasonable way. Objects in fact do exist outside our immediate perceptions of them—or at least it is useful to think about them that way. Given that the very young child does not know this but later comes to understand it, we must conclude that he has added some new element to his organization of the phenomenal field that allows his thoughts of objects to extend beyond his experience of the objects themselves. In other words, "out of sight, out of mind" no longer describes the child's experience.

At this basic level—the constructions of reality made by the young child—it is possible to understand readily the importance of each step a person takes in making his construction a useful and faithful copy of reality. If the child never developed the ability to perceive the constancy of objects, he would always live in a magical environment where things would capriciously appear and disappear all the time, and he would surely never be able to perform even the most elementary manipulations of common objects. Just imagine an adult who buys a new car, parks it in his garage, walks into his house, and is never able to find the car again. The simple constructions made by the infant are the foundations of all later constructions.

The exact nature of a cognitive construction is perhaps more clearly stated in another example, this one based on the research findings of Tracy and Howard Kendler (1961). A typical subject in one of these experiments, say, a four-year-old child, is seated at a desk and is asked to choose between pairs of objects. The experimenter is interested in training him to choose only certain objects every time; thus on each occasion when the child is asked to choose between a big black cup and a little white cup, the experimenter gives him a candy if he decides on the big black cup. Similarly, he is rewarded for choosing a big white cup over a little black cup. In Figure 1.1, you will note that this first phase of training involves rewards (+) for picking large cups and nonrewards (−) for picking small ones. After a number of training trials, the child learns quite well the distinction he must make, and tends to pick the larger cup on every trial.

Without telling the child, the experimenter then changes the problem so that the child must respond to the same set of stimuli in a new way. One possible change (Task A in Figure 1.1) is called a *reversal shift,* since the correct response now is to choose the small cup instead of the large one. Another change that might be presented to the child is the *nonreversal shift* (Task B in Figure 1.1), in which the large black cup is still the correct

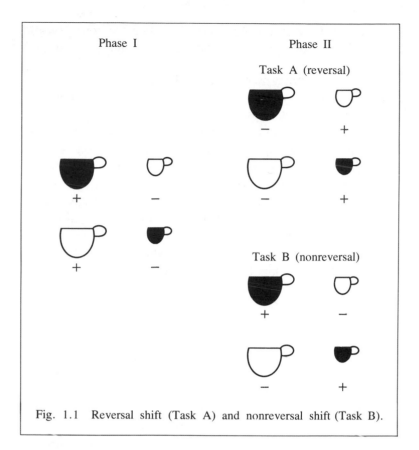

Fig. 1.1   Reversal shift (Task A) and nonreversal shift (Task B).

choice, but choice of the small black cup is now rewarded while that of the big white cup is not. There is an interesting difference between these two kinds of shifts. The reversal shift from Phase I to Phase II requires that the child learn to choose *two* new objects, whereas the nonreversal shift only requires that he learn to choose *one* new object (since the large black cup is still a correct choice). Thus it seems that the nonreversal shift should be an easier task and that it should take fewer trials for the child to respond correctly to the new situation. For the four-year-old child, this is indeed the case; he learns the nonreversal shift more quickly.

From another point of view, it can be argued that the reversal shift should be easier to learn. All it involves is a switch from large cups to small cups—a change within a single dimension—whereas the nonreversal shift requires a change from large cups to black cups—a shift to a new dimension. The interesting point here is that a child of seven learns the reversal shift more easily. From the ages of four to seven, something changes in the child's construction of reality that makes the reversal shift more understandable than the nonreversal shift. (It is interesting that, not unlike the four-year-old child, animals such as rats and chimps learn the nonreversal shift more readily.) The new understanding that comes with growth is the ability to think about objects in terms of *groups*. The younger child thinks about each object as a separate entity and therefore learns best when only one entity is changed. The older child thinks in terms of categories of objects, classifying them according to the large-small and black-white dimensions, and therefore learns best when the change occurs along a dimension of objects. A "construction" is, in this case, a new method of organizing observations of reality. Without the construction of dimensions, the person's phenomenal field contains many perceptions that must be dealt with individually; with the construction of dimensions, the person's phenomenal field contains perceptions that can be dealt with in terms of their membership in various classes or groups.

Although the few examples we have seen are by no means a complete list of all the constructions acquired by the individual, they do provide an introduction to a way of thinking about human beings. The philosophical stance we have been attempting to elaborate, and that we will continue to expand upon throughout this volume, is that *every person is a scientist*. This statement, a handy way of summing up the entire process of the construction of reality, has been the basis of writings by many philosophers and psychologists. The personality theorist George Kelly, for instance, developed his entire theory around this idea. He argued convincingly that psychologists—scientists themselves—were on the wrong track when they first explained their own motivations in life in terms of the pursuit of knowledge through science and then turned around and explained the motivations of the common man in terms of less noble goals such as pleasure, power, or the fulfillment of animal instincts. Kelly (1955), in envisioning human beings as scientists, assumed that each person has the need to understand, to predict, and to control his world; it is not at all difficult to make such assumptions. Everyday experiences tell us these motives are paramount in our lives.

People obviously are not scientists in the sense that they spend their days and nights in the lab amid racks of test tubes and flasks of percolating chemicals. They are scientists in the sense that they approach the world through a process of reality construction that is analogous to the theory construction process by which the scientist attempts to understand the world. According to Kelly, the individual's motivation in this endeavor is his need to anticipate the future. A study by Carlsmith and Aronson (1965), while not at all conclusive evidence for this point, is an unusual illustration of the motive for prediction. These researchers led their subjects to believe that a liquid they were going to be required to taste was either very bitter or pleasantly sweet. For some of the subjects, the liquid was just what the experimenters had claimed it would be; for the other subjects, the liquid was the opposite of what they had expected. This second group—whose expectancies about the situation were disconfirmed—rated both the bitter solution and the sweet solution as more unpleasant than did the group receiving the taste they expected. Apparently, unpredicted bitterness is worse than predicted bitterness; unpredicted sweetness is like taking the bitter with the sweet.

The Construction of Social Reality

Since none of us is in this world alone, everything we do, say, and even think is a product not only of our individual processes of construction, but also of our interaction with other people. People tend to affect our constructions in four major ways: they may change the way we see physical reality; they enter into our reality as objects in our phenomenal field; they themselves have phenomenal fields that we must consider in our interactions with them; and they have their own constructions of us. In short, the whole notion of the construction of reality becomes much more complex when we consider the possibility that more than one construction system exists. Statements such as "I think I know what you thought I was thinking" are not so ridiculous as they might at first sound.

Our first point is that other people affect the individual's construction of physical reality. Think back to an evening in late summer when you were lounging on an old blanket and looking up at the stars. Remember how it may have seemed that one of the stars was moving around? Just a little? Even if you don't remember, take it on faith that there is a perceptual illusion called the *autokinetic effect*, in which a pinpoint of light in a dark sky—or a darkened room—seems to move around although it is actually stationary. This effect was used to advantage in an experiment performed by Muzafer Sherif in 1935. He collected groups of people in a darkened laboratory room and asked them to describe the movement of the light. None of them were aware of the fact that the light source was actually mounted solidly on a table.

Every time the light was switched on for a brief interval, Sherif asked the subjects one by one to report the distance the light had moved. And though subjects experiencing this illusion of movement while alone generally arrive at estimates that differ widely, subjects who heard one another's judgments soon came to agree on a particular distance and to report that distance on each new trial. You might think that each individual in the experiment was just going along with the crowd and that while he really did see things differently, he was failing to report his true observations. Sherif also suspected this and arranged for subjects who had been tested in the group to return to the lab individually the next day. He found, surprisingly enough, that each subject stuck to the judgment he had made the day before in the presence of the group. The subject was seeing and reporting what he thought was a physical reality—the distance the light had traveled—in a way that was dictated by the judgments of other people. When physical realities become so ambiguous as to preclude clear judgments, people depend on one another to help clarify the situation by determining what is real for the group.

Questions about physical reality frequently do arise and are resolved by communications among people. Stanley Schachter (1959) has proposed that people have a need for *cognitive clarity,* which they often satisfy by finding out what other people think. If a person does not understand some aspect of his environment, he is likely to ask others what they think about it in hopes that their understanding will increase his own. When the "brilliant" comet Kohoutek passed the Earth in 1974, for example, not only were people talking about it in their homes and businesses, but they were hearing about it from television, magazines, and every tabloid on the newsstand. This unknown object was something for which most people had no handy construction system; they had never witnessed a similar event and had no way of knowing what to expect. The consequent uproar, while an excellent example of the contribution of interpersonal communication to the construction of reality, fell upon deaf ears only months later when it was learned that the astronomers had made poor calculations and that the comet would be visible only to the astronomers themselves.

As we noted earlier, there is a second way in which social processes impinge upon the individual's construction of reality. Other people are a part of the reality that we endeavor to understand and predict. Next to the mundane relationships we may have with physical objects (sitting in a chair, for instance, or hitting a tennis ball against a backboard, or watching an automobile rust), the relationships we have with other people are by far more exciting, more frightening, and more fulfilling. A social action as uncomplicated as a single kiss, for example, has been the basis of an overwhelming number of poems, rock and roll songs, street fights, pleasant daydreams, and lengthy novels, and may provide as much as six weeks' worth of material for a television soap opera. In short, other people provide us with our greatest rewards as well as our greatest costs; it is no wonder that we try to understand them. In the more technical terms we have defined, we can suggest that the individual's cognitive structure is needed to predict and control other people's behavior, and therefore must contain many thoughts about what people are like and what they will do.

That the individual has an organized set of thoughts about people seems beyond question. Just mentioning the names of a few people—Humphrey Bogart, Shirley Temple Black, Al Capone, Aretha Franklin, Howard Cosell—should point out to you that you have a detailed impression of even people you do not know personally. The name alone seems to call up a set of thoughts that enables you to make judgments of the person. Given the people listed, for instance, you could easily decide which were males, which were black, which were alive, and which were involved in shady activities. With a little more effort, you could no doubt even decide which of them might make a good friend, which might laugh at your jokes, or which might steal your stereo given the chance. We build up this detailed set of thoughts about people gradually from our experiences, and it allows us to predict what will occur in further experiences with people.

The third form of social impact on the individual's construction of reality can be summarized in this statement: sometimes it is necessary to understand what another person is thinking. Although we never have direct evidence telling us exactly what a person thinks or feels in a particular situation, we do have many sources of indirect information—the person's verbal and nonverbal communications to us, memories of our own thoughts in similar situations, and our general understanding of that person. Thus we can construct what we believe to be that person's construction of reality. At a very simple level, consider what happens when a friend is carrying groceries and asks you to take the car keys from his right pocket. If you were standing in front of him, and were completely unable to construct a copy of his reality, you would naturally reach to your right and end up extracting a handful of change, gum wrappers, and bottle caps from his left pocket. This course of events might seem unlikely, but it is a common behavior of young children. They seem unable to take the role of another person and consequently can neither understand spatial directions from another person's perspective nor understand the social motives of another person.

A particularly clever experiment performed by John Flavell and his colleagues in 1968 is helpful in elucidating the importance of role-taking in social interaction. Children of various ages (second through eleventh grade) were each brought into the laboratory and asked to play a game with the experimenters. Two plastic cups were placed upside down on a table in front of the subject, one with a nickel glued to the upturned bottom, the other with a dime. It was explained to the child that beneath each cup was a coin corresponding to the coin that was visible. One of the experimenters, Mr. Fry, left the room while the other experimenter conspired with the child to play a game with Mr.

Fry. They would remove a coin from beneath one cup and then ask Mr. Fry to choose which one contained the remaining coin. If he guessed correctly, he would be allowed to keep the money. Following these instructions, and before Mr. Fry re-entered the room, the experimenter said "Now we'll try to *fool* him—we'll try to *guess* which cup he'll choose and take the money out of *that* one. . . . Which one do *you* think he'll choose?" The child was obviously being asked to take the role of Mr. Fry. It is interesting that even second-graders were able to do this; they typically decided that Mr. Fry would opt for more money, the dime, and therefore removed the dime before he returned. Older children were more likely to follow the analysis further, reasoning that Mr. Fry would initially decide on the dime, but would suspect that the subject might have taken the more valuable coin for that reason. Thus, older children would choose to remove the nickel. Some of the oldest children were concerned that Mr. Fry might have gone so far as to follow even that reasoning, and therefore suggested that the opposite coin, the dime, be removed. All of this second-guessing (and third- and fourth-guessing) comes only as the child develops the ability to think about another person's thoughts. This ability is central to social interaction; without it, we could never communicate well with others, because we would never know how they were going to understand what we said. We must construct our own ideas about what other people think so that we can behave appropriately in their presence.

Yet we are not always solely concerned with what others think about things or about people; often we want to know what they think about us. This is the fourth central aspect of the individual's construction of social reality—his construction of himself. Although information about oneself is available from internal sources such as introspection and self-observation, some of the most important sources are external. What other people say about you, how they behave toward you, and what you believe they think about you are the primary kinds of information you have about yourself. When it comes right down to it, you only know what you are like, whether you are good or bad, and whether your actions are right or wrong, through social interaction. There exist no set standards, no exacting definitions, by which you can determine any of these things on your own. Suppose you believe that you are an excellent tennis player. How do you know this? You may observe, for example, that everyone you play against loses. This is a social definition of yourself in that you are comparing yourself with other people. You may, on the other hand, find that other people tell you that you are an excellent player. Again, a social self-definition. If we were to go even further, we could suggest that simply deciding that tennis is an activity by which you might be measured is another social self-definition. The game is entirely valueless unless people get together and agree that it is a worthwhile thing to do. In sum, a person alone in the world could not be a "good tennis player" because he could not play anyone, no one would know he was any good, and tennis would not even be an activity in terms of which a person's "goodness" could be assessed. And the social quality of self-definition extends well beyond the tennis court. If you were to sit down and write out a five-page description of yourself, most everything you would say could be traced to some sort of social foundation. Don't let this shake you, though. Remember that you play a central role in shaping what those around you think about themselves.

To summarize what we have said about the individual's constructions of social reality, let us extend the "person as scientist" idea to include "person as psychologist." All of the constructions we have discussed fit into a nice, neat package when we realize that human beings act like psychologists. The individual is continually striving to understand his social reality; the psychologist professes the same motive, and in addition, receives a paycheck for his work. In a sense, then, every person is a naive psychologist who goes about his activities—collecting data about people, testing his guesses about how people behave and think, building theories to explain the data and to predict and control future events—and yet is seldom aware that he is doing these things. To the individual, it all comes naturally and bears no comment; to us, it is a complex and intriguing process that deserves discussing at some length.

Implicit Theory   If the individual indeed behaves like a psychologist, why is he unaware that he is doing so? We have built a case for the idea that each of us spends a considerable amount of time involved in the cumbersome task of making observations, generalizations, and predictions about people. But if any of us were quizzed right now about the nature of our theories, we would most likely raise our hands and ask to leave the room. We would draw a blank. It may be that our theories are *implicit*—inaccessible to our immediate awareness—because they are so important in our everyday behavior. Since they are used again and again in almost every interpersonal setting, our notions about others become nearly reflexive in nature, in much the same way that repeated motor skills become reflexive. Imagine trying to describe in intimate detail the exact procedures you use in brushing your teeth—every upstroke and downstroke, each pause, which hand holds the brush, whether you start first on the uppers or lowers. Though you undoubtedly follow a very similar procedure each time you brush, it would take an observer several hours of watching you go through the motions to be able to list the rules governing your behavior. Obviously, your rules of tooth-brushing, although standardized and regular, are difficult for you to communicate and are difficult for others to observe. The individual's theories of psychology are similar to his rules of brushing. As we shall see, there is considerable organization and regularity in the naive psychologist's theoretical framework. Unfortunately, he is only dimly aware of its structure and application.

Formal Theory Building

As a part of this introduction to implicit theories, it is time for a short course in scientific method. To understand the workings of the naive psychologist's conceptions of humans, it is necessary to learn something about the process of theory construction as it is executed by the scientist. The first step is to define what is meant by a *theory*. This is best accomplished by noting that a theory consists of two parts, a set of *concepts* and a set of *relationships* that link the concepts together. Suppose we were attempting to build a theory about the following concepts: clouds, rain, blue skies, and wet socks. If we observe the environment carefully, we can note the following relationships among the concepts: it does not rain when the sky is blue; it sometimes rains when the sky is cloudy; when it rains, we sometimes get our socks wet. On a particular occasion—when we are wearing cheap socks that are not colorfast and that therefore may stain our ankles blue if they get wet—we may be especially concerned with the possibility of wet socks. The structure of the relationships allows us to make a prediction: If the sky is blue, it will not rain, nor will our socks get wet. One central function of theories is to make possible predictions of previously unobserved relationships.

A theory is a way of structuring observations of reality, of placing them in a rational system that specifies their interrelations. A theory is not reality itself. Instead, a theory is merely a single system that could be replaced by any number of alternate systems, each of which imposes a different structure on reality, and any of which might be true. Consider, for example, two theories that both predict that a certain individual, Fred, will have a bad day this Friday. One theory involves concepts such as "stars," "zodiac," "cusp," "date and place of birth," and so on. The other employs concepts such as "alcohol," "big party Thursday evening," "hangover," and so forth. Yet if each theory makes the same prediction for Fred, we cannot tell the difference between them in his case. They are equally true or equally false, depending on how Fred feels on Friday. If they each had predicted a different outcome for Fred, however, we could compare their predictions to the observed event and decide which theory better explained that event. If a theory is tested and retested in many different situations and the majority of its predictions come out wrong, it becomes less useful to the scientist, who is looking for a theory that predicts events correctly. But a tired old theory that seldom makes correct predictions is better than no theory at all. The old theory will be discarded only when a new theory is developed that explains more.

How do theories develop and grow? According to Abraham Kaplan (1964), they grow through two different processes, *extension* and *intention*. A theory develops through extension when a relatively simple set of relationships, derived from the observation of one set of events, is applied to new sets of events. So, for instance, a scientist might build a theory about the nature of sound by proposing that sound is generated by vibrating objects. To *extend* the theory, he might look for vibrations in objects that produce light or heat. Extension is generalizing a theoretical structure to fit new situations. But since sometimes a new situation can be different, extensions can sometimes be wrong. The other process of theory development, intention, takes place as the structure of a theory is changed to represent reality more adequately. This process may well include not only the addition of new concepts, but also the addition of new or different relationships among concepts. To add to the scientist's theory of sound through the process of intention, for example, we might suggest to him that the vibrations of the object are carried to the ear through the rapid compression and expansion of the air, that the frequency of the vibrations determines the tone of the sound, or that the amount of compression and expansion of the air determines the intensity of the sound. These added relationships and concepts refine the original theory. Theory building through intention, therefore, usually results in a better understanding of the original observations. Most scientific theories grow both through extension and intention—generalization and refinement; the important point is that this growth is always achieved through an interaction between thought and observation. The way in which reality is logically structured by a theory may change as new observations are made. A theory is not a rigid structure; to be useful, it must adapt to new evidence.

The structure of a theory guides the scientist in making decisions about what new evidence he should seek. As in our "wet socks" example, relationships that have been observed suggest relationships that have not yet been observed. These suggested relationships are called *hypotheses;* they have not yet been tested through the observation of reality. Hypotheses are central to the expansion of knowledge because they guide observation. A scientist does not observe everything there is to be observed. His observation is an active choice, not a passive exposure. In this sense, a scientist's theory can be seen as an agent that biases his observations. It makes him see less than the total reality to which he is exposed. He can be totally unaware of many possible observations, many possible concepts, and many possible relationships, because his theory requires that he focus only upon a certain subset. So in one way, a theory cuts us off from a full experience of reality; but in another way, it invites us to a full understanding of our experience.

The hypotheses generated from a theory allow the theory to be tested. We can never declare an entire theory "right" or "wrong," for the simple reason that it makes too many predictions for us to test. We can, however, decide whether it is right or wrong in particular instances. Does it predict a certain event correctly? This question, while perfectly reasonable, cannot be asked of some theories. It is possible that a theory can be constructed in such a way that it is not testable. One way to do this is to include concepts in the theory that are not observable; imagine trying to test a theory that proposes that a hundred snakes appear inside every refrigerator when the door is closed and that the snakes disappear when they are observed. A theory may also not be testable when it includes concepts that are too vaguely defined to be observed. So, for example, a theory suggesting that happiness causes the mumps might be very difficult to test—not because of the scientist's inability to observe the mumps, but because of his inability to specify exactly what happiness is. Happiness could be defined in a number of ways, none of which are prescribed by the theory. To make the theory testable, we might change "happiness" to "smiling," and, in so doing, reduce all of the concepts in the theory to easily observed events.

A theory may also not be testable when its faulty internal logic leads to conflicting hypotheses. An astronomical theory that predicted that the sun would burn out at noon on Wednesday and that the sun would not burn out at noon on Wednesday would not be testable. There is one other situation in which a theory is not testable. A theory may predict something that the scientist cannot feel free, morally, to test. Consider, for instance, a theory that predicts that the mutation of a certain virus will cause every first-born child in Canada to develop a facial tic. Any scientist with an ounce of morality would be aghast at the proposal that the theory be tested. Canadian scientists would be even more reticent. Thus, a theory may remain untested because the consequences of the test are too disastrous to consider. Since in this case the scientist can never learn the consequences of his hypothesis, he may well go on believing in the theory despite the fact that it cannot be verified.

Implicit Theory Building

Human beings, acting as naive psychologists, construct theories about social reality. These theories have all the features of the formal theories constructed by the scientist. They employ concepts and relationships derived from observation; they provide a structure through which social reality is observed; they enable the individual to make predictions. But, as we have pointed out, people are frequently unaware of the theories they employ. For this reason, they immediately assume that the structures they perceive and the predictions they make are correct. Probably the primary difference between formal scientific theory and implicit theory lies in this dimension of assumed correctness. Although even the most lofty scientific theories have their beginnings in the murky depths of scientists' own common-sense implicit theories, they are eventually written down and must stand the test of scrutiny by other scientists. Thus, while the scientist may place great trust in the structures and predictions of his pet theories, he is continually aware of their fallibility. The layman, on the other hand, lives by his theory; it is so much a part of him that he can see nothing else. This is an important point. The systems we call "implicit theories" are the individual's *reality*.

One "reality" shared by many individuals is that people of certain races are by nature bad, stupid, lazy, criminal, and generally undesirable. Although we might identify the individuals sharing this notion as racially prejudiced, they themselves would insist that their beliefs are correct and that their ideas about people of other races can be confirmed in reality. To draw the parallel between formal scientific theory and implicit psychological theory, let us explore in some detail the functioning of the implicit theoretical system constructed by a white individual who is prejudiced against blacks.

Suppose a white male child, Mel, is raised in a middle-class white suburban environment. The beginnings of his implicit theory of race would come when he was first able to tell the difference between black and white people—at about age four. In time, he would note that he is white, not black; his relatives and friends are white, not black; and eventually, that people who live in the inner city are often black, not white. The concepts of blackness and whiteness provide a theoretical structure that Mel uses to divide people into two kinds. Given this division, Mel proceeds to observe both kinds of people to find out what they are like. His observations of whites are made all day, every day. He interacts almost exclusively with white people, laughs with them, plays with them, and does the things they do. He develops a very detailed and faithful theory about whites. In contrast, his observations of blacks are infrequent and are made at a distance. He sees them occasionally on television; he sees them on the street in the city; he reads about them in newspapers. He probably receives quite a bit of information, secondhand, from all the white people he knows. In short, Mel makes all his observations of black people from his distant vantage point, never achieving the close interaction that is necessary to form an understanding that is similar to his understanding of whites.

At this point, it is likely that Mel will expand his theory of black people by *extension*. Since he has had such limited contact with black persons, he extends ideas gleaned from interaction with whites to increase his understanding of blacks. His implicit reasoning might go something like this: white people who exhibit behavior very different from mine usually have beliefs and values that are very different from mine; black people exhibit behavior that is very different from mine; therefore, blacks have beliefs and values that are very different from mine. The hypothesis generated by his theory is that blacks and whites tend to disagree about everything.

Had Mel constructed his theory of black persons through *intention*, he would have reached a different conclusion. By not observing black persons closely, he missed seeing many things that would have refined the structure of his theory. In particular, he failed to notice that blacks are typically exposed to a different reality; they are behaving appropriately to their world. In extending his theoretical structure rather than refining it, Mel has instead reached the conclusion that blacks are behaving inappropriately to *his* world.

Unfortunately, Mel's assumption that blacks' beliefs are incongruent with his own has dire consequences. Recall, if you will, a recent disagreement you had with another person. Very likely, it made you both uncomfortable. Even the most petty disagreement raises the alarming prospect that one of the people involved is completely and utterly wrong. The outcome of many such discrepancies between your beliefs and those of another person is that you end up disliking that person. To like the person and remain in his company often would be equivalent to admitting that your own perceptions of reality were incorrect. So instead of making a thorough revision of your theory, you hypothesize that the disagreeing person is the one who is stupid and misinformed. His opinions are outweighed by the evidence you have collected in the past.

Mel may never have interacted with a black person in his life, but his implicit prediction that he and the black would frequently disagree keeps him from ever approaching a black individual. Under these conditions, his theory cannot change. How can he understand and appreciate black people when his theory requires that he avoid them?

Mel is not atypical. Many whites have built theories similar to his. They do not even take the trouble to inquire whether a particular black person's beliefs are congruent or incongruent with their own. Studies by Milton Rokeach (1968) have shown, however, that when whites are presented with evidence that a particular black person has beliefs similar to their own, much of their racial prejudice toward him disappears. In one ingenious experiment, for instance, Rokeach arranged for white job applicants at a state employment center to be used as subjects. It was explained to each applicant that as a part of the application procedure, groups of applicants were being asked to meet and discuss how their prospective jobs might best be handled. The subject was then led to the discussion room and seated with four other applicants, two blacks and two whites. Actually, these other men were Rokeach's accomplices. As the discussion began, they listened closely to the subject and quickly determined his views. Shortly thereafter, a heated argument arose among the accomplices; two of them, a black and a white, violently disagreed with the subject's views, whereas the other two, again a black and a white, wholeheartedly agreed with the subject. Following this discussion, the subject was brought back to the main office, told that he was one of the top candidates, and asked which two of the other applicants he would prefer to have as co-workers. Sixty percent of the subjects chose the two accomplices who had agreed with them in the discussion, whereas only four percent made their choice solely according to race (by opting for the two whites). On the basis of this and many other studies, Rokeach concluded that white prejudice against blacks is not due to any deep-seated dislike for "blackness," but rather stems from the common tendency of whites to assume that blacks' beliefs are incongruent with their own.

Implicit theories take on added significance in this light. It is very possible for them to go wrong—wildly and irrevocably wrong. People can end up believing all sorts of strange things about the world, about each other, and about themselves. This is true because as an active observer of reality, a person can choose to ignore opportunities to make observations; prejudiced whites regularly choose to avoid contact with black people. Because the individual's implicit theory predicts that certain testing procedures will lead to unpleasant consequences, those tests are avoided. Such self-perpetuating systems bear a close resemblance to untestable scientific theories.

Behavioral Consequences of Implicit Theories

The only reason we are concerned with implicit theory is that an understanding of each person's implicit theory helps us to predict his behavior. In fact, it is erroneous to believe that things such as implicit theories, cognitive structures, or phenomenal fields truly exist in any physical form somewhere in a person's head. These concepts are part of the science of psychology. They are used as concepts in the theories of behavior that are developed by professional psychologists. Since a formal science like psychology can only be built on observations of reality that can be validated through the agreement of many scientists, many things that seem very real to the most people—their thoughts, feelings, experiences, and memories—cannot be "real" to the science of psychology. Another person's phenomenal field cannot be observed in the same way that his behavior—a heartbeat, a smile, or a drop kick—can be observed. However, it is possible for the scientist to infer the existence of a phenomenal field and to use such an inference to increase his understanding of behavior. Knowledge of the way in which an individual cognitively structures his world is knowledge about the organization of behavior, and as such, aids in predicting the occurrence of specific behaviors.

From this perspective, thought and behavior are intimately associated. The association takes place through particular thoughts that psychologists have variously called attitudes, evaluations, and sentiments. A thought such as "the campfire is dying," for example, really seems to have no relationship to behavior; the camper thinking this thought is simply acknowledging an aspect of his environment. However, a thought such as "I don't like dead campfires on cold nights" clearly has a behavioral implication; the camper will probably do something about the dying fire. Whether he will toss on some more wood, ask his camping companions to stoke the fire, or hire a roving Boy Scout to tend it is still in question, but in any case, the fire will be rebuilt. According to Carl Hovland and his colleagues (1953), this type of thought, an _attitude_, is defined as "an implicit approach-avoid response." If a person has a positive attitude toward a certain object, he will approach the object when possible; if he has a negative attitude toward an object, he will avoid that object when possible. Thus, although an attitude is not a behavior in any observable sense, it is an anticipation of a behavior. Knowing a person's attitudes toward politics, for instance, makes it quite likely that you will be able to predict how he will vote.

A person can have an attitude toward anything he can think about. In other words, every element in the individual's phenomenal field is potentially the target of an evaluation. So, while a thought such as $2 + 2 = 4$ may have no evaluative component for you (that is, you may neither like nor dislike it), it possibly could have one. If, for instance, you were a mathematician trying to develop new forms of arithmetic, you might look on such simple notions as $2 + 2 = 4$ with disdain. Or if your bank calculated your monthly balance on the basis of $2 + 2 = 3$, you might feel obligated to point out to the manager the virtues of good old $2 + 2 = 4$. Since many thoughts do imply behaviors, we can speak of a general _evaluative component_ of cognitive structure. The individual makes judgments of "good" or "bad" about nearly everything he experiences. These judgments are his anticipations of whether to approach or avoid such experiences in the future.

Evaluation is a major way in which thought is organized. In simple terms, the organization rule is "a thing cannot be both good and bad at the same time." This is true because the labels "good" and "bad" imply opposite and incompatible behaviors. Imagine, for instance, that someone is introduced to you as "sincere, warm, cruel, and stupid." You would be at a loss to know how to behave. You would like to make friends with him because he is sincere and warm, yet you would also like to run for your life because he is cruel and stupid. So what do you do? You might resolve the conflict by going completely one way or completely the other, choosing to approach or to avoid the person. In a similar way, the individual's cognitive structure acts to sort things out according to their evaluation. Since a primary purpose of the construction of implicit theory is to allow the individual to predict events, and, in so doing, to anticipate the behaviors he must enact, the implicit theory that is finally constructed must have clear implications for his behavior. It must tell him what to do in any situation. An implicit theory that predicts that two conflicting behaviors (approach and avoidance) would both be appropriate in a situation would be of no use to the individual. Therefore, as many psychologists have suggested, each person seeks to maintain consistency among his cognitions by making sure that he seldom has conflicting attitudes.

When a person's attitudes do conflict, he tends to restructure his thoughts to bring them back into a consistent pattern. The final product is a new set of attitudes, which, in turn, leads to a new set of anticipated behaviors. An example of this process is shown in a clever experiment performed by Knox and Inkster (1968). They interviewed people who were betting on horses at the two-dollar "win" window at a racetrack in Vancouver. Some of the people they interviewed were standing in line waiting to place their wagers (the "pre-bet" group); other people they interviewed were walking away from the window after placing their bets (the "post-bet" group). In each case, the interviewer approached the person and asked him to rate the horse on which he was betting according to the horse's chances to win. The interviewer asked the person to indicate the chances on a rating scale that ranged from "slight" to "fair" to "good" to "excellent." The pre-bet group most often rated their horses as "fair." The post-bet group most often rated their horses as "good." The only difference between these groups was that the post-bet group had already shelled out their money. Apparently, just placing a bet makes a person more likely to have a positive attitude toward his horse.

This experiment is a good illustration of the resolution of *cognitive dissonance* (Festinger, 1957). The person betting on a horse has thoughts about his actions, and these thoughts are incompatible (dissonant). We might look into the person's head for a minute and find these cognitions: (1) I bet money on this horse because it is a "fair" horse; (2) the other horses in the race are probably "fair," too, but I didn't bet on them. In order to justify placing the bet, the person must change these cognitions. Thought number one becomes: I bet money on this horse because it is a "good" horse. The individual has changed his attitude toward the horse in order to bring his dissonant cognitions into line. Knox and Inkster relate the story of one person, interviewed before placing his bet, who went so far as to seek out the interviewer on his way back from the window and try to convince her to change his horse's rating from "fair" to "excellent." We can be fairly certain that if the race had been called or rained out, he would have placed his money on the same horse at the very next opportunity. In this situation, and in many others, the individual's search for cognitive consistency—logic in his implicit theory—leads him to restructure his thought and change his behavior. This is probably the major process by which the mature adult's cognitive structure changes; although his general implicit theory is stable, the day-to-day conflicts he encounters frequently require him to make minor revisions.

the implicit psychologist

There are two important issues regarding implicit theories that we have not yet fully addressed. One, the changes in implicit theory that accompany the individual's growth from infancy to adulthood, we have discussed only briefly in the context of research studies that used children as subjects. The other, the differences among the implicit theories held by different people, we have not discussed at all. We have been reserving these discussions especially for this section of the chapter. The heading "The Implicit Psychologist" implies that our attention will be focused on the individual, rather than on his theories. Thus, while the body of this and each of the following chapters is devoted to outlining the elements of implicit psychological theories that are typically present in the adult, this special section of each chapter is concerned with how the implicit theories of both children and adults may differ from this general model.

The Development of the Implicit Psychologist

If there exists a general rule about the development of social thought, it is that the complexity of cognition is ever-increasing. Each new experience adds to the individual's understanding of all of his experiences. It is useful to talk about these changes in cognitive complexity in terms of two processes, *differentiation* and *integration*. Differentiation refers to the separation of thoughts or structures of thoughts, whereas integration refers to their combination. These terms may be applied to the processes of change that occur at many different levels of thought. So, for instance, at a very simple level, we can speak of differentiation when, at the age of eight months, the infant begins to cry every time he sees a stranger. He has differentiated between familiar faces and strange ones. At the same time, however, he has also made an integration. Familiar faces are seen as similar to each other because of the quality of familiarity; strange faces are seen as similar to each other because of their quality of strangeness. Any differentiation that is made between two sets of thoughts implies that an integration has been made within each set of thoughts.

Differentiation and integration are handy terms to use in analyzing the development of just about any thought process. Because of this, scientific psychologists sometimes use them too often in describing too many different events. Overuse has caused the meaning of these terms to become vague. Since we also plan to use the concepts frequently in discussing development, it seems important to clarify their meaning by recounting their origin. Psychologists Kurt Lewin (1935) and Heinz Werner (1948), both very influential theorists, borrowed these terms from biology and popularized their use in psychology. The biologist talks about the growth of an organism in terms of differentiation and integration. As a human embryo develops from one cell into many different kinds of cells, for example, it is said to differentiate. A human being is not, however, one big blob of cells. Certain groups of cells combine to form organs, nerve assemblies, bones, and so on. The formation of these systems is integration. Terms used in describing the development of the mind, therefore, are simply analogies to the development of the body.

Differentiation and integration in cognitive development, as in biological development, are adaptive processes. A lack of differentiation or integration in a particular area of thought usually means that the individual's construction is inappropriate to the reality he is attempting to understand. Piaget (1950) refers to these inappropriate constructions in terms of *centration*, the tendency to focus on irrelevant, concrete thoughts in trying to make judgments that really require more abstract (differentiated and integrated) thoughts. In defining this phenomenon, Piaget conducted a number of demonstrations to show its importance in the thought of the young child. He would, for example, show a child two water glasses, one that was short and wide and one that was tall and narrow. The short, wide glass was about three-fourths full of water. Piaget would pour all of this water into the tall, narrow glass and then ask the child, "Now is there more water? Or less? Or is it the same?" Young children invariably reply that there is more water. This response can be interpreted in terms of centration on the height of the glass. The young child pays attention—inappropriately—to the height of the glass in making his judgment of the volume of water.

Somewhat older children are able to differentiate between height and width, and therefore will sometimes answer "more" and sometimes "less." If they pay attention to height, they will say there is more water; if they pay attention to width, they will say there is less. Obviously, they must notice the conflict in their own judgments—it cannot be both more and less at the same time. This cognitive conflict helps to urge them on to new constructions. Later in their development, children are able to integrate their thoughts about height and width, noticing that the changes in height and width during the pouring compensate for one another and that the total volume of the liquid is conserved. Thus, the older child is able to understand this segment of the environment more completely because he has differentiated thoughts of height and width and has integrated these thoughts into the higher-level concept of volume. Older children and adults know that the amount of water is unchanged during the pouring operation, even if they pour it in their laps.

As we will note often in the following chapters, differentiation and integration take place in the development of social thought. To get a flavor of how these concepts are applied to social-cognitive development, let us consider one such application made by David Elkind in 1967. He has suggested that some of the problems peculiar to adolescence are traceable to the adolescent's inability to make a certain type of cognitive differentiation. The adolescent is able to differentiate between his own thoughts and those of other people, but he fails to differentiate between the *objects* of his own and others' thoughts. Thus, although he knows that other people have thoughts and attitudes that are different from his own, he thinks that their attitudes are all aimed at things that personally concern him. He believes that others are as obsessed with his appearance and behavior as he is himself. In a way, then, the adolescent is carrying around an imaginary audience in his head; even when there is no one around, he feels that people are all spending their time thinking about the same things he thinks about. This accounts for his extraordinary feeling of self-consciousness. Because the audience is his own construction, and thus has the privilege of knowing everything he knows about himself, it knows exactly what to pay attention to in the way of faults, improprieties, and blemishes. The audience knows that he has a nearly invisible stain on his shirt, that he has been biting his fingernails again, and that he has a particularly horrendous cowlick. And, the audience is appalled by these atrocities, as he is himself. When he is proud of a certain aspect of his image, however, the audience is also likely to be pleased. Thus, he will wear all sorts of strange clothes, shout at the top of his lungs at inappropriate moments, and otherwise behave in a typical adolescent way; the audience applauds him when he thinks his behavior is admirable. He cannot differentiate between his own likes and dislikes and what he believes is fashionable. Fortunately, the adolescent continues to make observations of others, and, after a while, finds that in reality other people are only infrequently occupied with his concerns. Thus, for most adults, the imaginary audience has left the auditorium.

Differences Among Implicit Psychologists   Many times the differences that appear between one adult's implicit theory of psychology and another adult's theory may be due to differences in their experiences. No two people live in the same skin, so no two people have exactly the same set of experiences. It is often true, nevertheless, that one person may communicate his ideas about his experiences to another person. The differences between their theories may be reduced through such communication. The girls reading *Confidential True Romance and Everlasting Love* magazine while giggling together during their first slumber party are forming implicit theories about love relationships by studying the (fictional and highly dubious) experiences of others.

Differences between adults' implicit psychology theories may also arise when the adults are at different levels of development. This is because there is no final, perfected implicit theory attained by all adults. There is, however, often an *ideal* theory attained by some adults that is thought of as the end product of development. The person you happen to meet at a bus stop may not even be near this final stage; his understanding of his social environment may well be incomplete. Because of this variation among adults, there is often a great deal of crossover between explanations of developmental processes and explanations of differences among adults. So, for example, we may speak of adults as differing in their overall level of differentiation or integration.

A program of research by Herman Witkin and his colleagues (1962) has focused on a very basic type of cognitive differentiation—the differentiation of perceptions. These investigators have found that adults differ in their ability to make fine distinctions among the objects they perceive. For example, in examining the drawing shown in Figure 1.2, some people would immediately notice all of the unusual objects embedded in it. Other people might take several minutes to find all of the objects. Others could stare at the picture until it burst into flames and still be unable to locate even the pumpkin. This last group Witkin has termed *field dependent;* their perceptions are strongly dominated by the overall organization of the perceptual field (the house, fence, and so on). People who *can* overcome this distracting field and perceive the embedded elements are *field*

Fig. 1.2 Embedded figures: a measure of field dependence. (Find the key, cat, ladder, moon, the letter C, broom, pumpkin, horseshoe, shamrock, screw, witch's head, and letter A.) Used by permission of *Highlights for Children*. Copyright © 1976, Highlights for Children, Inc., Columbus, Ohio.

independent. In formally assessing a person's level of field dependence, Witkin uses similar tasks—tests of the ability to see simple geometric forms that are embedded in more complex forms.

The individual's ability or inability to perceive differences between things has consequences for his implicit theory of psychology. Witkin has explained that the field independent person has a well-developed sense of his own identity and separateness from other people. This is true because of his propensity to see differences; this special ability to make distinctions among perceptions allows him to pay attention to a fundamental social distinction, the distinction between himself and others. Wegner and Vallacher (1975) have found that field independent people are likely to emphasize the differences between their own thoughts and attitudes and those of other people. In this study, each person was asked to fill out a questionnaire about his political beliefs, social behaviors, religious attitudes, and so on. He was then asked to read a description of a person, "Harold Warren," and to fill out the questionnaire again, this time the way he felt that Harold would answer it. People who were identified as field dependent (because of their poor performance on embedded figures tests) were likely to predict that Harold's answers would be the same as their own; they assumed similarity to him. On the other hand, the field independent people most often predicted that Harold's answers would be the opposite of their own; they assumed dissimilarity to him. It was also found, when the subjects were questioned later, that the field dependents felt they were similar to most of their relatives and acquaintances; field independents insisted that they were very different from their relatives and acquaintances.

The ability to differentiate among perceptions enables the individual to feel separate and different from other people. This feeling no doubt makes the social lives of the field dependent and the field independent markedly different. The field dependent, believing that he is quite similar to everyone he knows, is likely to accept many of their thoughts and attitudes as correct. The field independent person, in contrast, is likely to question others' reactions to situations, discount their attitudes and opinions, and resist their attempts to influence him. In a sense, the field independent person is like an ocean liner gliding through the tempest of social forces; the realization that he is different from others helps him keep a steady course. The field dependent person, in turn, is buffeted by those stormy seas like a dinghy.

Differentiation between self and others, as you can probably tell, is the first and most major differentiation made by the implicit psychologist. This differentiation provides the groundwork for all later social cognitive structures. Recalling that every differentiation also implies an integration, we can also point out that self-other differentiation creates two new systems of thought—one about self and one about others. We will turn to a discussion of the self system near the end of this book (in Chapter 6). Until then, the content and structure of thoughts about others will be our topic.

Summary   Each person actively constructs a cognitive representation of both physical and social reality. This implicit construction is similar to the theories developed by scientists and psychologists. Although less explicit than formal theories, the layman's implicit theories are similarly motivated by needs for understanding, prediction, and control. And, like the scientist, the layman satisfies these needs through the development of hypotheses about relationships between concepts in a theory. Both the scientist and the layman achieve better understanding through the extension and intention (generalization and refinement) of their theories.

Implicit theories about reality become especially important when people attempt to understand social phenomena. Often, it is not immediately apparent why others do what they do, what they are really like, or whether they are friend or foe. People construct implicit psychological theories in an attempt to answer these questions and thus achieve competence in their interpersonal worlds. Unfortunately, implicit theories about others and even about the self can be mistaken. Unlike the scientist, who would most often correct or reject an erroneous theory, the layman may sometimes live with a mistaken view of people. This is because he builds his theories for pragmatic purposes; he must act on the basis of his conceptions. His theories are translated into action through attitudes—the evaluative components of thoughts. Because a negative evaluation leads the individual to avoid contact with an object or person, it necessarily prevents him from achieving a better understanding of that object or person.

The basic differences among people's implicit theories can be traced in terms of developmental trends and personality dimensions. As the child matures, his implicit theories become increasingly complex—differentiated and integrated. These changes reflect the person's accommodation to new experiences, and allow him to make judgments of these experiences with greater abstraction and less centration. The theories held by adults may also differ in their developmental levels; field dependence-independence is an example of such a difference. Personality differences among adults may also result from their differing experiences with the world.

chapter two

We have argued that every person is a scientist. Just as the professional scientist looks for the lawful regularities underlying the apparent flux of reality, the implicit psychologist attempts to discover regularities in the behavior of other people. Regularity is of central concern to both the scientist and the implicit psychologist because it directly implies predictability, which in turn provides the potential for control. Thus, a working knowledge of regularities in human affairs allows the implicit psychologist to function with competence in a complex interpersonal world. But predictability is not the end state of scientific investigation. Any serious scientist does more than simply describe regularities in phenomena. Even a perfectly reliable relationship between events, one that can be predicted with one hundred percent certainty, is not a true scientific relationship until it has been *explained*. It is not enough to know that Event Y always occurs in the presence of Event X; the scientist wants to know why this relationship exists—what is it about X that causes Y to happen?

Consider, for example, the behavior of apples. Long before the time of Isaac Newton it was known that every time an apple breaks loose from a branch it falls—not up, not sideways, not in random circles, but down. This was a perfectly reliable observation, yet one that lacked a satisfactory explanation until Newton deduced mathematically the principle of gravitational force. According to this principle, the apple and the Earth are exerting force on each other. Thus, figuratively speaking, the apple and the earth are "falling" toward each other. It is only because the earth is more massive than the apple that the latter seems to do all of the falling.

implicit motivation theory

Attribution

As it turns out, of course, more than the behavior of apples can be explained by this principle; the mathematical formula expressing gravitational force has been fruitfully applied to the behavior of other objects, including the planets and stars. This example thus demonstrates an important point: by explaining one set of events we often find that we can explain and predict other sets of events that, prior to the explanation, seemed unrelated to the first set of events.

Explanation serves a similar function for the implicit psychologist. The layman, much like the scientist, looks for underlying causes that can account for the observed regularity in the behavior of others. Once the causes of a person's behavior have been determined, we can then predict other behaviors by the person, some of which may have important consequences for ourselves. In this sense, therefore, every person is an *implicit motivation theorist*. Each one of us attempts to understand the causes of behavior. Knowing *why* a person does what he does—knowing what has motivated his behavior—is far more useful to the individual than is the simple knowledge that the behavior has occurred. Imagine, for example, the following sequence of events. When you enter a friend's house, a stranger (Fred) immediately gets up and leaves. The following day, you arrive at a party and as you enter, this same person, Fred, gets up and leaves. Two days later, you see some friends on the street, and as you approach, Fred, who had been mingling with them, abruptly leaves. Suppose Fred engages in the same behavior in half a dozen other situations as well. You show up, he leaves. This state of affairs, while affording you perfect predictability of Fred's behavior, is brimming with uncertainty. *Why* does Fred leave when you arrive? Does he dislike you intensely? Do you remind him of his cruel and unusual stepfather? Or is there something about Fred that makes him react that way to strangers? Is he very insecure, for example? Prediction, then, is not enough. You probably would not be satisfied until you had identified some reason for his behavior. Your explanation would then allow you to predict some of Fred's other behaviors. If you decided that Fred was simply afraid of strangers, for example, you might predict that he would have an anxiety attack on a crowded bus, or that he would avoid public relations as an occupation. However, if you attributed his behavior to a personal distaste for you, perhaps because of some mistaken information regarding the soundness of your character, you might suspect the possibility of aggressive behavior on his part at some time in the future. In this case, your explanation would have led to personally relevant predictions of Fred's behaviors.

This process of inferring the causes of someone's behavior is referred to as *attribution* by social psychologists. When a person (the *actor*) engages in a particular act, the causes for that behavior may very well be unknown, both to someone who is watching (the *observer*), and to the actor himself. Thus, both the actor and the observer tend to attribute the behavior to certain possible causes. This is the attribution process. In one sense, it seems like attribution is just an elaborate guessing game: who can really know all the causes of even the simplest behavior? Yet in another sense, attribution is a complex, almost scientific, enterprise. The implicit motivation theorist uses a wealth of information about people, about behaviors, and about the situations in which behaviors occur in his search for explanations. Attribution represents a sophisticated example of implicit psychological theorizing.

Psychologists consider the study of attribution worthwhile because of the relationship between attribution and behavior. Often we react not so much to the fact of another person's behavior as to the perceived cause or intention underlying the behavior. If attributed to a "bad" motive (disdain, for example), even a very innocuous behavior (being patted on the head) might be reacted to violently (with a left hook). On the other hand, if attributed to an "innocent" motive (playfulness), an objectively harmful behavior (being poked in the eye) might be reacted to benignly ("thanks, I needed that"). Consider again the case of Fred. If you attributed his strange behavior (leaving when you arrive) to arrogance, you would probably react negatively and possibly bring about a heated confrontation. But if you attributed the same behavior to, say, shyness or feelings of inferiority, you would probably react sympathetically and possibly bring about a warm confrontation.

The central role of attribution in structuring our reactions to someone's behavior is nowhere more evident than in our legal system. Whether a given behavior is considered "criminal" depends not only on the nature of its consequences, but to a large extent on society's determination of *why* the behavior was undertaken. The distinction between murder and manslaughter provides a clear example. Both involve, to say the least, bad consequences—the death of a human being. But there is a critical difference in motivation between the two. Murder refers to the *intentional* killing of a person; the death would not have occurred if the actor had not desired it. Manslaughter, on the other hand, refers to the unintended taking of a person's life. Murder is therefore considered worse than manslaughter, and the societal reaction is more severe because of the greater personal responsibility attributed to the murderer. The "sanity-insanity" distinction is another familiar example where attribution processes play a central role in defining criminal behavior. Sanity and insanity are not psychological terms; they are legal terms pertaining to the actor's ability to distinguish between right and wrong at the time of his offense. A determination of insanity thus implies that the actor was not entirely responsible for the consequences of his actions. Extreme stress, for example, might be seen as the cause of someone's violent behavior if it interfered with the actor's thought processes to the point that he could no longer tell right from wrong. Again, the same behavior—the killing of a human being, for example—is interpreted in different ways if the suspect is perceived to have been sane (able to distinguish right from wrong) or insane (unable to make this distinction) at the time of his misdeed.

Internal and External Causes

For very good reasons, then, psychologists have become increasingly interested in the processes involved in attribution. As the result of a few theoretical explorations and dozens of empirical studies, several principles of attribution have been established. The most general principle was implicit in some of the attribution examples discussed earlier. We are referring to the distinction between the perception of *internal causes* and *external causes* of behavior. This distinction was first articulated by Fritz Heider (1958) and was later elaborated upon by Edward Jones and Keith Davis (1965) and by Harold Kelley (1971). According to this principle, behavior is seen either as caused by forces in the situation surrounding the actor or as caused by the actor's personal qualities or dispositions. An attribution to external causes means that the observer feels most people would behave in the same way as the actor if they were in the same situation. By contrast, if the observer makes an internal attribution for someone's behavior he is in effect assigning traits or motives to the actor that are more important than situational forces in accounting for the actor's behavior. Consider, for example, the case of a young man who comes home one evening and gives his wife a fish. The possible causes for this behavior can be classified as either internal or external. We might make internal attributions by suggesting motives or intentions on the part of the young man (he wanted fish for dinner), or by suggesting that he had a trait or disposition to behave in this manner (he has always loved fish). On the other hand, we could make external attributions by suggesting that his behavior was motivated by external forces (his wife asked him to bring home a fish) or caused by an event over which he had no personal control (someone handed him a fish on the street).

Whether an observer attributes behavior to properties of the person or to external factors depends on a number of things. First of all, there are some specific sources of information to which the observer attends when he infers the cause of someone's behavior. Harold Kelley (1967) has specified these sources of information and indicated how they are processed to yield an attribution. Second, attribution depends on the attributor's expectancies and biases. These factors were outlined by Edward Jones and Keith Davis (1965) and have been supported by several investigations. And third, attribution sometimes depends on the attributor's focus of attention. The search for potential causes is not exhaustive; in some circumstances, the individual simply attributes causality to whomever or whatever he directs his attention. Each of these influences on attribution will be considered in turn.

Sources of Information

Basically, Kelley argues that in making a causal attribution, the individual analyzes information about a person's behavior in much the same way that a scientist would. The attributor notices whether the behavior in question occurs in the presence or absence of a limited number of potential causes. The potential causes of a behavior include the *actor* himself, the *person or entity toward which he is behaving,* and the *setting* in which the behavior occurs. In a two-person interaction, for example, a sarcastic comment by Andy directed to Walter can be attributed either to characteristics of Andy (he is sarcastic), to characteristics of Walter (he invites sarcasm), or to some feature of the setting in which they are interacting (they are in a room full of back issues of *National Lampoon*).

To identify which factors or combination of factors caused Andy's sarcasm, the attributor attends to three sources of information—*consensus, consistency,* and *distinctiveness.* The behavior is said to have high consensus if other people besides Andy behave sarcastically toward Walter. If Andy is the only one who does it, then the behavior has low consensus. In thinking about this source of information, try to keep in mind the idea of *consensus among actors.* Thus, yelling and cheering at a football game is a high-consensus behavior. Yelling and cheering at a funeral is not. The second source of information—consistency—refers to *consistency across time.* Thus, if Andy has been sarcastic toward Walter on many other occasions, Andy's sarcastic behavior is highly consistent. If this is the first time it has happened, even though Andy and Walter have been together many times, then Andy's sarcastic behavior is low in consistency. The third source of information—distinctiveness—refers to *distinctiveness among targets.* There are a variety of other people besides Walter to whom Andy might be sarcastic; these are the possible targets of sarcasm. If Andy is sarcastic only toward Walter, then his behavior is high in distinctiveness. If Andy is sarcastic to almost everyone he knows, then Andy's sarcastic behavior is low in distinctiveness.

The particular combination of answers to these questions will determine for the observer whether the cause of Andy's sarcasm is attributable to Andy, to Walter, or to the particular situation. Specifically, an attribution will be made to Andy under conditions of low consensus (no one else is sarcastic toward Walter), high consistency (Andy is always sarcastic toward Walter), and low distinctiveness (Andy is sarcastic toward others as well). In other words, if Andy is the only one who does it, if he is always doing it, and if he does it to everybody, then there is probably something about Andy that makes him do it; Andy is sarcastic. An attribution to Walter, on the other hand, is likely under conditions of high consensus, high consistency, and high distinctiveness. This combination of the three factors says that everyone does it to Walter, Andy always does it to Walter, and Andy does it only to Walter. Therefore, Walter is apparently the type of person who invites sarcasm. Finally, the particular situation will be seen as the cause of Andy's sarcasm under conditions of low consensus, low consistency, and high distinctiveness. In everyday terms, if Andy is the only one who is sarcastic to Walter, if he has not behaved this way toward Walter in the past, and if he does not often behave this way toward others, we decide that there is something unusual about the present situation that has caused the sarcasm.

For purposes of simplification, let's say that the attributor has eliminated the particular situation as a likely cause of Andy's sarcasm. This would be the case, for example, if the attributor were observing Andy and Walter interact for the first time. In effect, this eliminates consistency as a source of information for the attributor. It is then possible to portray the remaining two factors, consensus and distinctiveness, in the form of a simple table (Figure 2.1).

In this table, the names listed vertically—Andy, Bruce, Chris—represent the consensus factor (the different potential actors). The names reading across—Walter, Xavier, Yvonne—represent the distinctiveness factor (the different potential sarcasm targets). S designates a sarcastic comment by an actor to a target. Examination of Figure 2.1 suggests that sarcasm is attributable to Andy: it occurs under conditions of low consensus (no one besides Andy is sarcastic toward Walter) and low distinctiveness (Andy is sarcastic toward everyone). An attribution to Walter would be made if S were distributed as portrayed in Figure 2.2. That is, everyone is sarcastic toward Walter (high consensus) and Andy is sarcastic toward Walter but not others (high distinctiveness.)

The layman's approach to causal analysis, as portrayed in these tables, is strikingly similar to a sophisticated statistical technique known as *analysis of variance,* which is often used to analyze the results of psychology experiments. While there is much in common between the implicit psychologist's informal

	Potential sarcasm targets		
	Walter	Xavier	Yvonne
Andy	S	S	S
Bruce			
Chris			

Potential sarcastic actors

Fig. 2.1   Identifying the cause of sarcasm: attribution to Andy.

	Potential sarcasm targets		
	Walter	Xavier	Yvonne
Andy	S		
Bruce	S		
Chris	S		

Potential sarcastic actors

Fig. 2.2   Identifying the cause of sarcasm: attribution to Walter.

analysis and the professional psychologist's more formalized approach, there exist nonetheless some basic differences, which in turn lead to vastly different conclusions regarding the causes of behavior. We shall document these differences and attempt to explain them later in this chapter in the section entitled "divergent perspectives."

Expectancies and Biases

Sometimes we do not have consensus, consistency, and distinctiveness information available when we are trying to explain someone's behavior. This is especially true when we are observing a person for the first time; we have no way of knowing how he behaves in different circumstances or how consistently he has behaved in his present fashion in similar circumstances. According to a model of attribution devised by Edward Jones and Keith Davis (1965), the individual often makes confident attributions for an actor's behavior without the benefit of such information. Central to this analysis is the assumption that individuals have a pretty good idea of what behavior is expected or socially desirable in a given situation. The individual in a sense has an "implicit situation theory," a set of expectations concerning the rules of behavior in various settings. We expect people to be quiet in church, to drink at parties, to obey traffic lights, and to do what they are told when threatened with physical harm. But behavior that is in accordance with situational expectancies is of little use to us when we are trying to judge the particular qualities of a person. According to Jones and Davis, it is only when someone is perceived as violating the *situational demands* that an internal attribution is made to him or her. There is no basis for attributing characteristics to a person who sits quietly in church, for example, since the situational demands alone are sufficient to account for such behavior. But if the same person were to tell ribald tales during the liturgy, many of those present would instantly form a negative judgment about his character. Violations of other situational expectancies can, in a similar manner, lead to internal attributions. For example, the individual who risks governmental disapproval by expressing politically controversial opinions may be perceived by some people as having such attributes as integrity, conviction, and courage.

An example of this principle is provided in an experiment by Jones, Davis, and Gergen (1961). Subjects in this study were asked to make judgments about the personality of a person who either complied with or deviated from expected responses in a job interview. One group of subjects observed a person— actually, an accomplice of the experimenter—being interviewed for a job as a submariner. It was made clear to both the subject and the interviewee that because submarines confine many people in close quarters, a good submariner should be a "team player." For effective team performance, it is important that a submariner not only enjoy the company of others, but also be willing to conform—in short, a good submariner doesn't rock the boat. During the subsequent interview, some of the subjects saw the interviewee presenting himself as extroverted and conforming. Other subjects saw him portray an individual who was more autonomous and independent. Assuming the interviewee wanted the job, it follows that he would describe himself in terms of "good submariner" qualities, that is, as extroverted and conforming. Thus, situational expectancies alone could account for this type of self-presentation but would be insufficient to account for an interviewee's description of himself as independent and autonomous. Yet another group of subjects viewed a person—again, an accomplice—being interviewed for a job as an astronaut. In contrast to the "good submariner" description, a "good astronaut" was said to be independent of other people (introverted) and able to make his own decisions (nonconforming). Again, some of the subjects observed an interviewee who conformed to the situational demands (in this case, by presenting himself as introverted and nonconforming), while others observed an interviewee who violated the situational demands (by presenting himself as extroverted and conforming). As with the submariner, subjects were asked to judge the interviewee's personality and to rate their confidence in their judgments. As predicted, subjects made more extreme judgments of the personalities of the interviewees who deviated from situational expectancies than of those of the interviewees who did not. For example, the conforming would-be astronaut was described as more conforming than was the conforming prospective submariner. Subjects also indicated greater confidence in their ratings when they were judging someone who was not behaving in the expected fashion. Behavior alone is usually not enough to generate an internal attribution; rather, behavior is interpreted in the context of situational pressures.

In the study just described, the situational expectancies for the interviewees' behavior were made clear to the subject. Most people, however, have a pretty good idea about what sorts of behavior are expected or considered appropriate in most situations without having to be told by a psychologist. And most of us are aware of how people in certain positions or roles are expected to behave. A teacher is expected to smile less than a waitress, for example, and no one expects either a politician or a used-car salesman to be particularly candid. An experiment by Thibaut and Riecken (1955) provides an example of this implicit understanding and demonstrates how attributions are determined in part by these expectancies. Using written messages, each subject tried to persuade two men to carry out a certain activity. The subject was led to believe that while one of the men had a relatively high status in the university (as an instructor), the other had a much lower status (as a freshman). The behavior of both men was identical: they complied with the subject's request. But when subjects were questioned as to why each man complied, different reasons were given for their compliance. An internal attribution was made for the high-status man's compliance—he complied because of some personal quality. Because of his status, the external force (the subject's request) was perceived by subjects as an insufficient cause for his behavior. Thus, he must have complied because he was a helpful person or just a nice guy. But the freshman did not receive credit for his own behavior; the subject's persuasion was seen as a sufficient cause for the compliance of this lower-status person. That is, his behavior was attributed to external causes rather than to his personal characteristics.

In addition to deviations from situational expectancies, Jones and Davis have pointed out biasing factors that lead an observer to make internal rather than external attributions for a person's behavior. An internal attribution is likely to be made, for example, when the actor's behavior is rewarding or costly to the attributor. In psychological jargon, this factor is referred to as *hedonic relevance*. Think of the reaction you might have to someone who stepped on your foot on a crowded bus. Though you might not act on your immediate impulse and return the favor, you would probably attribute clod- or oaf-like properties to the person. In contrast, a neutral observer of this episode might see it simply as a consequence of the crowded conditions—an external attribution. A closely related factor is *personalism*. This refers basically to the observer's perception that the act was intended to have hedonic relevance for him. In other words, not only does the behavior have good or bad consequences for the attributor, but the attributor feels the act was specifically directed at him. Imagine your reaction to a foot-stomper who picked you out of the crowd on purpose! Not surprisingly, personalism is associated with extreme internal attributions.

Focus of Attention
From Kelley we have learned that the implicit psychologist identifies the causes of behavior by attending to and integrating information about consensus, consistency, and distinctiveness. Jones and Davis, in turn, have shown how expectancies for behavior and biases stemming from self-interest influence attribution. The application of these principles, however, does not always result in the identification of a single cause. Quite often it is difficult to figure out why something occurred. If a behavior is characterized by high consensus and low distinctiveness, for example, both an external cause (because of high consensus) and an internal cause (because of low distinctiveness) might seem plausible. Acknowledging that social behavior often has complex causes may be insightful, but it is not of much help to the individual who is attempting to understand and predict the

actions of others. Multiple plausible causes thus are a source of uncertainty; the individual tries to identify a single cause, discounting the others.

The identification of a single cause in settings where there are several plausible causes often depends on the attributor's *focus of attention*. When one observes an event, one tends to assign causality to that element of the setting that occupies one's attention (see, for example, Duval and Hensley, 1976). To understand why attribution follows the focus of attention, consider two basic features of causality—spatial and temporal contiguity. One thing (object, person, or event) is perceived as causing another when they occur close together in time and space. Lighting a match in Ethiopia is not likely to be seen as a cause of a forest fire in Patagonia—particularly if the match was lit in 1794 and the fire occurred last week. Temporal contiguity is especially relevant to focus of attention and attribution. If you pay attention to some stimulus (looking at or listening to a person, for instance) when an event occurs, the stimulus and the event are linked in a temporal sense—they are in your awareness at the same time. If the stimulus is as plausible a cause as any other feature surrounding the event, you will probably see the stimulus as the cause of the event.

Suppose, for example, you observe a group discussion and are asked to indicate which member of the group was most responsible for the way in which the discussion was proceeding. If there are no obvious behavioral differences between the members (one person talking continually while the others are silent, for example), you will probably attribute causality to the person who most occupies your attention (the man with the Hawaiian shirt, perhaps). Just such a finding has been reported by McArthur and Post (1977). Thus, when the cause of some behavior or sequence of behaviors is unclear—for instance, because of insufficient information about consensus, consistency, and distinctiveness—the individual assigns causality to whatever he is focusing on.

Causes of Success and Failure

Many of the things people do represent attempts to achieve a goal or accomplish a task. The problems to be solved are sometimes intellectual (solving a puzzle, for example, or understanding concepts in a psychology text), sometimes physical (winning a tennis match or eating fifty eggs in an hour), and sometimes social (getting someone to like us or persuading a friend to lend us money). Many of the things people do, in other words, end in success or failure. In attempting to explain why someone succeeds or fails at a given task, the implicit psychologist employs a number of implicit rules. Before elaborating these, however, it is necessary to introduce a new attribution principle. In addition to the distinction between internal and external causes, a distinction can be made between causes that are *stable* over time and those that are *variable*, or likely to change over time. Being insulted, for example, would be a variable cause of hostility, since this cause is not everpresent. But paranoid thinking, or the feeling that everyone is out to get you, is more than a temporary state or mood, and thus could be considered a stable cause of hostility. In the same vein, generosity might be caused either by a stable condition, like a well-paying job, or by a variable condition, like a good mood. Note that the stable-variable distinction is independent of the internal-external distinction. As should be apparent in the examples just described, stable causes can be either external (a well-paying job) or internal (paranoid thinking), and the same can be said for variable causes: being insulted is a variable external cause, whereas a good mood is a variable internal cause.

Possible Causes

The stable-variable distinction in combination with the internal-external distinction provides a tidy framework for specifying the potential causes of success and failure. This framework, shown in Figure 2.3, was first suggested by Bernard Weiner and his colleagues (Weiner, 1974).

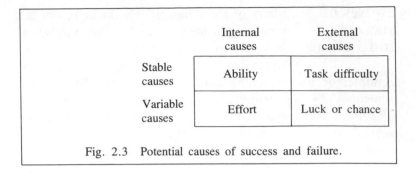

Fig. 2.3   Potential causes of success and failure.

Listed in the divisions of this table are four potential causes of success or failure. Suppose, for example, you observe a person finish first in the 100-yard dash at a track meet. Your attribution for his success would probably correspond to one of these four general causes. You might, for example, note his superior co-ordination and strength, thereby making an ability attribution. Or you might note his intense motivation and concentration, factors that fall under the general category of effort. Another possible explanation for his success is the relative ease of the task—he won the race because of the weak competition. Or, finally, you might simply attribute his success to luck, feeling that on another day he could easily have finished last.

Attribution to each of these four causes is based on different sources of information. The amount of ability we attribute to a person depends largely on the person's degree of success at similar tasks in the past. In terms of Kelley's model of attribution, high consistency leads to an ability attribution; we tend to see the person as having high ability if he or she has done consistently well, low ability if consistently poor. Another term from Kelley's model—consensus—is useful for understanding when ability is seen as the cause of success or failure. Consensus, you will recall, refers to the proportion of other people who behave in the same manner as the actor in situations similar to that of the actor. In the case of performance at a task, high consensus means either that most people succeed or that most people fail at the actor's task. According to Weiner and his colleagues, ability is attributed when the actor's performance is at variance with high consensus. High ability, in other words, is attributed when the actor succeeds at a task at which most people fail; low ability is perceived as the cause of an actor's performance when he fails at tasks at which most others succeed.

Ability is a stable attribution; once a person has been labeled as having high or low ability, this label tends to stick—even if the person's degree of success changes drastically in the future. An ability attribution, in other words, generates expectations for continued performance at the same level of success. Rather than revise one's ability estimates if these expectations are then contradicted, one tends to attribute the change in performance to a change in effort or to luck. Support for the persistence of an ability attribution is provided in a study by Edward Jones and his colleagues (1968). Subjects in this study observed a person perform thirty difficult IQ-type questions. This person was actually an accomplice of the experimenters, and he performed according to prearrangement in one of three ways. One-third of the subjects saw him start out quite well, answering ten of the first fifteen questions correctly and then decline in his performance, answering only five of the last fifteen questions correctly. A second group of subjects saw him perform in the opposite way; he answered five of the first fifteen questions correctly and then improved on the remaining fifteen, answering ten correctly. The remaining subjects also saw the person answer fifteen of the thirty items correctly, but his pattern of success was random, showing neither decline nor improvement. All subjects were asked to rate the person's IQ, predict how well he would do on another series of items, and recall how many he had answered correctly on the first series. Keep in mind that in all cases the person's total performance was identical—fifteen correct responses out of thirty.

Results showed that the person's performance was perceived quite differently in each of the conditions. When the person declined in his performance, doing well at first but poorly on the later items, he was judged to have a higher IQ than when he improved or performed randomly. Moreover, when his performance declined, he was actually recalled as having done better than when he improved or performed randomly, and he was predicted to do better on a later series. To take an example from everyday life, imagine a student who earns nothing but A's his first year in college, but earns only C's for the next three. Extrapolating from the study by Jones and his colleagues, this person is likely to be seen as bright even though his overall academic average is mediocre. To account for the decline in his performance, an observer might label him a "high-potential under-achiever," attributing his unspectacular grades to poor motivation. In the eyes of those around him, he is still bright and simply needs encouragement to do better. Thus, first impressions count. The aspiring student might want to keep this in mind the first day of class.

Like ability, effort represents an internal locus of causation for success and failure. Unlike ability, however, it is variable rather than stable—at one moment we may be motivated to master the subtleties of quantum physics, but at the next moment the subtleties of sleeping. Effort is thus used to account for fluctuations in performance, particularly if the fluctuations correspond to changes in the incentive for success. If the student described above were promised a four-year scholarship if he earned straight A's his first year, an observer would probably attribute his performance to effort rather than to ability.

Task difficulty differs from ability in that it represents an external locus of causation, but like ability, it is considered to be a stable rather than a variable cause of success and failure. As noted above, ability is perceived to be the cause of success or failure when the person's performance is different from that of most other people—that is, when it is at variance with high consensus. But if a person's performance is consistent with high consensus, the performance is likely to be attributed to the difficulty (or ease) of the task. Task difficulty, in fact, is a common attribution for our failures, whether in athletic endeavors ("Nobody could have beaten them today!"), scholastic situations ("That test was impossible"), or social encounters ("She probably tells everybody they're as stupid as paste").

Attributing a person's success or failure to luck is a curious phenomenon. In effect, the attributor is claiming that neither the person nor the difficulty of the task were important. The fact that it is such a common attribution suggests that quite often we simply cannot account for someone's successes or failures. In our more lucid or insightful moments, of course, we know that every outcome has a cause; but some causes are more subtle than others. Person- or task-related causes are particularly difficult to identify when the pattern of successes and failures for a person is highly variable, appearing to be random.

Self-interest and Attribution

Identifying the causes of someone's success or failure is not always a detached undertaking. Sometimes we want or expect a person to do well. In other instances, we hope for and anticipate someone's failure. Such motivational states and expectancies can influence the way in which a person explains another person's success or failure. Consider how you might react if someone you disliked intensely got a very desirable job: "I can't believe it; why is he always so lucky?" But if a good friend got the same job under the same circumstances, your reaction might be: "Her talent was obviously recognized." Or think of the way you might console a friend after a failure: "Anyone could lose forty-eight handball games in a row; there were a lot of close calls." To have enemies succeed and friends fail is rather discomforting, even threatening, since it implies that we may fail as well. Attributing such outcomes to luck lessens this discomfort and allows us to maintain our belief in a just world.

Sometimes, however, things do go sour for us. At one time or another, each of us has failed at something. Failure can take many forms, from flunking out of college to falling down while helping a little old lady across the street. Blaming bad luck or making some other external attribution is a likely response to such events. If we flunk out of college we might explain to anybody who will listen that the instructors were lousy and the grading unfair. And who can blame us for tripping over the little old lady; there's no way we could have seen that pebble.

Striking evidence for the self-serving nature of attributions for success and failure is provided in a study by Johnson, Feigenbaum, and Weiby (1964). Students taking educational psychology courses participated in a trial program involving the teaching of mathematics skills to fourth-grade boys. Each aspiring teacher explained to two pupils how to multiply by ten. According to prearrangement, one of the pupils did quite well, but the other did poorly. Each teacher then taught the same students to multiply by twenty. For half the teachers, the two pupils maintained their earlier level of performance: one of them continued to do well, the other poorly. But for the other teachers, there was a change in performance by one of the pupils: while the one who had done well continued to do well, the other pupil, who had performed poorly, now improved to the level of the first pupil. The teachers were then asked to explain the performance of the two pupils. Those teachers who worked with the improving student attributed his improvement to their skills—an internal attribution. If the pupil did not improve, however, the teachers blamed his continued failure on his own poor motivation or low IQ—an external attribution from the teacher's point of view, somewhat akin to task difficulty. That the teacher's explanations for the students' performance were self-serving is shown in a later study by Beckman (1970). She found that observers watching a similar teacher-pupil situation made just the opposite attributions: they blamed the teacher if the pupil did not improve, and credited the pupil if he did improve. Other recent investigations have also demonstrated that individuals tend to attribute causality to themselves after successful performance on a task but attribute causality to other factors when they are unsuccessful (see, for example, Miller, 1976). Clearly, then, self-interest can bias our explanations of success and failure. We attribute success to our ability or our effort, but attribute failure to bad luck or task difficulty.

Divergent Perspectives: Actor and Observer

Our concern so far has been with the general process of inferring the causes of someone's behavior. We have distinguished between types of perceived causes and have indicated, through theory, research findings, and examples from everyday life, the conditions under which one type of cause or another is likely to be invoked. For the most part, attribution has been described as a logical affair—not exactly without an emotional component, but certainly dependent on our powers of reasoning. Yet it is painfully obvious that people often see the causes of behavior differently. It seems, in fact, that people disagree less about what happened than about why it happened. To help understand why people can make different attributions for the same behavior, let's consider a basic difference in perspective—the difference between actors and observers.

Actor versus Observer

Many if not most disagreements about why something happened can be traced to actor-observer differences. The person engaged in the behavior—the actor—quite often sees things differently from an observer—someone who sees or hears about the behavior. Edward Jones and Richard Nisbett (1971) have offered a way of summarizing actor-observer differences: actors tend to attribute their actions to external factors, whereas observers tend to attribute the same actions to personal dispositions of the actor. It's easy to think of examples where this generalization seems to hold. Consider how a parent might respond upon discovering that Junior put sand in someone's gas tank ("You're naughty, irresponsible, and cruel") and contrast it with Junior's explanation ("The guys made me do it"). Lovers' quarrels are similarly characterized quite often by actor-observer differences. A man, for example, may neglect to buy a birthday present for his woman friend, attributing his oversight to a heavy schedule and pressures at work. The woman might come up with her own explanation, namely, that his character is flawed by traits ranging from laziness to a marked deficiency of passion. It is important to note that the actor's tendency to attribute his behavior to external factors is not necessarily the same thing as making excuses for his misdeeds. Suppose, for example, that the man had bought a present for his lover. Duly impressed, she might comment on his loving nature, warmth, generosity—and obvious color-blindness. He, in turn, might note (though not to her) that he bought the pink and green striped dress because he knew she would be hurt and angry if he didn't get her something. In other words, his behavior was motivated by pressure, not passion.

A significant event in recent history—the Watergate scandal of the early 1970's—clearly demonstrates actor-observer differences in causal inferences about the actor's behavior. Many of the participants in that affair maintained that they were simply following executive orders, while the "higher-ups" argued that they acted out of a concern for national security. All the actors, in short, made external attributions. But by the summer of 1974, a majority of citizens—observers via the press—saw the participants as corrupt, power-hungry, and paranoid. The observers made internal attributions.

Of course, it might seem that Watergate is too special a case to tell us anything of general value about actor-observer differences in attribution. After all, the Nixon Administration hardly constituted a representative sample of citizens—most were lawyers—and their occupation, running a country, was certainly unique. It may come as a surprise, then, that some psychologists recently replicated a Watergate-type situation and found the same sort of actor-observer differences. West, Gunn, and Chernicky (1975) conducted an elaborate study in which college students were enticed to participate in an illegal burglary. The experimenters wanted to see if students would agree to participate in such an activity when provided with rationales ranging from "national interest" to an opportunity to make money. Also of interest was whether the explanations given by subjects for accepting or declining the offer would correspond to the explanations observers would offer for such a decision.

Each subject was approached by a "private investigator" who told him about a "project you might be interested in." If the subject expressed an interest, the investigator suggested that they meet later at a local restaurant. At this meeting, the investigator was accompanied by another man carrying a briefcase that contained elaborate plans for burglarizing a local advertising firm. At this point, the subject was given one of four stories. Some subjects were told that the burglary was for the Internal Revenue Service (IRS), and that the purpose was to microfilm an allegedly illegal set of accounting records that were being used to defraud the government of $6.8 million in taxes. The microfilmed records were said to be necessary to get search warrants so that the original records could be seized. The subjects were promised immunity from prosecution if they agreed to participate. A second group of subjects were given the same story, but were not promised government immunity. Subjects in a third condition were given a quite different story. The investigator told the subject that a rival advertising firm had offered him $8000 for a copy of designs prepared by the target firm. The subject was offered $2000 of the $8000 if he agreed to help the investigator microfilm the designs. A final group of subjects was given a story that provided virtually no incentive for participation. The investigator was simply interested in finding out whether his plan would work. He assured the subject that no theft would be committed, but at the same time he offered no money for the subject's participation.

In all conditions, the investigator presented the same plan in considerable detail. A four-person team was required: the investigator, who would monitor police calls in an office outside the building; the man with the investigator, who would serve as a lookout; a lock and safe expert with extensive background in military intelligence; and the subject, who would be the inside lookout and do the microfilming. The subject was shown impressive evidence of the planning that had gone into the operation, including aerial photos of the building and surrounding area, blueprints, and a list of police cars in the area.

After being thoroughly familiarized with the details of the plan, the subject was asked whether he wished to participate. The results of the study showed that overall, about 20 percent of the subjects agreed to participate in the burglary. This figure is somewhat misleading, however, since compliance differed vastly between the four conditions. Not surprisingly, of those subjects asked to participate simply to see if the plan would work, only 10 percent agreed to do so. Agreement was even lower (5 percent) when the plan was IRS-sponsored but did not provide for immunity from prosecution. Agreement was somewhat higher when $2000 was promised—20 percent. But by far the most agreement was obtained for the IRS-sponsored plan that included a promise of immunity from prosecution: 45 percent—nearly half of the subjects—agreed to take part in the break-in.

Another group of subjects functioned as observers; each was given a detailed description of one of the four conditions. Among other things, they were asked whether they themselves would have agreed to participate. Overall, the percentage of hypothetical agreement for observers (16 percent) did not differ greatly from the actual agreement of the subjects (20 percent). Unlike the actors, however, the percentage of agreement varied little between the four conditions for the observers; that is, no condition generated much more agreement than any other condition. The observers, in other words, were less sensitive to the differences in situational forces between the four conditions than were the actors, a result that follows from the Jones and Nisbett actor-observer distinction.

Further support for the Jones and Nisbett hypothesis is established by the differing attributions given for compliance by actors and observers. Some of the observers were asked to imagine that one of the subjects (John) had agreed to participate, while others were asked to imagine that John had refused. In both cases, they were asked to describe why John had made the decision he had. Observers' answers were classified as either dispositional (for example, "he likes to take risks" if he agreed, or "he's honest" if he refused) or situational (for example, "the plan was foolproof" if he agreed, or "it was illegal" if he refused). Actors' actual explanations for their agreement or refusal were similarly classified as either dispositional or situational. Analysis of observer and actor explanations showed that both for agreement and for refusal to participate, observers' attributions were more dispositional than were actors' attributions; actors tended to attribute their decision to the situational forces rather than to their own personal characteristics.

Though not as unusual as the Watergate experiment, several

other studies have demonstrated that different explanations for the same behavior are given by actors and observers. One procedure that has been employed is to turn the actor into an observer of his own behavior by presenting him with a videotape of his performance in a setting involving social interaction (for example, Storms, 1973). When asked why they behaved the way they did, actors who observed themselves on videotape tended to make dispositional attributions to a greater extent than did actors who were not afforded the chance to see themselves as an outsider might have. In a variation on this procedure, other studies have, in a sense, turned observers into actors (for example, Regan and Totten, 1975). To accomplish this, observers are told to "empathize" with the actor—that is, to see things the way the actor might. The results of these studies show that "empathic" observers tend to find situational reasons for the actor's behavior to a greater extent than do observers who view the actor without special instructions. To explain nervous laughter, for example, the uninstructed observer might say the actor is "an anxious sort of person," whereas the empathic observer (and the actor himself) might say the nervous laughter was caused by the person with whom he was interacting or by the strangeness of the experimental setting.

Reasons for Actor-Observer Differences

Having established that actors and observers usually give different explanations for behavior, how are we to explain these differences? An immediate and simple answer would be to attribute these differences to nonrational, self-serving biases on the part of the actor, the observer, or both. But we've taken considerable care to point out that, except for certain special cases (such as explaining the success and failure of friends and enemies), attribution is basically a rational process. And as it turns out, actors and observers seem to differ, in large part, for rational rather than nonrational reasons. In the first place, the actor has more information available to him about his behavior in past situations than does the observer. The actor knows, in other words, how he or she usually behaves in similar and not-so-similar situations, while the observer has to infer the actor's typical behavior. In terms of Kelley's model, the actor has more consistency and distinctiveness information on which to base an attribution than does the observer. Lacking such information, the observer is more likely to generalize on the basis of one observation—to assume that if the person behaves this way now, then he probably behaves this way most of the time. Given this assumption of low distinctiveness and high consistency, a dispositional attribution seems quite rational from the observer's perspective.

In addition to having differing amounts of information about the actor's past behavior, the actor and observer differ in their perceptual information in the present. Unless there are mirrors present, it is physically impossible for the actor to watch himself when he is interacting with someone or is engaged in a task. Instead, other people or characteristics of the setting stand out in his perceptual field. But from the observer's vantage point, the actor is highly visible and tends to dominate the perceptual field. The situational cues that are important for the actor are only pieces of background information for the observer; for him, the actor occupies center stage. Actor and observer, in other words, differ in their focus of attention. While the actor is noticing and inferring things about the situation, the observer is noticing and inferring things about the actor.

However, even if the actor and the observer *did* attend to the same information, their explanation for the actor's behavior might differ anyway. There are two reasons for this; again, they are fairly rational reasons. First of all, the observer might feel that he would have behaved differently from the actor in that situation. The observer might feel that his response would have been more forceful, perhaps, or less emotional than the actor's response. If this is the case, the observer will probably consider his likely response to the situation to be more appropriate or normal than the actor's response. Thus, not seeing the logic in the actor's behavior, the observer may infer that the actor's behavior stems from unique motivations or traits. As we shall see in Chapter 4, the perception of behavioral differences between ourselves and others is often a basis for assigning traits to others—traits, unfortunately, that are often negative or derogatory.

A second reason follows from our understanding of why we bother to explain someone's behavior at all. As emphasized earlier, we endeavor to explain phenomena since a good explanation allows us to predict other phenomena that are as yet unobserved. In this light, consider the difference between dispositional and situational causes from the observer's point of view. If we see the situation as causing someone's behavior, we cannot with confidence predict the person's behavior in a different situation. But if we see the behavior as caused by a powerful disposition in the person, we can predict how the person will behave in a variety of settings, including those that are likely to involve us. In short, inferring a trait in someone else fulfills the function of attribution—it provides an explanation with considerable predictive value. Now consider attribution from the actor's point of view. Successful transaction with the world requires that the individual remain flexible and accommodating to changing circumstances. But if the individual perceived his own behavior as caused by powerful dispositions, he would in effect be saying that he is not free to approach new situations flexibly. To define oneself as invariably friendly, for example, suggests that one might smile and crack jokes while being robbed. The individual is concerned with the outcomes of his behavior and thus is likely to conceive of himself in terms of goals and values rather than in terms of response dispositions. To direct his own behavior—and later to explain it—he attends to the rewards and costs in the situation.

That individuals are willing to assign traits to other people but reluctant to do the same to themselves has been demonstrated in a study by Nisbett, Caputo, Legant, and Maracek (1973). As in many studies of person perception, subjects were asked to describe several people, including themselves, in terms of various adjectives. Each person was to be described along twenty bipolar scales—scales expressing an adjective and its opposite—such as reserved versus emotionally expressive, lenient versus firm, and honest versus dishonest. Unique to this study, however, was the inclusion of another response option following each scale: "depends on the situation." Thus, subjects could either describe a person in terms of a trait or indicate that the person's behavior regarding that trait might vary from situation to situation. Descriptions were obtained in this way from the subject for four persons (his best friend, his father, a person of the same sex whom he liked but did not know, and Walter Cronkite) and for himself. Results showed that when describing the four other people, subjects quite readily made trait judgments. But when it came to their own self-description, subjects tended often to mark "depends on the situation" rather than define themselves in terms of traits.

In sum, actors and observers differ consistently in their explanations for behavior, and they do so for fairly sound reasons. Within the limits of consensus, consistency, and distinctiveness information, observers are inclined to attribute the actor's behavior to internal causes, often inferring personality traits, while the actor himself sees his behavior as a response to circumstances. Since both the actor and the observer have a fairly rational perspective, it is difficult to label one perspective "right" and the other "wrong." Questions about accuracy can be considered, however, when we examine another difference in perspective, namely, the difference between the layman—the amateur observer of human behavior—and the psychologist—the professional.

Divergent Perspectives: Layman and Psychologist   If the individual looks for the causes of behavior in a rational, scientific manner, then the typical attributions given by the layman for behavior should be similar to the explanations offered by professional psychologists (assuming, of course, that professional psychologists are rational and scientific!). Examples from our daily lives, as well as many of the research studies cited so far, demonstrate that attributing traits to other people in order to explain their behavior is quite common. Do psychologists similarly assign traits to people in order to explain their behavior? Or are psychologists convinced that external factors—situational forces, role expectations, rewards and costs—are the important determinants of behavior?

For many years, psychologists focused almost exclusively on the use of traits to predict behavior. Personality theorists such as Gordon Allport (1937) hypothesized that traits were directly traceable to specific systems of neurons in the brain. This is about as internal as an attribution can be. Extreme internal attributions also typify the theories of Freud, Jung, Cattell, Murray, and a host of other influential psychologists. Although these theorists vary in the extent to which they see personality traits as innate versus acquired, in every case the behaviors of adults are seen as determined by their inner nature—their traits. The history of psychology, therefore, is a history of observer-like attributions.

The Psychologist's Approach

Psychologists in recent years have explicitly examined the usefulness of traits for explaining social behavior. Much of this research has focused on a behavior that is often attributed to persons, namely, anxiety. No doubt each of us has at one time or another described someone as "anxious," "tense," or "a nervous sort of person." Again, this characterization implies that in most situations this person would demonstrate greater nervousness or anxiety than would other people. Psychologists have pitted this hypothesis against an alternative hypothesis that says that anxiety is brought about by particular settings, and that the most anxious person in one set of circumstances might be the least anxious in another. In tackling this issue, psychologists have performed many studies, the designs of which are similar to the tables presented earlier in our discussion of Kelley's model of attribution. In Figure 2.4, for example, a table is presented that portrays three persons and four settings. The num bers in each division of the table represent the degree of anxiety experienced by each person in a particular setting; the higher the number, the greater the anxiety. Keep in mind, of course, that these results are imaginary.

A statistical analysis of Figure 2.4 would reveal what is apparent on inspection: that anxiety varies more between persons than it does between settings. Stated differently, the table is characterized by low consensus (within each setting the persons differ from one another in anxiety) and low distinctiveness (a

	Setting				
Person	With mother at home	With male friend at school	With employer at work	With female friend at party	Average
A	1	1	1	1	1.0
B	3	3	3	3	3.0
C	6	6	6	6	6.0
Average	3.33	3.33	3.33	3.33	3.33

Fig. 2.4   Identifying the cause of anxiety: attribution to persons.

person's anxiety doesn't change from setting to setting). If results such as these were actually obtained, one could conclude that anxiety is indeed a trait, that is, an internal characteristic of persons.

A completely different pattern of imaginary anxiety scores is portrayed in Figure 2.5. In this table, the variability in anxiety is greater between settings than it is between persons. In Kelley's terms, there is high consensus (within each setting the persons are similar to one another in anxiety) and high distinctiveness (a person's anxiety changes from setting to setting). Such results would lead to the conclusion that the cause of anxiety is external (in the setting) rather than internal (a property of the person).

Yet a third pattern of imaginary anxiety scores is portrayed in Figure 2.6. Here we see that anxiety depends on both the person and the setting. First of all, there is low consensus (within each setting the persons differ from one another), which supports the person-centered view of anxiety. And, averaging across settings, it is clear that Person A is slightly more anxious than Person B or Person C. But at the same time, the matrix is character-

	Setting				
Person	With mother at home	With male friend at school	With employer at work	With female friend at party	Average
A	1	2	5	3	2.75
B	1	2	5	3	2.75
C	1	2	5	3	2.75
Average	1.0	2.0	5.0	3.0	2.75

Fig. 2.5   Identifying the cause of anxiety: attribution to situations.

Person	Setting				
	With mother at home	With male friend at school	With employer at work	With female friend at party	Average
A	5	3	7	3	4.5
B	2	1	6	7	4.0
C	1	6	3	2	3.0
Average	2.67	3.33	5.33	4.00	3.03

Fig. 2.6   Identifying the cause of anxiety: attribution to the interaction of persons and situations.

ized by high distinctiveness—each person's degree of anxiety changes from setting to setting. And averaging across persons, note that some settings produce greater anxiety than others. Interacting with one's employer, for example, produces greater anxiety than spending time with one's mother. In this sense, the table supports the notion that anxiety is dependent on the setting. Even closer inspection of this table shows that the most anxious person in one setting is not necessarily the most anxious in another. Person A is more anxious than Person B or Person C when interacting with either his mother or his employer, but Person B is the most anxious person when talking to a female friend at a party and Person C is the most anxious when talking with a male friend. To predict anxiety, then, we would have to know the particular *combination* of person and setting, rather than either the person or the setting alone. In statistical terms, a result analogous to this is referred to as an *interaction*—the effect of one variable depends on, or interacts with, the other variable. In this case, the effect of person depends on, or interacts with, the effect of settings.

The Psychologist's Conclusions

Experimental psychologists have conducted many studies that approach the causes of social behavior in just this fashion (see a review of these studies by Bowers, 1973). Many individuals are observed in a variety of different settings or are asked to report how they typically respond in these settings. If the study is concerned with anxiety, for example, trained observers might record each person's behavior in several settings and rate him or her according to how anxious he or she was in each setting. The results of such a study are then portrayed in tables similar to those presented in Figures 2.4, 2.5, and 2.6, and a statistical analysis is performed.

The results of these studies most often resemble the pattern portrayed in Figure 2.6—the table supporting the interaction notion. While there is some variability between persons across all settings, and between settings across all persons, usually the largest source of variability can be traced to the interaction between persons and settings. This finding, repeated in many studies, suggests that the use of traits to explain a person's behavior is probably not warranted. Knowing that someone is more anxious than others in one setting does not help you predict if he or she will be similarly anxious in a different setting. This is true not only for anxiety, but for other behaviors as well. Largely because of these findings, and because of the poor ability of "personality" tests to predict actual behavior (see Bem and Allen, 1974; Mischel, 1968), experimental psychologists have become cautious about assigning traits to people. They emphasize instead the situational forces on our behavior, noting that whether we demonstrate a trait-like behavior depends on the setting.

In short, there are discrepancies between implicit psychology and the findings of experimental psychology. In our daily lives we routinely assign traits and dispositions to people in order to account for their actions. But from the perspective of many experimental psychologists, an individual's behavior can usually be traced to stimuli in the environment that affect all of us in one way or another and in varying degrees. Though each of us responds uniquely to the forces in a given situation, we all show considerable variability in even the most trait-like behaviors (anxiety, honesty, friendliness, etc.) from one situation to another. An attribution to internal factors simply reflects the observer's inability to detect subtle situational factors that direct behavior. Ideally, if an observer were experienced enough in observing others and/or had taken the right psychology courses, he or she would make internal attributions rather sparingly. In this sense, it is useful to remember that insensitivity to external forces can even lead one to attribute internal properties to inanimate objects in order to explain their "behavior". Consider, for example, the type of attributions often made by a child—a person without the benefit of experience or sophisticated knowledge. Let's say the child is walking home from school, passes next to a tall building, and notices a leaf dancing in the wind. His past experience leads him to expect things to fall down, not up or in crazy circles. And he's had no courses in meteorology generally, or wind tunnels in particular, so again he has trouble inferring the causes of the dancing leaf. Unable to detect the external force causing the movement of the leaf, the child might attribute special qualities to it; perhaps he sees it as magically alive. The leaf, after all, is overcoming gravity and seemingly directing its own motion. But of course we know better; the particular combination of external forces (wind currents) in this particular situation (an area next to a tall building) is producing the leaf's strange behavior (dancing instead of falling like most leaves do).

Of course, there are many other examples where internal attributions are made because the "real" external causes are less immediately obvious. Primitive religion is interesting in this regard since an entire culture can be built upon what is essentially a misattributed phenomenon. Imagine yourself in a dark cave about ten thousand years ago. Suddenly a strange flash of light zigzags across the sky, followed a second later by a deep rumbling sound in the sky around you. Then you notice fire in the distant forest. Soon it becomes a raging fire that threatens your safety. Knowing nothing about the causes of lightning and thunder, your natural tendency might be to attribute human or god-like qualities to the thunder and lightning. Because of their terrifying properties (wicked-looking bolts of light, ominous claps of thunder) and because of their dire effects (forest fire), they could easily be seen to represent "anger" or "vengeance." But of course you are not in a cave ten thousand years ago. And you probably have at least rudimentary knowledge of the external causes of thunder and lightning. You know this because over the years science has sensitized us to the subtle and complex pattern of causes underlying natural phenomena.

Reasons for Layman-Psychologist Differences

From the perspective of contemporary psychology, attribution to combinations of internal and external factors is the appropriate way to view behavior; a person's behavior changes considerably from one setting to another. But for the implicit psychologist who resides in a world full of other people whose behavior has important consequences for himself, attribution to internal factors alone is just as appropriate. It would be difficult indeed for any of us to respond to certain behaviors with any other than an internal attribution to the actor. Suppose you and every member of your family have just narrowly escaped serious injury by a speeding car that cut in front of you on a city street. Do you make an external attribution: "That person was responding to certain factors that everyone would respond to; the death of a loved one, perhaps, or maybe somebody offered him a million dollars to get across town in 12 minutes"? In this case, it is more likely that you would make an internal attribution, noting an analogy, perhaps, between his ancestry and that of male puppies. Internal attributions are necessary if we are to hold others accountable for their actions.

The tendency to assign traits to others, and thereby explain their behavior, reflects more than insensitivity to situational forces or a desire for restitution and vengeance. In fact, there are some rational reasons why the assignment of traits is so common. For one thing, as noted in the discussion of actor-observer differences, internal attributions quite often allow the observer to predict an actor's behavior in varied situations with greater confidence than do external attributions. Suppose, for example, that you notice someone shoplifting in a department store. If you attributed this act to the actor's basic dishonesty, you might predict that, given the chance, he would cheat on an exam, or lie to his friends. But if you attributed his behavior to extreme poverty, you would feel less confident of these predictions. Given the importance of predictability in our dealings with others, it is not surprising that we look for characteristics and motives in people to account for their behavior.

Assigning a trait to someone also makes sense when you consider the well-established relationship between expectancy and behavior. If we expect a certain behavior or attitude from someone, we often act in such a way so as to make the person do or say what we expected. For example, if we expect to be treated with hostility by someone it is unlikely that we will greet him or her with wet, warm kisses; instead, the chances are that we will adopt a defensive posture, indicating quite clearly that we won't put up with much. Such a posture, in turn, is likely to bring about the very thing we expected—perhaps irritation at first, turning to anger and hostility. This behavior thus confirms our expectation, and hence our trait attribution. Self-fulfilling prophecies like this are common in social relationships; we will consider them in greater detail in Chapter 4.

It should be kept in mind as well that we usually see others in narrow contexts. We simply do not interact with or observe most people in a great variety of situations. Even observations of one's parents are limited; one may rarely see them in other than family-related settings. And, of course, within a situation, an individual not only behaves consistently, he also behaves somewhat differently from others in that situation—this is implied directly by the interaction notion that was portrayed in Figure 2.6. And as we can recall from Kelley's model, low consensus leads, logically, to an internal attribution. Imagine the traits a child might attribute to his father, for example. At home, where most of the father-child contact occurs, Dad may appear strong and dominating, perhaps even intimidating family members once in a while. On the basis of observations such as these, it is quite rational for the child to attribute certain qualities to Dad, such as toughness, dominance, and maybe even the capacity for violence. Of course, at work he may be just the opposite—gentle and submissive, apologizing to the janitor for using the wastebasket. But unless the child sees him in that and other settings, he or she has no reason *not* to attribute Dad's at-home behavior to traits. In short, because we typically see others in a limited number of settings, we are not aware of the variability in their behavior across settings. Lacking distinctiveness information, then, we base our attributions, quite rationally, on consensus information. And since individuals are likely to differ from one another in the same situation (i.e., there is likely to be low consensus), we tend to attribute traits to them.

For understandable reasons, then, the implicit psychologist over-attributes behavior to internal causes. And because we see behavior as caused by traits or dispositions in a person, we hold others responsible for the consequences of their acts. Not only is this reasonable from the attributor's point of view, it is advantageous for society as a whole. If people were not made to feel personally responsible for their behavior, excuses or rationalizations could easily be invented to justify even the most destructive behavior. It may be that aggression is a "natural" response to frustrating circumstances, for example, but knowing that others would blame you, not the situation, if you reacted to a two-hour traffic jam by pummeling the nearest pedestrian, is likely to prevent such an act. Paradoxically, then, it is the layman's relative insensitivity to situational forces that keeps most of our behavior within conventional moral standards, requiring us to resist impulses that psychologists might see as natural responses to external stimuli. Given the psychologist-layman difference in attribution, it is not surprising that psychologists are often excluded from juries in criminal trials; because of their sensitivity to situational forces, they are sometimes reluctant to cast their votes against a defendant.

Of course, many people besides psychologists feel that much so-called deviant behavior is not a manifestation of sin or weakness of character, but rather is an inevitable response to intolerable conditions such as poverty and inequity. Well-intentioned liberals, either because of their learned awareness of societal forces or because of their capacity for empathy (adopting the perspective of the actor), blame crime, drug abuse, and violence on the oppressive and alienating conditions of inner cities. This is a sensitive interpretation, and to a very real extent it is probably true. But at the same time, such an interpretation may serve to aggravate rather than relieve the problem, particularly when it is communicated to the "victims" of those forces, since it amounts to giving justification for behavior that might otherwise be inhibited. In the final analysis, it may be that the feeling of personal responsibility is simply an illusion (see B. F. Skinner, 1971); nonetheless, it seems to be a useful illusion as far as social control is concerned.

the implicit psychologist

In answering the question, "why do people do what they do?", the implicit psychologist usually is quite rational, demonstrating fairly complex thought processes. However, it is only after years of maturation that a person is capable of highly sophisticated thinking.

This implies directly that children perceive the causes of behavior differently from adults. On the other hand, it should not
be inferred that there are no common aspects to the ways children and adults explain behavior. Cognitive development is an
orderly transition; as we shall see, this is also the case for developmental changes in attribution.

Developmental Changes In 1932, Jean Piaget conducted a series of simple
yet intriguing studies of the child's moral judgments. As we
have already noted, a person's judgment of whether a particular
behavior is good or bad depends in large part upon his perception of the causes of that behavior. Thus, studies of the child's
developing moral judgments tell us something about his developing perception of causes.

Piaget noted a number of interesting changes that occur in the
developing child's ideas about what is moral. In one study, he
gave children the job of determining which of two little girls,
Mary or Elizabeth, was naughtier. Piaget described the two
children in stories something like this:

1. There once was a little girl called Mary. She wanted to help
her mother set the dinner table one evening, so she started to
carry a big tray of cups to the dining room. As she went through
the door, she lost her balance and dropped all the cups, breaking
most of them.
2. Elizabeth was a little girl who went to the kitchen one day to
get a cookie. Since she didn't want her mother to know, she
climbed on top of the counter very quietly. Just as she was
reaching for the cookie jar, she brushed a cup from the shelf and
it fell to the floor and broke.

Very young children thought that Mary was naughtier—she

broke all those cups; older children thought that Elizabeth was naughtier—she was trying to steal a cookie. Apparently, the very young child pays special attention to the objective seriousness of the act—the damage. The older child notes instead that the individual's intentions are of prime importance.

Piaget noted the same kind of developmental sequence in other types of moral judgments. He found, for example, that young children think a tall tale such as "Your front yard is knee-deep in raisin pudding" is much more serious and punishable than a white lie like "I just love your taste in ties." The child focuses on the "size" of the lie and ignores whether or not the liar intended his lie to deceive. From our lofty perches as adults, we can see the clear absurdity of such judgments. It matters a great deal what a person's intentions are. If someone says "I am now going to dislocate your shoulder," your major concern is whether he *means* to do it. The young child, in attending only to the consequences of a moral action, is missing the important cue of intention. The development of the ability to attribute intentions to others, and of the ability to consider such internal attributions in making moral judgments, is a major addition to the child's understanding of his social world.

Other researchers since Piaget have also been concerned with the development of attribution processes. One study by Weiner and Peter (1973) is particularly notable because it shows that some types of attributions do *not* change with development. These researchers pointed out that the distinction between *intentions* and *consequences* in moral situations is similar to the distinction between *effort* and *performance* in achievement situations. Very simply, when a person is engaged in an achievement task, the "goodness" or "badness" of his actions can be determined either according to how hard he tried or how successful he was. His effort or trying is an internal attribution made by an observer, and therefore is much like an internal attribution of intention. His success or failure in the task is an objectively observable event, and therefore is much like the consequence of a moral act. If these two systems of judgment are in fact quite similar, then we would expect that judgment of achievement by young children would be based on actual performance, while judgment of achievement by older children would be based on perceived effort. This was not the case. Weiner and Peter examined the achievement judgments made by over 300 children ranging from four to eighteen years of age and found that both younger and older children pay much more attention to performance than to effort. The conclusion we can draw from this study is that young children, older children, and even adults judge achievement according to success or failure. They ignore effort in making their judgments. Thus, whether you win or lose seems to be more important than how you play the game.

Individual Differences

The adult, with his or her complex perception of causes, has experienced many years of cognitive maturation. If this development has not gone wrong somewhere along the way, the mature individual possesses the capacity to perceive the causes of behavior in a logical manner. In spite of the logical processes underlying attribution, however, it is not uncommon for two individuals to explain the same event in vastly different ways. As pointed out earlier, in many cases these differences are attributable to the different perspectives held by actors and observers. But quite often the disagreement is not between actor and observer, but between two observers of the same behavior. To explain such disagreements, psychologists have attempted to isolate basic differences between individuals that are relevant to attribution. We shall examine two such differences, one involving attributors and one involving the targets of attribution. Differences among attributors can be traced to a personality variable that was "discovered" fairly recently. The difference among targets can be traced to a more familiar variable with a considerably longer history; namely, the difference between males and females.

Internal Versus External Locus of Control

Earlier in this chapter, we argued that the use of traits to characterize individuals often reflects insensitivity to external forces. Internal attributions are useful from the layperson's perspective, but to the psychologist—the professional observer of the human condition—the use of traits to explain behavior rarely leads to successful theories. This does not mean, however, that psychologists have not devoted considerable time and energy to the task of identifying basic dispositional differences between people. But the effort has generated few significant variables. One personality variable that has met with success is one that, somewhat ironically, is related to the attribution process. This variable, labeled *internal versus external locus of control* by Julian Rotter (1966), refers to two contrasting views of causality that people hold. Some people, those labeled *internal,* believe that the outcomes they experience—their successes and failures, pleasures and pains—are a result of their own actions. Other people, identified as *external,* believe that their outcomes depend very little on their own acts, but rather are attributable to the actions of powerful others or to chance. The internal person feels that he is able to effect changes in his life; the external person is fatalistic, feeling powerless to determine anything of real consequence. Of course, most people are somewhere between the two extremes; the average individual recognizes both the external and the internal causes of his outcomes.

This basic difference in attributional tendencies has been shown to have important effects on the way people think and behave. Consider, for example, the way each type of person—internal or external—might react to succeeding at a particular task. If you asked each one of them whether he would succeed the next time he tried, what would he say? According to a study by Battle and Rotter (1963), the internal and external would make strikingly different predictions. These researchers found that children classified as internal reacted to success by predicting that success would occur again, and reacted to failure by predicting more failure. Externals, in contrast, expected that after a success, they would fail, and that after a failure, they would succeed. These two different strategies seem to be based on two different views of the world. The internal individual behaves as though the world is predictable and stable, and as though his success or failure is determined by stable factors. If he finds that he is good at something, he predicts that he will succeed at that task in the future; if he experiences failure, he decides to avoid that situation because he expects to fail again. The external person, however, behaves as though the world were a set of dice where successes and failures happen by chance. In a sense, he follows what is known as the "gambler's fallacy," the idea that the occurrence of a particular chance event lessens the probability that that event will occur again. So, given a successful experience, the external person feels that the dice will not roll "success" again; given a failure, he predicts that his luck will change.

Under certain circumstances, internals and externals also differ in their attributions for the behavior of others. This difference between internals and externals is apparent when they attempt to change someone's attitude about something. When the internal successfully influences someone, he is eager to take credit for this success since it reinforces his internal locus of control. He should feel particularly competent if he judges the person he persuaded to be bright and therefore not easily persuaded. On the other hand, when the internal fails to influence someone, this is threatening to his internal orientation; with enough experiences of failure, the internal may come to feel that he is unable to effect changes in his environment. One way of defending against this threat is to attribute low intelligence to the unpersuaded other—to say "the person simply wasn't bright enough to understand what I had to say." In short, an internal should attribute greater intelligence to someone he can persuade than to someone who resists his influence attempts.

Considering how externals view themselves in relation to the world, just the opposite prediction seems reasonable for them. The external doesn't expect his behavior to have much effect on anyone; he sees little relation between his acts and their effects. If his behavior does have an effect, he is likely to explain it in a

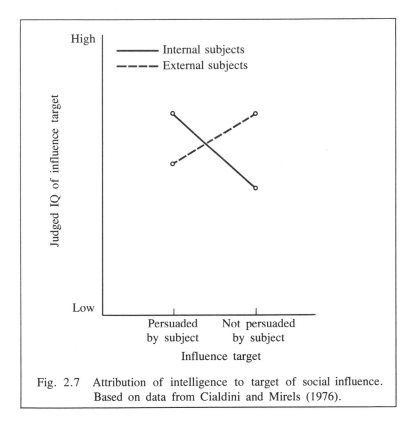

Fig. 2.7   Attribution of intelligence to target of social influence. Based on data from Cialdini and Mirels (1976).

way that is consistent with his expectations. So if he successfully influences someone, he may attribute low intelligence to
the person—"it doesn't take much to change that dummy's
mind." On the other hand, if he fails in his attempt to influence
someone, there is no need to derogate the intelligence of the
person; his expectancies have simply been confirmed. In short,
an external should attribute less intelligence to someone he can
persuade than to someone who is unaffected by his influence attempts. A study by Cialdini and Mirels (1976) demonstrates this
very difference between internals and externals. As can be seen
in Figure 2.7, internals in this study attributed higher intelligence to a person they could persuade than to someone they
couldn't persuade, while the opposite was the case for externals.

Male and Female
It's no secret that males and females differ in ways other than
the obvious anatomical ones. Starting early in infancy, boys and
girls behave differently, largely because they are expected to
behave differently. Parents have clear ideas about what is desirable, or at least tolerable, behavior for a "little man," and this
differs in essential ways from what is considered right for a "little lady." Of course, difference in and of itself is not bad; one
way of behaving is not necessarily superior to another. But as it
turns out, the expected behaviors for a "well-adjusted" female,
at least in our culture, hardly represent the *human* ideal. Males
are expected to be active, logical, independent, and forceful—
traits associated with positive mental health. By contrast,
females are expected to be passive, emotional, dependent, and
submissive—characteristics we also admire in a pampered pet
poodle. Of course, this description is exaggerated; in real life,
females can deviate greatly from the feminine stereotype,
realize successes in "masculine" areas, and still be regarded as
normal. And there is evidence that the stereotypes are beginning
to fade in our society, with both males and females feeling freer

to express themselves in different ways.

Despite the changes, however, the effects of female socialization continue to manifest themselves, often in subtle ways. One such way is in attribution—specifically, in the attributions for success and failure. Several studies in the past few years have converged on a somewhat dismaying finding: successful performance by a male is typically attributed to ability, but a similar success by a female is more often attributed to luck or motivation. Evidence suggests that both males and females share low expectations for female success in almost every endeavor, from simple games to life-long careers. And, as indicated earlier in this chapter, when an actor's performance violates the observer's expectations for performance, the observer is likely to attribute the performance to variable or external factors rather than to ability.

Consider a study by Deaux and Emswiller (1974), for example. Males and females first overheard either a male or female perform considerably above average on a perceptual discrimination task. They then were asked to indicate whether the testtaker's success was due to his or her ability, to luck, or to some combination of the two. Analysis of subjects' responses showed that ability was perceived to play a larger role in the males' successes than in identical performances by females. Furthermore, this pattern of results obtained for both male and female subjects. Apparently, both sexes employ a double standard when it comes to explaining their successes: if a male succeeds, it's skill; if a female succeeds, it's luck.

Of course, it could be argued that unexpected success by a female in a one-hour laboratory session is easy to explain away as the result of luck. But what of female success in a profession? It would seem difficult to attribute the success of, say, a respected and successful female doctor to luck. A recent study by Feldman-Summers and Kiesler (1974), however, shows that there is a bias against crediting successful professional women with high ability. In their study, male and female undergraduates read a description of a highly successful physician. Among other accomplishments, the physician was involved in community activities to improve health care, had an expanding practice, and had just been named Doctor of the Year in Santa Clara, California. In some of the descriptions, however, the physician had taken over the practice from the physician's father, himself a highly regarded doctor. The descriptions differed in another way: the name of the physician was either "Mark Greer" or "Marcia Greer." After reading the description, subjects were asked to indicate why the physician was successful. Attributions could be made to ability as a doctor, motivation to be successful as a doctor, the ease of the goal, or good luck. Results showed that when the physician assumed the father's practice, male subjects attributed the male physician's success to ability, but the female physician's success to ease of the goal—after all, Daddy gave her a practice! For both male and female subjects, there was a tendency to attribute less ability but more motivation (effort) to the successful female than to the successful male. Apparently, as the authors contend, those who are number two try harder. Or, stated differently, perhaps those who try harder are number two.

Summary   Like the psychologist, the layman attempts to understand and predict behavior. Central to this endeavor is the attribution of causality. To determine whether a behavior was internally or externally caused, the individual processes a considerable amount of information—the consensus, consistency, and distinctiveness of the act. Even if such information is absent or conflicting, the individual still may confidently explain an act if it violates his expectancies for behavior in that situation. Confident attributions also may be made if the act in question has personal relevance for him or if his attention is focused on a plausible causal agent.

Attributions for success and failure are of particular interest. Through the processing of consensus, consistency, and distinctiveness information, the individual isolates causes that vary not only in the degree to which they are internal or external to the actor, but also in their stability over time. Despite reliable information to the contrary, sometimes success and failure are explained in a self-serving manner. People explain their own performance, as well as that of their friends, by ascribing internal causation for success and external causation for failure.

Because they have different perspectives, actors and observers sometimes perceive different reasons for the actor's behavior. While actors typically find situational causes for their behavior, observers are more likely to infer traits in the actor to account for his actions. Another significant difference in perspective is that between the layperson and the psychologist. Although the layperson is scientific in his approach to attribution, he typically does not observe the actor in a wide variety of settings. Hence, he is less likely than the psychologist to attribute behavior to situational factors or to person-situation interactions. Laypersons are biased toward trait explanations for another reason: if a person is made to feel personally responsible for his actions (because of an internal attribution), he is likely to resist situational forces that would produce antisocial behavior.

Because attribution involves sophisticated theorizing, there are developmental changes in attribution. The young child does not consider whether an act was internally or externally caused when judging its goodness or badness; the consequences of the act are all that matter. For the adult, the causes of the act— whether it was intended by the actor or caused by factors beyond his control—are more important than the consequences of the act. When it comes to achievement, however, adults as well as children seem to be more concerned with outcomes than with causation when judging an actor; winning or losing is what counts.

Mature adults differ from one another in their characteristic perspective on causality, particularly when it comes to explaining their own outcomes. Some individuals favor internal attributions; they see their outcomes as due to their ability or effort. In contrast, other people are inclined toward external attributions for their successes and failures. The sex of the actor also affects causal attributions. If a male succeeds in some endeavor, whether a simple task or a life-long career, ability is perceived to be the cause. But if a female succeeds in the same endeavor, luck or effort is seen as the major reason.

chapter three

In 1920, L. Hamilton McCormick published a book entitled *Characterology: An Exact Science*. In it, he described the methods by which an individual's character could be determined from facial features, coloring, head shape, and body shape. He noted, for example, that thick, bushy eyebrows are a sign of a severe, uncompromising nature, that red hair denotes sensitivity and vivacity, and that small ears indicate a poor memory, little musical ability, and a very short life. Since his statements about personality were not based based on scientific investigation, but were drawn from his experiences with different people, his book is an excellent example of an implicit personality theory made explicit.

The originators of the term "implicit personality theory," Jerome Bruner and Renato Tagiuri (1954), used it to refer to the idea that each individual has his or her own theory of what people are like. In the last chapter, we pointed out some of the processes whereby an individual's implicit motivation theory is used to determine the causes of behavior. But the implicit theorist does not just see a person as a bundle of unrelated causes. Instead, people typically see other people as having *personalities*, entire sets of enduring dispositional or physical qualities that determine many of their behaviors. Implicit personality theory, then, is the individual's theory of how the attributes of a person are related to each other. McCormick's notion that "small ears indicate a poor memory" is just such a relationship.

In this chapter, we will focus on four aspects of implicit personality theory. The first section will center on how information about other people is *selected*. Since there are many different facets of a person's ap-

implicit personality theory

Impression Formation

pearance and behavior that might be considered as contributing to the individual's personality, it is necessary to know how the implicit theorist selects certain kinds of information while neglecting other kinds. The second section covers the processes by which information about personality is *generated* by implicit theory. The implicit theorist often looks at one piece of information (red hair, for example), and then infers other characteristics (such as a hot temper) on the basis of that information. The third section discusses how information is *organized* in an implicit personality theory: how all the separate pieces of information, selected as well as generated, are related to one another in an overall pattern. The final aspect to be discussed is how conflicting pieces of information are *combined;* for example, when an implicit theorist meets someone who is both friendly and conceited, he tends to resolve the conflicting characteristics into a single, unified impression of the person. In discussing all four of these components of implicit personality theory, we will be talking about processes that are analogous to tasks undertaken by a scientific psychologist. The scientist makes some basic observations (selects information) and develops hypotheses (generates information) on the basis of these observations. He also develops a theory (organizes information) that ties together his observations and hypotheses. The scientist's theory, however, may be hard-pressed to account for certain observations; when this happens, he must do some fancy theoretical work to reconcile the new findings (combines information).

Selecting Information   Observing a person is much like listening to a radio. Usually, instead of listening to every station on the entire dial, you pick a few that you like and listen to them most of the time. When you observe a person, you also tend to tune in only a small part of the spectrum of information available to you. Here, for example, is a description of a friend given by Sara, a senior in high school:

Randy is a rather tall, nice-looking boy who is immature and very aggressive. He is constantly hitting me or grabbing my things to get attention. He is very nice about it, but he can get obnoxious in a crowd and the whole thing can get very embarrassing. I ignore him and he does it even more.

Obviously, Randy has many more qualities that Sara failed to mention. In forming her impression of Randy's personality, she has tuned in to one set of related characteristics, and has tuned out many other possible kinds of information.

As we pointed out in Chapter 2, one major way in which information is selected is through the processes of attribution. Much of the actor's behavior is not particularly useful to the observer in his attempt to determine the dispositions of the actor. Behavior that is in accord with situational expectations, for example, or acts that have little relevance for the observer, are given little attention and are soon forgotten. The observer selects those pieces of information about the actor that might prove useful in explaining his behavior. To some extent, then, the selection of information is determined by the actor, his particular actions, the effects of his acts, and the situation in which the acts occur. This is not the full story, however; the selection of information is not entirely dependent upon the person being perceived. Would the high school principal have written the same description of Randy that Sara did? Certainly not. The realization that different observers may select different information about the same actor requires that we consider the impact of the observer's unique cognitive structure and his particular situation upon the selection of information.

Observer's Cognitive Structure

A classic study performed by Sanford Dornbusch and his colleagues (1965) demonstrates that the observer's unique cognitive structure is an important component in the information selection process. These researchers interviewed a large number of children from the ages of nine to eleven who were all at camp together one summer. Taking each child aside for an hour or so, the interviewers asked the child to describe two of the other children at camp. Later on, recordings of the interviews were analyzed to find out what kinds of things the children had said about each other. Sixty-eight different categories of statements (such as "age," "race," "mental ability," and "generosity") were used to classify everything the children had said.

Dornbusch and his co-workers then performed an interesting analysis. First, they calculated the amount of overlap in the use of categories between descriptions of the same child given by two different children. If, for example, both children noted that the child they were describing was the son of a doctor, an instance of category overlap was scored. Across all the pairs of descriptions, is was found that there was 45 percent overlap in categories of information: two children describing the same child talked about the same things 45 percent of the time. The researchers then calculated the category overlap between descriptions of two different children made by the same child. It was found that categories overlapped 57 percent in these pairs of descriptions; one child describing two others mentioned the same kinds of information about them 57 percent of the time.

The conclusion to be reached from these findings is simple and striking. Apparently, the selection of information about a person depends more on the perceiver than on the person being perceived. Two people perceiving one person agree about his important attributes only 45 percent of the time, whereas one person perceiving two different people selects the same attributes in each person 57 percent of the time. Each perceiver selects a consistent set of categories of information in each person he attempts to understand. Every time he meets someone new, instead of just noticing the particularly outstanding features or behaviors of that person, he also notices whether the person has a certain set of qualities that he looks for in everyone.

These frequently selected kinds of information about people are called *general attributes* (Wegner, 1977). A general attribute is one that the implicit psychologist notices in many different people; in contrast, a specific attribute is one that he selects in only one or a few people. For most observers, an attribute such as "intelligence" is probably general, in that each observer typically makes an estimate of the brightness or dullness of each person he meets. Attributes such as "the ability to make chocolate pudding," on the other hand, are likely to be specific for the observer. Only a few observers—perhaps managers of restaurants serving pudding—would frequently select this information. And even then they would only do it when hiring kitchen help.

Specific and general attributes differ in a very significant way. Because a specific attribute is used to characterize only a few people, it is of no use in comparing a wide assortment of people. Suppose an observer, Charlie, has a specific attribute, "provides money," which he employs to judge only two people, his mother and father. Though he can distinguish between Mom (soft touch) and Dad (blood out of a turnip), he cannot compare Mom and Dad with others. If different attributes were always used for judging different people, comparing people would be like comparing apples and campaign slogans. Fortunately, this is not the case; the individual has general attributes at his disposal, and can thus compare many different people according to common criteria. A general attribute—"considerate," for example—is a quality held in varying degrees by practically everyone the individual judges. The individual can therefore assess the relative considerateness of most of the people he encounters.

Wegner (1977) has demonstrated that these two kinds of attributes, specific and general, reflect different amounts of judgmental *articulation*. Articulation is the number of intervals that can be discriminated along a dimension (Bieri et al., 1966). Black-white judgments are not articulated. An articulated judgment is one in which the objects being judged are assigned to intervals along a dimension such as black, dark grey, medium grey, light grey, white. Judgments of specific attributes tend to be unarticulated; a person either has or does not have the attribute. Judgments of general attributes, in contrast, tend to be articulated. The observer can assess *how much* of the attribute a person has.

In this regard, it is interesting to note that young children typically use specific attributes in describing other people, and that the proportion of general attributes employed to describe others increases as the child grows older. Initially, the child notices the unusual things that are specific to each person he encounters. But eventually the child develops the ability to think about people in terms of the same general attributes, and in so doing, he becomes more capable of making fine discriminations among people. Perhaps as Charlie matures, for example, his "provides money" attribute will change from a specific to a general one; in addition to Mom and Dad, various friends, lovers, and bankers will be discriminated in terms of their willingness to provide money. By adulthood, the person's cognitive structure for selecting information about people is both simple and complex. It is simple in that the same kinds of information are sought in each experience with a new person. Rather than being sensitive to all the unique features of a person, we look only for those attributes that permit us to compare him with everyone else. At the same time, however, this apparent simplicity provides the potential for more complex judgments about others. The greater articulation of general attributes allows the adult to make precise differentiations among persons.

Situational influences
Although the observer's implicit personality theory does provide a rather stable perspective from which people can be viewed, it is also true that the observer's perspective can change

as his situation changes. Information is not only selected differently by different observers, but is also selected differently by the same observer on different occasions. Imagine, for instance, the kinds of information you might select about someone you meet in your living room as opposed to the information you would select if you were to meet the person in your shower stall. Your impressions of the same person would be different because of your own circumstances. Indeed, it has been found that both the content and the articulation of information selected can depend on the observer's situation.

Changes in information content were found in an ingenious experiment conducted by Seymour and Norma Feshbach (1963). Two groups of boys at a YMCA were asked to make personality judgments of men and boys. The subjects were shown facial photos of each individual and were asked to rate the person on a series of descriptive scales. For one of the groups of boys, this was all that occurred; they were ushered into the experimental room, given their instructions, allowed to make the judgments, and ushered out. For the other group of boys, the situation was arranged differently. As they were entering the experimental room, the experimenter commented that there were two phases to the experiment, one involving judgments of pictures, and another having "something to do with the equipment over in the corner." The equipment consisted of a black stool draped with wires, a bank of impressive electrical gadgetry, and, near the stool, a long hypodermic needle placed conspicuously on a white napkin. As the subjects were given their instructions and began to make their judgments, the experimenter—in a white lab coat—slowly and deliberately filled the hypodermic with a milky fluid. All this was arranged to arouse fear in the subjects. The experimenters wanted to know how fear arousal affected the selection of personality information.

Compared with the personality judgments made by the first

group of boys, the judgments made by the fear-aroused group were quite unusual. When judging the pictures of other boys, subjects in this group more often said that the boys they observed looked "scared" and "unhappy." Apparently, their fear-arousing situation affected the content of the information they selected. They believed that the boys they were observing had the same feelings they did. When this group made judgments of men, however, their impressions differed from those of the first group in another way. The fear-aroused subjects felt that the men were more likely to be "bad" and "cruel." They attributed qualities to the men that could be seen as causes for their own feelings of fear. This experiment shows, then, that the kinds of information an observer selects can be affected by the situation he is in, as well as by the type of person he is observing in that situation.

The observer's situation not only affects the kind of information that is selected, but the amount of information as well. The amount of information an observer selects is reflected in the articulation of his or her judgments of people. Unarticulated, either-or judgments ("she is fat," "he is short") convey much less information than articulated, dimensional judgments ("she weighs 162 pounds," "he is four feet, nine inches tall"). A study by Vallacher (1976) has demonstrated that the articulation of an observer's judgments can change depending on his situation. Vallacher attempted to simulate a basic element of many situations in which we observe others—the awareness that we are being observed in return. In a typical interaction between two people, each person observes and tries to form an impression of the other person. Each person, then, is not only an observer, but an object of observation as well. Does the awareness that we are being observed affect our ability to select information about other people? It seems likely that being observed produces a certain amount of self-consciousness, anxiety, and apprehension. Under these conditions, we might pay less attention to the other person, selecting only a limited amount of information about him.

To test the validity of this reasoning, subjects in this study were assigned to either a self-conscious condition or a non–self-conscious condition. All the subjects viewed five short videotapes, each of which presented a different person being interviewed for a job. After observing each job interview, the subjects rated the interviewee on each of twenty descriptive scales (such as "competence," "aloofness," and so on). The subjects in the self conscious condition were told that, in addition to making these judgments, they themselves would be videotaped as they watched the job interviews. It was explained that for purposes of another study, their nonverbal behavior—facial expressions, body movements, etc.—would be recorded by two TV cameras. Thus, while they were observing each interviewee, they were aware that they themselves were being observed.

The manipulation of self-consciousness made quite a difference. Compared with the subjects who observed without being observed themselves, the self-conscious subjects exhibited less articulation in their ratings of the interviewees. On a rating scale such as "competence," for example, the self-conscious subjects tended to rate each interviewee as either very competent or very incompetent—a categorical, either-or judgment. The non–self-conscious subjects were more likely to use many intervals along the "competence" dimension, assigning each interviewee a different degree of competence. Apparently, the awareness of being observed can reduce the amount of information we attend to in someone, and this can prevent us from effectively discriminating between different people. Imagine how you might feel, for example, upon entering a party that has been going on for some time. The room becomes quiet; all eyes are on you. It is unlikely that you will note a great deal of information about each of the people present. Even if each person wore a different funny hat, they would all appear to be the same because you would be too conscious of how you appear to them to discriminate effectively among them.

In summarizing our comments about the selection of information, there are three important points to keep in mind. First, the particular kinds of information selected are determined more by the observer than by the person being observed; the observer's unique implicit personality theory determines the intake of information. Second, the attributes of others that the observer selects may differ in their generality and articulation; categorical, either-or judgments are made with respect to specific attributes, whereas more articulated judgments are made with respect to general attributes. And, finally, an individual's implicit personality theory is sensitive to many external influences; both the kind of information and the amount (articulation) of information selected can be affected by situational changes.

Generating Information

Many times it is necessary to make educated guesses about people. Suppose, for example, that a young man comes to your door collecting donations for a charitable organization. You have never met him before and therefore have no idea whether he is a trustworthy individual—someone you could depend on to turn your donation over to the charity. But you do have some information about him. Suppose the man were wearing silvered sunglasses, black leather pants, and holding a riding crop in his teeth. Though none of this evidence is directly related to his level of trustworthiness, it is likely that you would send him away. Your decision to do so would be based on an *inference* about his personality.

Inferences

That people do make inferences about one another has been

demonstrated in a variety of experiments. A study by McKeachie (1952), for instance, was designed to find out if the wearing of lipstick by a college female would affect college males' impressions of her personality. Six males were asked to interview each of six females; for each male interviewer, three of the women wore lipstick and three did not. Each of the females wore lipstick for three of the interviews and did not do so for the other three. After the males filled out a series of personality ratings of the females, they were asked what things had influenced their ratings. Although all of them mentioned the womens' answers to questions and the topics discussed, and some of them mentioned clothing and speech, none of them mentioned lipstick. Yet when the ratings were analyzed, it was found that the females wearing lipstick were rated as more frivolous, more talkative, more anxious, less conscientious, and more likely to have a marked interest in the opposite sex than females without lipstick. Since the same group of females was rated in each case, we must conclude that the male interviewers made inferences about their personalities on the basis of lipstick.

In another study dealing with perceptions of women, a different kind of inference was examined. Goldberg, Gottesdiener, and Abramson (1975) showed five-by-seven-inch black and white glossies of thirty different women to a group of subjects and asked the subjects to identify which of the women were supporters of the women's liberation movement. When subjects chose the fifteen women they believed were feminists, they typically chose the least attractive women in the group. Their judgments reflected the underlying inference "feminists are ugly." Since this is a shocking put-down of the women's movement, the researchers decided to find out if it was indeed true. They asked the thirty women whose photos had been used to rate their own enthusiasm for the feminist movement, and, in addition, asked a group of people to judge the physical attractiveness of each woman's photo. The physical attractiveness ratings of the actual feminists were no different from the ratings of nonfeminists. Thus, while people do tend to infer that feminists are unattractive, there is no basis in reality for such an inference.

One way to interpret these findings—that observers often make far-reaching inferences on the basis of minimal information about another person—is to suggest that each observer has expectations about how characteristics are related in other people. This notion was the major principle in Bruner and Tagiuri's (1954) original definition of implicit personality theory. They reasoned that the implicit theorist sees certain personality traits as related and other traits as unrelated. An implicit personality theory is the entire pattern of expected relationships. Once the observer has selected some types of information about a person, he can construct an impression of the whole person through inferences based on expected relationships. This portion of the impression is, as we have said, an "educated guess."

Guesswork is at its maximum when we have only a little information about a person. It has been found that the strength of inferences is greater when the observer is rating strangers than when he is rating familiar individuals (Koltuv, 1962). Faced with a complete stranger, the observer must fill in many gaps in his conception of the person by making frequent and often extreme inferences from relatively little actual information. In rating a familiar person, on the other hand, the observer has much more knowledge about the actual attributes of the person and so relies less heavily on predictions and more heavily on solid observations. The individual's conceptions of familiar persons are more highly developed and refined, whereas his conceptions of unfamiliar persons are simple generalizations from his past experiences.

Central Traits
What kinds of information about a person would lead an ob-

server to make extreme inferences? A classic investigation by Solomon Asch (1946) was one of the first to address this question. His subjects were asked to form impressions of a person based on very little information—a list of traits. Their task was to read the trait list, write a paragraph or so describing their impressions, and then select from a long list of pairs of opposite traits (such as wise-foolish) the ones that would best characterize the person. Different groups of subjects were given different initial trait lists. One group, for instance, was asked to describe a person who is intelligent, skillful, industrious, cold, determined, practical, and cautious. Another group was asked to describe a person who is intelligent, skillful, industrious, warm, determined, practical, and cautious. Since the only difference between lists was the substitution of "warm" for "cold," Asch reasoned that any difference between impressions would reflect subjects' inferences based on the "warm-cold" trait.

The impact of these different lists on subjects' impressions was substantial. The "warm" person was seen as more generous, good-natured, popular, wise, happy, and imaginative than the "cold" person. Of course, some of these differences reflect similarities in the meanings of the trait names; "warm" is similar in meaning to good-natured, for example. But other differences, such as in wisdom or imaginativeness, are not traceable to similarity in meaning. Instead, such differences seem to reflect major inferential leaps made by the subjects.

Asch then conducted another study in which the words "polite" and "blunt" were substituted for "warm" and "cold" in the trait lists. The differences in impressions between these two lists were much less pronounced than the differences generated by the "warm-cold" lists. On the basis of this finding, Asch suggested that some attributes (such as warm-cold) are *central* to impression formation while others (such as polite-blunt) are *peripheral*. Observers make more extreme inferences on the basis of central traits than on the basis of peripheral traits. Although this distinction is helpful, Asch offered little in the way of explanation for this difference. What is it about a central trait that causes the observer to make extreme inferences?

One characteristic of central traits that helps to account for their importance is their evaluative nature. Over a half-century ago, Edward Thorndike (1920) commented on the importance of evaluation in judging persons. He noted that when observers made judgments of people, their ratings of persons on many different attributes tended to be related. It was as if the observer saw a strong relationship among traits such as intelligence, friendliness, honesty, happiness, competence, trustworthiness, ambitiousness, and so on. Thorndike did not believe that these relationships really existed and suggested instead that observers were susceptible to a *halo effect*. Once the observer perceives someone as having any good or positive trait, he sees that person as more likely to possess many other good or positive traits. Similarly, when someone is seen as having a negative trait, his "halo" disappears, and he is seen as foolish, dishonest, lazy, unhappy, and probably surrounded by a swarm of flying pests. The halo effect, then, describes the tendency of an observer to rate other people in accordance with his evaluation of them.

From this perspective, the centrality of "warm-cold" is due to the strong evaluation that it implies. The inferences that subjects made from "warm" (generosity, good-naturedness, popularity, wisdom, and so on) are all positive in evaluation. Inferences the subjects made from "polite" were also positive, but were not so numerous or extreme. Since "he is warm" seems to be a more positive statement about a person than "he is polite," and since "he is cold" seems more negative than "he is blunt," the centrality of "warm-cold" can be traced directly to the strong evaluation of a person that the words "warm" and "cold" call forth.

Another reason for the centrality of certain attributes has to do with their *stability*. In Chapter 2 we introduced the *stable-variable* distinction. Some internal attributes—ability, for example—are perceived to be *stable* over time, while other internal attributes, such as effort or concentration, are thought to be *variable*, or likely to fluctuate over time. Gifford (1975) reasoned that perhaps the central-peripheral dimension reflects this stable-variable distinction. To test this idea, he asked subjects to rate a variety of traits according to their stability over time and across situations. In an analysis of these ratings, he found that some attributes were considered to be very stable and dispositional, while others were considered quite fleeting and changeable. Later on, he asked another group of subjects to make inferences about persons described by lists of either stable or unstable attributes. The stable attributes included words such as "intelligent," "dominating," and "warm"; the unstable attributes included terms like "happy," "restless," and "dissatisfied." It was found that stable attributes were much more central than unstable attributes, in that subjects made stronger inferences from them. It seems, then, that another reason for the centrality of certain attributes (such as warm and cold) is that they imply lasting, dispositional qualities in a person. Suppose you observe someone accepting a glass of water from someone and enthusiastically offering thanks. You could more confidently infer other characteristics of the person if you knew his ready acceptance reflected a stable quality (like friendliness) than if you knew the act reflected a temporary state (his shirt was ablaze).

To summarize our discussion of central traits, let us return to one of the major themes of this book—that every person is a scientist. Our examination of trait centrality has focused on the importance of evaluation and stability. These two factors are important to the implicit psychologist because they help him to achieve the greatest understanding of how to behave toward others. It is not surprising that evaluative traits are central;

evaluative information tells the individual whether he should approach or avoid the person he is observing. Nor is it surprising that stable traits are central; stable, predictable events are especially useful to the individual as he tries to anticipate future situations and the behaviors he must enact. Knowing, for example, that a person is bad, has always been bad, and forever will be bad, is good. It allows for complete predictability. Knowledge that a person is always good would have similar value. The individual, as an implicit scientist, makes the strongest inferences about people on the basis of information that affords him the greatest amount of prediction and control.

Origin of Inferences

Unfortunately, the individual's needs for prediction and control sometimes obscure his understanding of others. This is the case when the relationships an observer expects among attributes are markedly different from the real relationships among attributes. Examples of this discrepancy are not difficult to find. The notion "feminists are ugly," as we have seen, is wrong. Similar notions relating membership in certain racial and national groups to characteristics such as thriftiness, laziness, or drunkenness are also likely to be mistaken. Even the idea that warmth implies wisdom, an inference made by many of Asch's subjects, is probably wrong. Where do all these harebrained ideas come from?

The inferences an observer makes about attributes come from two major sources—communication from others, or the observer's own experiences. But in either case, the inferences originate in *someone's* experiences. This was the explanation of the origin of inferences given by Donald Campbell in 1967. He suggested that *stereotypes,* patterns of characteristics we ascribe to various groups of people, arise from the observer's experience with those groups. According to this explanation, someone somewhere once observed a Scot who was extraordinarily thrifty; someone met a black who was lazy; someone knew an American Indian who drank. In other words, a stereotype has a grain of truth. At one time, the characteristic attributed to the group actually was an attribute of some group member or proportion of group members. Later, through the process of communication, the inference was established as a truism in the minds of many observers. Stereotypes, from this point of view, are the residue of past truths.

Recent research has shown that the "grain of truth" hypothesis itself has a grain of truth. But it also has a grain of falsehood, because it assumes that the observer (at one time in a particular situation) did make a perfectly logical inference. Let us examine the relative truth and falsity of the hypothesis by reviewing two experiments. The first of these, a study by Wegner, Benel, and Riley (1976), shows that people do make inferences that correspond with their experiences. To investigate this issue, these researchers provided groups of subjects with experience designed to cultivate certain inferences. In particular, one group received a series of personality descriptions (telling about a person's life situation, interests, abilities, and traits) in which the traits of "persuasiveness" and "realism" were closely related: when a person was described as persuasive, he or she was also described as realistic. Another group read similar descriptions in which the traits were negatively related: when a person was described as persuasive, he or she was also described as not very realistic. Later, these two groups were asked to read still other descriptions that made no mention of persuasiveness or realism. They were also asked, however, to rate each person who was described in terms of how realistic and how persuasive he seemed to be. When these ratings were analyzed, it was found that the group given experiences suggesting a positive relationship between the traits now perceived a more positive relationship than the group given experiences suggesting a negative relationship. Apparently, an individual's experiences do change his or her expectancies. This much of the grain-of-truth hypothesis seems to be true.

Now for the false part. If individuals do develop expectancies and later make inferences solely on the basis of their experiences, it seems that their expectancies and inferences should reflect their experiences exactly. There is evidence that this is not the case, however. People sometimes see things as related when in fact they are not; this tendency is referred to as the *illusory correlation* (Chapman and Chapman, 1969). Hamilton and Gifford (1976) have examined a particular type of illusory correlation—the tendency to see two sets of infrequent or distinctive events as being related. Their research suggests that stereotyping—generating evaluative inferences about groups of people—may in part reflect this basic perceptual tendency. In one experiment, subjects were asked to read short statements about a variety of different people. Two-thirds of the individuals they read about were identified as members of "Group A." The remaining third were identified as members of "Group B." Thus, there were twice as many Group A members as Group B members. The statements read by the subjects were of two kinds: desirable (for example, "John, a member of Group A, visited a sick friend in the hospital") or undesirable (for example, "Roy, a member of Group A, always talks about himself and his problems"). The statements were arranged such that within each group the majority of the people (slightly over two-thirds) were described by desirable qualities. Thus, although the desirable statements outnumbered the undesirable, neither Group A nor Group B had a higher proportion of desirable (or undesirable) persons. Yet, when subjects read about all the people and then reported their impressions of the typical member of each group, they rated the Group B member as less desirable than the Group A member. There was no real relationship between group membership and desirability, but subjects thought that there was.

In a second study, Hamilton and Gifford presented another group of subjects with similar information. But in this case, the proportion of desirable and undesirable qualities was reversed. Thus, two-thirds of the people in both Group A and Group B were described as having undesirable qualities, and one-third as having desirable qualities. Under these conditions, subjects reported that Group B was more desirable than Group A. In order to interpret the findings of these two studies, it is necessary to note that in both cases, the *smaller* group (B) was seen as having the *less* frequently occurring quality (undesirable in the first study, desirable in the second). The *larger* group (A), in turn, was seen as having the *more* frequently occurring quality. The illusory correlation the subjects saw was a heightening of the perceived relationship between distinctive (infrequent) events.

This method of forming expectancies is common among observers. Unfortunately, it represents a bias in the processing of information about others. It is possible, because of the illusory correlation, for observers to believe strongly that they have actually experienced a relationship between two characteristics when in fact no such relationship exists. This bias is similar in some respects to the bias toward dispositional attributions discussed in Chapter 2. Just as it is easy to explain a behavior by attributing it to the actor's disposition, so also is it easy to explain an odd behavior by attributing it to an actor's membership in an unusual group of people. When two distinctive events occur together one or a few times, the observer concludes that they must be related. Our conclusion about the grain-of-truth hypothesis, then, is this: although an observer's system of inferences is built from his transactions with reality, in some instances his interpretations go awry. He develops expectancies and makes inferences about relationships that were never there at all.

All in all, the importance of the inferences an individual makes about others cannot be emphasized enough. We have noted in this section that such inferences are made with great regularity, that the strongest inferences are based on central traits because of their evaluative, dispositional nature, and that the inferences a person makes are based upon his sometimes correct and sometimes incorrect interpretations of his experiences with people. Although these points do describe the inference process, they do not address the enormous impact that inferences have on interpersonal relations. People fall in love, they beat one another over the head, they live happily ever after, they lob grenades at one another, they erect monuments to each other, and in general carry on life as we know it—all on the basis of inferences. Often, one person knows very little about the other, but they go ahead and smooch or pummel each other anyway. Inferences, although they are only educated guesses and can be utterly wrong, are a focal point of social interaction.

Organizing Information

Professional psychologists frequently harbor the dream that one day they will be able simply to open up a person's head, painlessly, and trace the wiring inside to find out why he behaves as he does. That dream is not likely to come true. It would be like trying to locate a particular street in Philadelphia using a map of the Milky Way. In lieu of the ability to trace circuits, psychologists have turned to methods of building theories about internal relationships. Noting a variety of related thoughts and behaviors, psychologists hypothesize about the organization of internal systems that might function to produce them.

In the case of implicit personality theory, researchers have investigated the organization of two such systems—the system of *attribute inferences* and the system of *personality judgments*. In each case, researchers have taken advantage of the fact that a very handy way to represent an organized system is to draw a map. In other words, the organization is shown in *spatial models* of implicit personality theory. In mapping the organization of attribute inferences, *attributes* are used as points on the map. In mapping the organization of personality judgments, *persons* are used as points on the map. We will discuss each of these types of organization in turn.

Models of Attribute Inference

Since people see some attributes as related to one another and others as quite unrelated to each other, we can start to understand the total picture of attribute inferences by constructing a spatial representation of the similarities and differences among attributes. Attributes close to each other on such a map are seen as similar; attributes distant from each other are seen as different. In a series of inventive studies by Seymour Rosenberg and his colleagues (1968, 1972), just such a procedure was used.

Rosenberg and Jones (1972) used a mathematical method called *multidimensional scaling* to develop a spatial representation of the attributes of people that were employed by a particular person, the novelist Theodore Dreiser. These researchers scoured one of Dreiser's works, *A Gallery of Women*, taking note each time Dreiser used an attribute to describe a person. They developed a measure of the author's belief that pairs of attributes were related to one another by calculating the number of co-occurrences of each pair of attributes. For example, when a character was described as both "young" and "beautiful," the researchers scored a co-occurrence between the two traits. In essence, it was assumed that this measure tapped the amount of perceived similarity between attributes—the likelihood that one would be inferred from the other. If a pair of attributes always occurred together and never in isolation, then they could be considered as functionally the same.

The computer program for multidimensional scaling used by Rosenberg and Jones developed a spatial representation of the attributes Dreiser used. This map was arranged such that attributes that co-occurred frequently were near each other, while at-

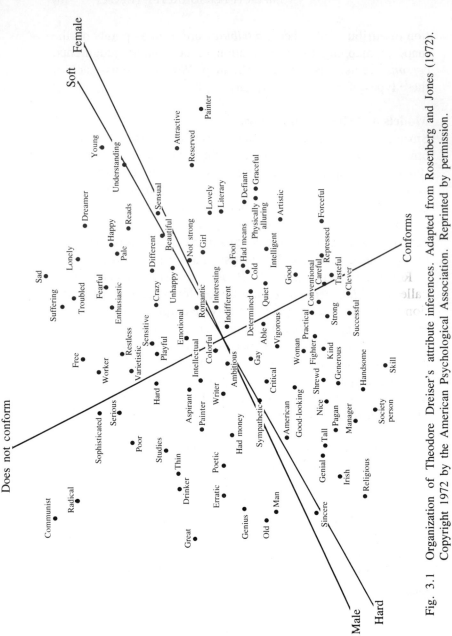

Fig. 3.1 Organization of Theodore Dreiser's attribute inferences. Adapted from Rosenberg and Jones (1972). Copyright 1972 by the American Psychological Association. Reprinted by permission.

tributes that did not co-occur frequently were distant from each other. A representation generated by the computer program is shown in Figure 3.1. Some major dimensions (conforms-does not conform, male-female, and hard-soft) have been drawn on the map to aid in interpreting the many attributes that are displayed. In general, it seems that Dreiser saw two major dimensions of attributes. The conformity dimension, with "communist" and "radical" and "free" at one end and "tasteful" and "repressed" at the other, defines one major axis of the representation. The other major axis, male and hard versus female and soft, has at its extremes words like "sincere" and "great" to describe males and "charming" and "sensual" to describe females.

The striking feature of this representation of Dreiser's perceived relationships among attributes is how well it fits what we know of the style of his own life. Dreiser's sexual involvement with women, for instance, was often scandalous. According to his biographers, he was compulsively promiscuous and often carried on affairs with several women at a time. Yet these women were not just sex partners, since he also depended on them for a great deal of intellectual stimulation. They frequently served as his literary agents and editors. This aspect of his relationship with women shows up in the map with female attributes such as "reads," "defiant," "cold," "intelligent," and "clever." It seems that the sex of a person was a very important attribute for Dreiser; many other attributes were seen as closely related to maleness and femaleness.

The conformity dimension was a second major theme in Dreiser's life. From the beginning of his literary career, he fought the forces of convention in society. His first book, *Sister Carrie,* was accepted for publication by Frank Doubleday, who later tried to cancel publication because Mrs. Doubleday found the novel offensive. For Dreiser, the conformist was seen as "successful." The map also captured what Dreiser saw as the

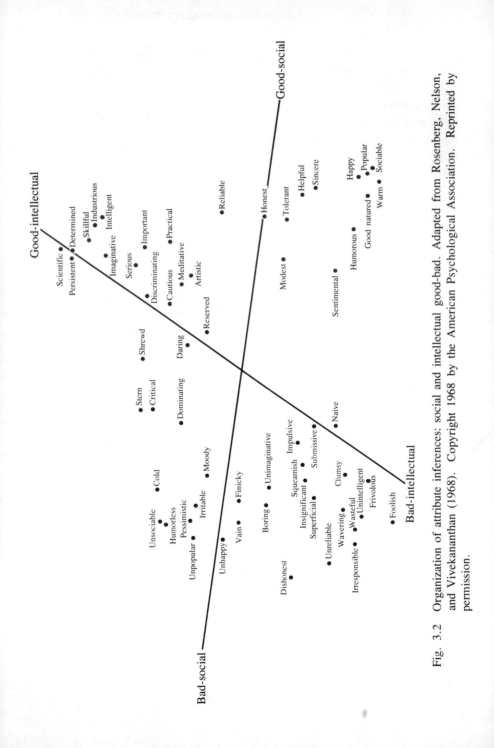

Fig. 3.2 Organization of attribute inferences: social and intellectual good-bad. Adapted from Rosenberg, Nelson, and Vivekananthan (1968). Copyright 1968 by the American Psychological Association. Reprinted by permission.

frequent results of nonconformity—"sad," "suffering," "lonely," and "troubled."

This map of the relationships Dreiser perceived among attributes is informative because it tells us about the major dimensions of his implicit personality theory. Apparently, he saw sex and conformity as important characteristics of people—characteristics from which information about many other attributes could be inferred. Knowing a person's sex or their level of conformity was, for Dreiser, knowing the person. But this is not necessarily true of other perceivers. The dimensions of attributes that Dreiser saw were no doubt built from his experiences with people, but since none of us have had those same experiences, our conceptions of attributes are not likely to coincide with his. To investigate the conceptions of attributes held by others, Rosenberg and his colleagues (1968) asked a group of people to make judgments of attributes. A two-dimensional representation of this group's judgments is shown in Figure 3.2.

If the pattern of attributes is inspected, it is evident that two major dimensions can be identified. Going from the lower left corner to the upper right, the attributes increase in their desirability for intellectual activities. Moving from the upper left corner to the lower right, the attributes increase in their desirability for social activities. It appears that the dimensions of intellectual ability and social ability account for the organization of attributes on the map. These two dimensions—intellectual good-bad and social good-bad—represent the two major kinds of information on which inferences are based. In each case, it should be noted that the information is evaluative. Thus, the two dimensions are not strictly independent in the sense that they cannot be predicted from one another. Rather, you will note that the dimensions on the map are not at right angles; it seems people typically believe that intellect is somewhat related to social skills. In a sense, then, this representation shows a very clear halo effect. All the good qualities, both intellectual and social, are on the right side, while all the bad qualities, again both intellectual and social, are on the left.

In addition to representing the halo effect quite clearly, the map also offers a smartly packaged way of thinking about Asch's "warm-cold" research. Look, first of all, at the attributes "warm" and "cold" on the map. They are located at the extremes of the social good-bad dimension. Now recall the other words that accompanied "warm" and "cold" in the trait lists Asch gave his subjects: intelligent, skillful, industrious, determined, practical, and cautious. These words all fall at the good end of the intellectual dimension. The traits "warm" and "cold," therefore, were the only information subjects in Asch's experiment had as to the social good-bad dimension. It is no wonder that they made many extreme inferences. They were inferring all the other attributes that accompany warmth—social goodness—when "warm" appeared in the list, and all the attributes that accompany coldness—social badness—when "cold" appeared. In each case, extreme levels of social goodness or badness were attributed to the person described by the list because "warm" and "cold" have extreme positions on the social good-bad dimension.

In general, attribute maps are extremely helpful in understanding how a person makes inferences about others. The maps show us the relatedness or lack of relatedness of many of the terms people use to describe others, and in addition, provide depictions of the general dimensions of these terms. Attribute maps are, however, representations of how people see attributes, not representations of how they see persons. An alternative method of viewing the organization of implicit personality theory is to develop spatial representations of the perceived similarities and differences among persons.

Models of Personality Judgment

We have argued that when an observer forms a cognitive representation of another person, he or she sees that person in terms of attributes. Using a map to represent this idea allows us also to represent a number of other important features of personality judgment. Consider for a moment the cognitive representation of persons that might be developed by a very simple-minded fellow, Rollo, who knows only two attributes that other people could possibly have—their height and their lovableness. These arc the two kinds of information that Rollo selects in his interactions with everyone. A map of Rollo's implicit representation of people might look like Figure 3.3. The people he knows are all classified according to height (the taller they are, the more northerly on the map) and according to lovableness (the more lovable, the more easterly). As you can see, Rollo thinks his mom is moderately short and very lovable, his sister Lulu is moderately tall and very lovable, and his Uncle Marmot is very tall and not lovable at all. This map is useful because it represents three properties of cognitive structure—similarity, articulation, and dimensionality. The *similarity* of the different persons is simply their closeness on the map; people Rollo sees as similar are near each other, whereas people he sees as different are far apart. The *articulation* of each attribute (height and lovableness) can be thought of as the number of segments along each dimension; in our map of Rollo's theory, wc have shown his cognitive structure to be somewhat articulated, since there are four possible levels of height and six possible levels of lovableness. The *dimensionality* of the cognitive structure is the number of dimensions required to represent the individual's thoughts about people; in the case of Rollo, only two dimensions suffice because only two kinds of information are selected.

It is possible to become gravely concerned about the usefulness of a map of personality judgment when we consider the cognitive structure of an average (non-simple) person. Isn't it true that people typically select many more than two attributes? How can we draw a spatial representation with 500 or 1000 di-

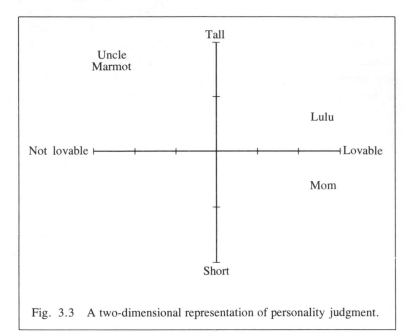

Fig. 3.3   A two-dimensional representation of personality judgment.

mensions? Fortunately, such a complex map is not necessary. As we noted in our discussion of models of attribute inferences, people frequently see attributes as closely related to each other. The finding that *warmth* implies *generosity,* for example, suggests that it is not really necessary to represent these two attributes as separate dimensions on the map. If an observer believes that someone is warm, he probably also believes that the person is generous; if he believes the person is cold, he also believes him selfish. The two attributes are functionally equivalent, since judgments of persons on one attribute tend to order persons in the same way as judgments on the other attribute. Even though the observer may have different names for the two attributes, they are not different in the way he uses them to judge people.

Given this analysis, we can begin to reduce the complexity of the map by determining which of the attributes selected by an observer are similar to each other and then by representing each group of similar attributes as a single dimension on the map.

Suppose that in addition to height and lovableness, Rollo also selected information about his acquaintances' strength, weight, shoe size, cuteness, warmth, and cuddliness. It would not be necessary to develop a map with eight dimensions because some of the dimensions would be redundant. It is likely, for instance, that Rollo's judgments of an individual's strength, weight, and shoe size would correspond closely to his judgment of the individual's height. Similarly, his judgments of lovableness would be closely related to his judgments of cuteness, warmth, and cuddliness. Thus, while it would appear that Rollo has eight different attributes upon which to base judgments of people, he actually has only two major dimensions of judgment.

How do we know that Rollo doesn't have just *one* dimension of judgment? Why have we included both height and lovableness in this model of his cognitive structure? In fact, two dimensions are needed because the two dimensions are *independent,* unrelated to each other in the way Rollo uses them to characterize people. Knowing that Rollo thinks his mom is lovable tells us nothing about her height. If the two dimensions were not independent, then Rollo's judgments of people on one dimension would be systematically related to his judgments of the same people on the other dimension. This is the state of affairs shown in Figure 3.4. Since all of the points on the map—the people Rollo knows—fall in a line, the height of each one can be predicted directly from his or her lovableness; the taller the person, the less lovable. If this were the case for Rollo, then his two dimensions of judgment would collapse into a single dimension of short and lovable versus tall and not lovable. As you can tell, the dimensionality of cognitive structure is not determined by the number of different attributes the person uses to comprehend people, but rather by the number of independent dimensions required to represent the person's judgments of people. In practice, researchers use a mathematical technique called *factor analysis* to determine the number of dimensions and the types of dimensions an individual uses to judge people. This method determines the relatedness of the personality judgments the individual makes on all the different attributes he uses, and then determines which groups of attributes are used in the same way to describe people. Each group of functionally similar attributes is called a *factor*; each of these factors represents an independent dimension of judgment.

What are the typical dimensions of judgment that people use? The answer to this question appears to be: it depends. In most of

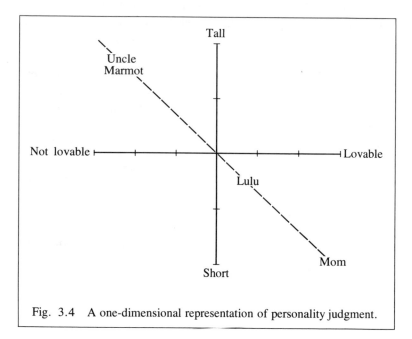

Fig. 3.4   A one-dimensional representation of personality judgment.

the studies of personality judgment, researchers have identified three general dimensions—*evaluation* (good-bad), *activity* (active-passive), and *potency* (strong-weak). Evaluation is conveyed in attributes such as warm and cold, smart and stupid, or friendly and unfriendly. Activity refers to attributes like fast and slow, or energetic and lazy. Potency, meanwhile, is reflected in attributes such as hard and soft, or dominant and submissive. As you might suspect, the evaluative dimension is the most important of the three. Some recent studies of personality judgment have shown, however, that the use of these dimensions of judgment seems to vary from one situation to the next and from one person to the next. In a study of the personality judgments made by a group of psychologists judging each other (Jones and Young, 1972), the major dimensions of judgment were status, political persuasion, and professional interests. In other studies (Reed, 1972; Kuusinen, 1969), still other major dimensions were identified. Our conclusion here must be, then, that the major dimensions of judgment are different for different individuals and also differ according to the situation in which the judgments are made.

Personality judgments, regardless of their underlying dimensions, reflect the individual's ability to conceptualize people in different ways. William Scott (1969) has suggested that the two properties of cognitive structure represented in this model, articulation and dimensionality, are types of cognitive differentiation. The cognitive map is actually a picture of how the perceiver differentiates among people. When a dimension is articulated (has many intervals), the observer can differentiate people into many groups according to that dimension. When the observer's cognitive structure has many independent dimensions, he can differentiate among people in many ways. Returning to Rollo and Figure 3.3, we can note that height, the dimension with four intervals, allows him to differentiate people into four different groups. Lovableness, in turn, allows him to differentiate people into six different groups. But the combination of the independent dimensions of height and lovableness affords him the opportunity of differentiating people into twenty-four discernible groups. He could reliably tell the difference between twenty-four different kinds of people; a very lovable, moderately tall person is different from a somewhat lovable, very tall person, for example. Thus, both articulation and dimensionality are measures of the complexity of an individual's implicit personality theory.

We have shown in this section that the organization of implicit personality theory can be represented in at least two major ways. Models of attribute inferences represent the organization underlying the individual's conception of attributes. Models of personality judgment represent the systematic way in which the individual differentiates among persons in terms of their attributes. Both forms of organization are important for understanding the overall scheme of implicit personality theory. In summarizing this scheme, it should be pointed out that the individual can see *attributes* as similar or different, and can see *people* as similar or different. The maps we have explored are simplified pictures of the cognitive structures that allow the individual to differentiate among attributes and among people in terms of their attributes.

Combining Information   The organization of information within cognitive structure becomes evident when we insert new information that must be combined with the old. When incoming information does not properly fit the structure, some type of restructuring takes place to allow the new information to be integrated into the structure. Just as every star on the flag had to be moved when Hawaii became the fiftieth state, so every cognition held by a person is juggled slightly when something new pops into his head. But some cognitions require little juggling while others require circus-act skill. Suppose we were to introduce you to two people, Spike and Rock, by telling you two attributes of each. Meet Spike; he is kind and considerate. Meet Rock; he is cruel and wise. What are your impressions of these two characters? Our bet is that it takes you less mental juggling to form an impression of Spike than it does to form an impression of Rock. It seems difficult to conceptualize a person who is both cruel and wise, whereas it is quite easy to think about someone who is both kind and considerate.

Incoming information can be inconsistent with one's cognitive structure. When we describe a person by using two (or more) traits, it is likely that you will assume the traits go together. This is because people typically see others as integrated, whole personalities, not clusters of unrelated attributes. But when a pair or group of attributes that are seen as similar (because they are held by one person) are also seen as dissimilar (because the observer differentiates among them), conflict occurs. The kinds of inconsistencies that may arise correspond directly to the kinds of differentiations that the observer makes among attributes of persons. Our description of Spike holds little conflict because most observers do not differentiate between kindness and consideration. Our description of Rock is more conflicting because observers usually do differentiate between cruelty and wisdom.

It is useful to distinguish between two general types of trait conflict, *evaluative inconsistency* (conflict along the good-bad dimension) and *descriptive inconsistency* (conflict along any other dimension). Rock, the fellow you met a moment ago, has evaluatively inconsistent traits because cruelty is bad while wisdom is good. Some other hypothetical characters, Duke and Buck, have descriptively inconsistent traits. Duke is cautious and bold. Buck is alert and relaxed. The attributes characterizing each of these persons, although similar in evaluative tone, are conflicting on other dimensions. If you often differentiate among people on a dimension from *cautious* to *bold*, it will be difficult to form an impression of Duke because he cannot be located on the cautious-bold dimension; he belongs at both ends. If alert-relaxed is a dimension you use, Buck will seem strange. In the case of such descriptive inconsistencies, the amount of conflict the observer experiences depends entirely on whether the particular dimension of inconsistent information is one that the observer uses to comprehend people. But since everyone uses an evaluative dimension of judgment, evaluative inconsistency provides difficulties for everybody. Researchers have generally focused on evaluative conflict for this reason.

What happens when we perceive evaluatively inconsistent information about a person? The answer depends on how that information is received. We can divide the occasions on which we receive conflicting information into two types—occasions when we must form impressions of strangers ("Darling, I'd like you to meet my parents"), and occasions when we add new information to our store of knowledge about familiar people ("Darling, there's something in my past I think you should know"). Research has been conducted about each of these cases.

Meeting strangers

There are a number of different ways in which you might receive information about a stranger. An acquaintance might tell you about the person; you might simply meet the stranger on your own; you could even receive reports from a number of different people before meeting the stranger yourself. However you receive the information, though, your tendency is to form a unified impression of the individual. You attempt to fit the pieces of the puzzle together in a meaningful way. Somewhere along the line, you, the observer, decide on an overall evaluation to assign to the complex of differently evaluated bits of information you have received. You decide on how much you will like or dislike this stranger who is described by a number of attributes. If these attributes are evaluatively conflicting (some are good and some are bad), what is the nature of the process whereby you decide on your final evaluation of the person? This process has been the subject of many studies, most of which have attempted to predict the observer's final evaluation on the basis of some mathematical model of the judgment process.

Two simple models, *adding* and *averaging,* have most often been used in these attempts. An example helps to show the difference between these models of judgment. Suppose that we assign numbers from $+3$ to -3 to attributes according to their evaluative quality; the most positive numbers refer to the most positive evaluations, the most negative numbers indicate the most negative evaluations, and zero refers to a neutral position. Now suppose we tell you that Millie, a woman we know, is healthy $(+1)$ and happy $(+2)$. An adding model would predict that you would evaluate Millie very positively $(+3)$ because your total evaluation would be the sum of the evaluations of her attributes $(1 + 2 = 3)$. An averaging model would predict that you would evaluate Millie as only moderately positive $(+1.5)$ because your total evaluation would be the average of the evaluations of her attributes $(\frac{1 + 2}{2} = 1.5)$. This is an important distinction. If adding models are correct, it would be possible to make an observer increasingly positive toward a person simply by alerting him to many moderately positive attributes of the person. If averaging models are correct, we could increase the positivity of the observer's attitude toward the person only by telling him about attributes of the person that were themselves more positive than the average of the person's known attributes.

Over the last fifteen years, much controversy has raged over the relative validity of these two models. Some studies support one; other studies support the other. Norman Anderson (1965) has developed yet a third model—the *weighted average model*—that has been found to predict evaluation as well as or better than either the adding or averaging models. This model assumes that an observer begins with a neutral impression, and that this impression is averaged in a more positive direction by positive attributes and in a more negative direction by negative attributes. Essentially, this model says that we begin to form an impression of a person slowly. Even if the person had an attribute that was extremely positive (+3), our initial impression of him would be a weighted average of zero (the starting point) and +3 (the attribute). By *weighted,* it is meant that the components are given different weights in forming the final average. It could be, for example, that we might place a good deal of weight on our initial bias of seeing the person as neutral, but place only little weight on his single positive attribute. The average, instead of being 1.5 (because $\frac{0+3}{2}$ = 1.5), could be only 0.5 if we weighted the neutral value by a factor of two-thirds and the attribute value by a factor of one-third. The equation for computing this evaluation would look like this: $\frac{2/3(0) + 1/3(3)}{2}$ = 0.5.

The weighted average model, while quite complex for those not handy with mathematics, has a deceptively simple meaning. All it says is that your liking for a person is determined by your general liking for any person (the neutral starting point), by your evaluation of that person's attributes, and by the importance (weight) you assign to the starting point and each successive attribute. It is unfortunate that the model does not always work. In gathering data to test this model, Anderson and other psychologists interested in evaluative judgments have almost always used a very simple technique. They typically give a subject a brief list of attributes (for example, *cruel, happy, friendly*), and ask him to rate the person on a scale from "likable" to "not likable." This technique probably oversimplifies the situation in which such judgments are usually made. People are encountered as people, not as lists of words. The way we process words may not correspond to the way we process a person's behavior.

Studies that have examined impression formation in a more naturalistic way have found that inconsistency is not simply averaged away. In an early study by Eugene Gollin (1954), su jects were shown a film of a young woman engaging in evalua tively inconsistent behaviors. Two scenes suggested she was promiscuous and immoral, a middle scene was neutral, and two final scenes portrayed her as kind and considerate. Instead of a simple likability rating, the measure of impression formation in this study was the subject's written description of the woman. Gollin found that these descriptions fell into three general categories. Some of the subjects blatantly ignored one or the other kinds of information and formed a unified impression based upon either promiscuity or kindness. They simply blocked out one of the conflicting sources of information. Other subjects included both types of information in their descriptions, but made no attempt to resolve or explain the inconsistency. They merely noted that she appeared kind and promiscuous. A third group of subjects were successful in their attempt to form a unified impression of the woman that included both positive and negative qualities. They introduced integrative themes such as "she's easy-going" or "she's happy-go-lucky" to explain the conflicting attributes. These three modes of resolution, *univalence* (either good or bad, but not both), *aggregation* (unintegrated good and bad), and *integration* (good and bad tied together by a new idea) have also been found in other more recent studies.

Research reported by Kaplan and Crockett (1968) has substantiated the findings of Gollin and has also shown the lengths to which observers will go in the search for consistency. Subjects were given eight paragraph-long descriptions of a person, John G., each of which was purportedly written by one of his acquaintances. The paragraphs variously described him as loyal, responsible, generous, fair, inconsiderate, sarcastic, unenthusiastic, and stubborn. In other words, half Boy Scout and half boy scoundrel. When subjects wrote their descriptions of John G., they exhibited much the same behavior as Gollin's subjects. Univalent, aggregated, and integrated impressions

.re found. But Kaplan and Crockett reported that there was considerable variation within each of these modes. Some observer's, deciding that John G. was generally bad, proceeded to interpret all of his positive qualities in a negative light. They decided, for example, that his responsibility was really an overly great concern for picky details. His loyalty was blind, foolish faith in authority. Other subjects squeezed out of the conflict by taking special note of the experimenters' remark that the original paragraphs were written by different persons. They pointed out that these people might well have formed different impressions because John behaved differently in the presence of each. Still other subjects claimed that John G. acted differently in different situations. Both of these latter groups of subjects were denying the conflict by pointing to the possibility that John's characteristics might not really reflect stable traits, but rather temporary behaviors. To top it off, a small group of subjects threw in the towel and diagnosed John as a split personality.

The conclusion to be reached from all this is that evaluative inconsistency in impressions of others is not something we can brush off lightly. When we are given conflicting attributes presented only as lists of traits, as in the adding and averaging models research, we can readily form simple, unified impressions. But when we receive large quantities of information, all of which points to a glaring inconsistency in our cognitive representation of a person, we squirm. We discount information, forming univalent impressions; we aggregate information, forming clusters of attributes that we cannot reconcile; we integrate information, forming impressions on the basis of our own ideas of why such conflict could occur. All in all, it appears that the combination of information about others is not at all a simple process.

Primacy-recency
When we encounter a stranger who has conflicting attributes, we are at a temporary loss to know how to behave. This also

seems to be the case when we discover conflicting qualities in someone we already know. Often we meet someone who makes a good first impression, but upon later contact, we discover bad qualities. People we see first as bad can also, upon further examination, demonstrate good features. What do we believe? Conventional wisdom has it that first impressions count the most; dropping food on your lap on a first date is not usually considered good form (or particularly nutritious). Early research suggested that this was in fact the way impression formation worked. When Luchins (1957) asked subjects to read two conflicting one-paragraph descriptions of a person, he found that the contents of subjects' descriptions of the person were flavored heavily by the information they read first. The descriptions, whether they were univalent, aggregated, or integrated, tended to lean in the direction of the initial paragraph. This dominance of early information is called a *primacy effect*.

Do first impressions always count the most? Isn't it sometimes true that people revise their first impressions when later information becomes available? Luchins and others have addressed this issue in later research. They reasoned that it is seldom in our daily lives that we receive information about a person that is *immediately* contradicted by other information. Rather, considerable periods of time often pass between the occasion of our initial impression and the occurrence of new information. Indeed, we could argue that Luchins' experiment demonstrating a primacy effect was not really a faithful model of the acquaintance process because the two sets of information were given so close together in time. In research designed to replicate more nearly the conditions of real life, a delay was imposed between the two conflicting blocks of information. Under these conditions, a *recency effect* was found. Subjects' impressions were dominated by the most recent information they obtained.

Other experiments have shown that when subjects are asked to write down their impressions of the person after receiving the first block of information and then are given the contradictory information and asked to indicate their final impressions, a recency effect occurs. We can interpret the findings of both kinds of experiments—those with a delay between blocks and those with an intervening impression written between blocks—by suggesting that both activities tend to solidify a first impression in the observer's mind. This unified and stable impression is difficult to change once new, contradictory information is obtained. Thus, the observer tends to discount it entirely and base his final impression on the new information. A recency effect occurs. This is probably also the case with our impressions of acquaintances. Although we have a general idea of the evaluative quality of the people we know, the occurrence of new information can often lead us to revise our impression drastically.

The combination of information about others, as we have seen in this section of the chapter, is required when incoming information is inconsistent with the observer's cognitive structure. In studies of the resolution of evaluative inconsistency, a weighted average model has been found to predict overall evaluation when the observer is given minimal information about a stranger's conflicting attributes. Given more information, observers tend to use univalence, aggregation, and integration as strategies for the resolution of conflict. And given information that is inconsistent over time, observers exhibit a primacy effect when the inconsistency occurs in a brief time and a recency effect when the inconsistency occurs after an appreciable interval.

the implicit psychologist

The general patterns of implicit personality theory we have sketched in these last few pages are just that— general patterns. Here and there, we have given you hints that not every person's theory is the same, and that theories tend to change as a person grows up. These are tremendous understatements. The observer's implicit personality theory, because it is unique, because it reflects his experiences with the social world, and because it determines how he perceives every human being, is the nucleus of the observer's own personality. This was the major contention of personality theorist George Kelly (1955). He saw that the individual's "personal constructs"—the dimensions of his implicit personality theory—were entirely and uniquely the belongings of the individual. Moreover, they subsumed the individual's past because they were built on his experiences and held a view toward his future because they served to help him anticipate events. Kelly argued that the individual's interpersonal reality—the way he sees those around him—is the total of all the individual has been and will be. Many other researchers and theorists, excited by this view of implicit personality theory, have gone on to investigate the way it develops and becomes unique.

Developmental Changes   Implicit personality theory develops in some obvious, important ways and in some not-so-obvious but equally important ways. The obvious changes become evident when we read descriptions of people given by young children. Here, for example, is JoAnn (eight years, four months old) describing her boyfriend:

> He is nice. I like him. He doesn't beat on girls. He is all right. He wears cool clothes. His handwriting is all right. He says I wear pretty clothes. He likes me. He gives me candy.

Studies aimed at investigating the developmental changes that occur in the individual's descriptions of others (see, for example, Peevers and Secord, 1974) have found that the young child makes simplistic characterizations of people. As is the case with JoAnn, the young child typically uses just a few attributes to describe a person. Praising or condemning the person freely, the child talks mostly about actions and surface characteristics, not personality traits. And many of the attributes refer to the relationship between the person and the child-observer. In short, the young child's impressions of others seem almost impoverished in their simplicity. But as the child grows up, many intriguing changes take place. Successful transaction with a complex, multifaceted interpersonal world requires an implicit personality theory that is equal to the task.

Earlier in this chapter, we discussed attribute generality and pointed out that the attributes employed by the individual to comprehend others become more general as the individual develops (Wegner, 1977). Since we also noted that general attributes allow the individual to make more articulated judgments of others, it is not surprising to find that articulation also increases with development (Signell, 1966). These structural changes in the way information about people is selected reveal an important underlying pattern in the development of person perception. We can illustrate this pattern by comparing the way an observer builds a conception of a person with the way a mechanic might build an automobile. Consider first a mechanic who has never seen a car before (these are quite common), and who is left alone for three months in a room filled with materials and equipment. He might emerge with a vehicle sporting one square cement wheel, no engine, nine mufflers, and ashtrays filled with potted palms. In contrast, imagine a modern industrialist planning next year's model. He knows all the parts that go into a car and must only consider how big the car should be, what color, how many cylinders it should have, and so on. The difference between these two auto-makers is much like the difference between the child and the adult building conceptions of persons. The child's conception is built from unarticulated categories of information; the adult's conception is built from articulated dimensions of information. The child must select anew the parts for each person conception he builds; the adult knows what the parts are and must only decide on their specifications—the relative amounts of each attribute. The changes in implicit personality theory that accompany development allow the individual to take an "assembly line" approach to the understanding of others. This approach is not only more efficient, but also has greater capacities for differentiating among people.

With growth, the individual is also more likely to make inferences about others (Gollin, 1958). Instead of just reporting the observable facts (this woman is fat), the developing observer begins to explain the facts and understand their relationships (this woman is putting on weight because she has been taking solace in Twinkies ever since her husband called out to someone named "Bubbles" in his sleep). The importance of these higher-order conceptions of people is especially evident when we compare the younger and older child's ability to resolve inconsistent information about others. In some studies, very young children shown a person engaging in evaluatively inconsistent acts (helping in one scene, hurting in another) actually become so confused by the inconsistency that they insist two different persons are shown in the film. They will not believe that one person is capable of such disparate behaviors. In general, the ability to resolve inconsistency successfully appears to increase with development. Studies by Crockett (1970) and Biskin and Crano (1973) have shown that univalent impressions are typical in young children, that aggregated impressions become apparent in somewhat older children, and that integrated impressions occur most often among adults. The young child is totally unable to understand or appreciate the possibility that a person could be partly good and partly bad; the adult knows that this can happen.

The developmental changes we have discussed thus far—attribute generality, articulation, and inconsistency resolution—are all cognitive structural changes. They represent the successive reorganizations of the developing individual's concepts of persons. Another change discovered in recent research is a change in the *content* of implicit personality theory. If you will recall, earlier in this chapter we discussed Rosenberg's findings regarding the intellectual good-bad and social good-bad dimensions underlying attribute inferences. Do these same dimensions appear in the child's implicit representation of attributes? An experiment by Olshan (1974) was designed to answer this question. She used methods somewhat similar to Rosenberg's in developing maps of the attribute inferences made by third-, sixth-, and ninth-graders. These maps were remarkably similar in one respect—they all had an evaluative dimension. Thus, much like adults, children exhibit strong good-bad inferences in their attribute inferences. Important differences among age groups were found, however, in some other dimensions of judgment. Third-graders, for example, based many inferences on an *adult-child* dimension. This dimension was similar to the intellectual good-bad dimension in that adults were seen as smart, children as stupid.

The dimensions of attribute inference used by sixth-graders no longer included such heavy emphasis on *adult-child*. Apparently, this distinction becomes less important as the child grows up. A major new dimension, *male-female,* entered the picture for sixth-graders and also remained an important dimension for ninth-graders. In each case, this dimension was relatively independent of evaluation; neither males nor females were seen as more likely to be good or bad. These findings, all in all, reflect quite well some of the major changes that accompany growing up. If you can recall third grade, you will remember that the sex of a person made little difference. What was important was whether a person was your age or not. Then with the onset of adolescence came a subtle yet pervasive awareness that people were of two kinds—male and female—and that this difference made all the difference in the world. It is no wonder that sex enters the organization of implicit personality theory at this point.

Individual Differences   The way in which an individual sees people, according to George Kelly, determines what the individual himself is like. Recent studies by William Scott (1969, 1974) have provided substantial support for this contention. Scott has developed ways of measuring some of the important properties of implicit personality theory (articulation and dimensionality, for example), and has found that each individual reliably displays a certain level of each property. Probably the most interesting of Scott's findings are those regarding a particular property—*ambivalence*. Ambivalence is the extent to which an observer uses equal numbers of both good and bad attributes to describe a person. In a sense, ambivalence represents the observer's continued failure to locate persons he observes on an evaluative dimension; every person is seen as having both good and bad properties. First, let us look at some of the consequences of ambivalence. Then, we will focus on the possible causes.

Scott has repeatedly found that ambivalence toward acquaintances and toward the self is related to maladjustment. People who display great ambivalence in their implicit personality theories tend to be very critical of themselves and to express dissatisfaction with their lives. When students in New Zealand, Japan, and Colorado who were identified as maladjusted (on the basis of their own reports and assessments made by their friends) were given tests of their ambivalence, it was found that they were more ambivalent than the average student toward themselves, their acquaintances, and the interpersonal relations in the families in which they grew up. When tests of ambivalence were given to psychiatric and surgery patients at a hospital in Denver, it was found that the psychiatric patients, many of whom were diagnosed as schizophrenic, were more frequently ambivalent about their acquaintances than were the surgery patients.

Ambivalence, in its broadest sense, means that the individual does not know how to behave toward people. Since the ambivalent person sees people as having both good and bad qualities, he is seldom extremely attracted to anyone or repelled by anyone. He is always looking at the other side, finding bad points in the good person and good points in the bad person. Although this strategy might seem almost Buddha- or Christ-like, transcending earthly notions of goodness and badness, it does not work for mere mortals. Surrounded by his friends and family, the "good" people in his life, the ambivalent person suspects that they may be fools and charlatans, but cannot decide. Surrounded by a gang of criminals and cutthroats, some "bad" people he should probably avoid, the ambivalent person might note how witty, charming, and kind they seem. He cannot decide what to do. His relations with others are indecisive, confused, and anxiety-provoking.

This peculiar feature of poorly adjusted persons has been commented on by a number of clinical psychologists and psychiatrists. In fact, it forms the core of one of the major theories of schizophrenia. Although it is still not known whether schizophrenia stems from genetic, biological, or social factors, or from some combination of the three, a frequent supposition is that certain individuals, genetically or biologically predisposed to schizophrenia, develop the syndrome when they are exposed to particular social and interpersonal conditions. According to some theorists, one of the most important of these conditions is *double-bind communication*. Bateson, Jackson, Haley, and Weakland (1956) have proposed that frequent or severely conflicting messages from others can contribute to schizophrenia. This factor has been blamed as a source of other kinds of maladjustment as well.

Most often, theorists have suggested that double-binding messages from parents start the child in the direction of maladjustment (McCulloch, Wegner, Heil, and Vallacher, 1976). Mom says "I'm doing this because I love you" as she spanks the child; Dad encourages the child to be independent and then is hurt and irritated when the child behaves independently; Mom praises the child's accomplishments in a sarcastic, negative tone of voice. Double-binds may not even be this obvious. Dad, for example, might hit the child because the child hit his little brother. But Dad's act communicates a double message: Hitting is OK (when I hit you) and hitting is not OK (when you hit Ralphy). These are examples of single incidents—they may well have occurred in your own childhood. But what happens when conflicting communications become a matter of course in a household, when the whole family is trading in double messages? It seems that this sort of discourse could well lead the child to think about his parents—and himself—in ambivalent terms. As we have noted, the young child is especially incapable of dealing with conflict. When the child is repeatedly confronted with conflicting evaluations of himself and with conflicting evaluative actions and communications by his parents, he has to develop ambivalent representations. This tendency, then, contributes to the continued inability to predict other people's behavior and to deal with people effectively. The failure of implicit personality theory seems to have unfortunate consequences for the individual's personal adjustment and happiness. Because ambivalence is an important aspect of implicit psychology, we shall consider it again in Chapters 4 and 5.

Summary The individial's implicit personality theory is his cognitive structure for forming impressions of persons. In his initial selection of information about a person, the observer is guided not only by principles of attribution, but also by his tendency to select similar kinds of information about everyone. These frequently selected qualities—

general attributes—allow the observer to compare the particular person with a variety of others and thus to make articulated judgments. The observer's own situation also affects the nature of the information he selects.

Information that is selected serves as the basis for inferences about other, unobserved qualities of a person. Such inferences are often evaluatively consistent with previously selected information; this is the halo effect. Since central traits such as *warm-cold* are both highly evaluative and stable, they lead the observer to make many extreme inferences. In constructing an implicit theory to guide his inferences, the individual sometimes gathers correct information about relationships between attributes (the "grain of truth"), and at other times, identifies relationships incorrectly (the "illusory correlation"). The inferences about relationships among attributes and about the characteristics of persons are organized in a way that can be represented in spatial models. Such models are used to investigate and display the various dimensions of judgment the observer employs.

The individual becomes concerned with combining information about others when such information is evaluatively or descriptively inconsistent. Some studies of the combination of evaluatively inconsistent information have attempted to model this process through adding, averaging, and weighted average models. Other studies have found that individuals form univalent, aggregated, or integrated impressions when they are asked to write a detailed impression of a person. In addition, it appears that observers may place greater weight on first impressions under some conditions (the primacy effect), but weigh later information more heavily under other conditions (the recency effect).

Many changes in implicit personality theory accompany an individual's development. Attribute generality and articulation increase, as do a variety of other indices of the complexity of the individual's theory. Among adults, differences in implicit personality theories are important. The ambivalence of the individual—his tendency to see others and self as both good and bad—is related to his level of adjustment. Ambivalence in a person's implicit personality theory represents the failure to differentiate people in terms of their evaluative qualities.

chapter four

Evaluation is the most important dimension by which we perceive others. The individual does not describe others so much as he evaluates them, judging whether they are good or bad, whether they are attractive or repulsive. Evaluations can be specific, involving nothing more than the attribution of a single "good" or "bad" trait to a person to explain a "good" or "bad" act. More commonly, however, evaluations are general—the person as a whole is judged to be good or bad. Evaluation in this latter sense is in our concern in this chapter. The individual's evaluation of other people is analogous to the explicit concern with normality and adjustment on the part of professional abnormal and clinical psychologists. Just as these psychologists must daily assess healthy versus unhealthy functioning, the implicit psychologist must also judge whether someone is a good or bad person.

To understand how the implicit psychologist goes about deciding whether someone is good or bad, it is first necessary to consider these concepts in some detail. Because they are so basic to our construction of social reality, the terms "good" and "bad" are frequently and casually employed in many different contexts. For this reason, the meanings of these concepts are implicitly assumed rather than explicitly examined by most people. In the following section, our aim is to make the meaning of good and bad more explicit. As will become apparent, good and bad are not simply opposite ends of the same continuum; rather, they function somewhat independently in a psychological sense.

implicit abnormal psychology

Evaluation

Good and Bad   The words good and bad suggest different ideas and evoke different images, depending on one's orientation. From a religious perspective, good and bad represent two opposing forces that ultimately divide mankind into saints and sinners. Philosophically, good and bad are often seen as complementary opposites; just as hills would be flat without valleys, good and bad depend on each other for their existence. To an experimental psychologist concerned with person perception, however, these terms take on far less lofty meaning. Stimuli that have reward value for the individual elicit approach responses; "good" is the individual's cognitive representation of his approach response. "Bad," meanwhile, is the cognitive representation of an avoidance response to an aversive stimulus. Judgments of good and bad, then, represent behavioral tendencies of the perceiver.

Specifying good and bad in this way may be decidedly unpoetic, but it does have advantages. For one thing, it reminds us that these notions are a function of the perceiver, not of objective or even consensual reality. Because goodness and badness are thought to be properties of objects, much like weight or length, it is easy to forget that they are only the observer's labels for his own actions toward those objects. Statements of *liking* or *disliking*, on the other hand, are a bit more conservative. If a person says "I like seed catalogues," for example, he is acknowledging that the evaluation is his own opinion; if he says "Seed catalogues are good," however, his attribution of this property of "goodness" to the object itself carries with it the implicit assumption that other people at other times and in other places would agree. In this sense, evaluations of the goodness or badness of objects, events, and persons are typically stable, internal attributions. The first step in understanding evaluations comes in recognizing their subjective nature; even your worst enemy has friends.

Just as important, specifying evaluative judgments in terms of response tendencies allows us to garner insights from other areas of psychological research. Neal Miller and his colleagues (Brown, 1948; Miller, 1944), for instance, have demonstrated a striking difference between approach and avoidance behaviors that has implications for our understanding of evaluative judgments. By attaching a harness to a laboratory rat, they determined how much effort the rat would exert as it approached a rewarding stimulus or avoided a punishing one. It was found that the *gradients* of approach and avoidance (the amount of effort exerted at different distances from the stimulus) were quite different. As can be seen in Figure 4.1, the rat gradually exerts more effort as it nears the rewarding goal. In contrast, the rat's avoidance gradient is very steep; the animal exerts maximum effort to get away when it is close to a punishing stimulus, but its effort drops off dramatically as it moves away from the stimulus. These results, confirmed in many studies, demonstrate that responses to negative stimuli follow different patterns from responses to positive stimuli. When positive and negative elements are combined in the same object or location, the animal's response to the stimulus is not a simple averaging of his responses to the positive and negative elements separately. Instead, the animal's response depends on its distance from the stimulus. If far away, the animal will move toward the stimulus. As the animal approaches, however, its avoidance tendencies increase more rapidly than its approach tendencies; beyond a certain point, avoidance outweighs approach and the animal may move away from the stimulus.

As an example of what happens when a stimulus has both positive and negative qualities, imagine that you have decided to take up sport parachuting. As you slowly approach the day of your first jump, you take lessons, rent equipment, arrange for the airplane, and so on. But eventually, the day of the jump ar-

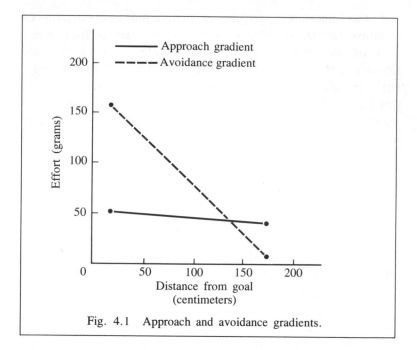

Fig. 4.1   Approach and avoidance gradients.

rives. Your avoidance tendencies begin to balance your approach tendencies, and you experience considerable ambivalence and hesitation. Finally, in the plane at several thousand feet, your avoidance tendencies are paramount. As your instructor forces you out the door, you take along a handful of his hair.

Good and Bad Characteristics

Because approach and avoidance gradients are different, conceivably there is an analogous difference in our response to the perceived positive and negative aspects of a person. At a distance—for example, when we judge a stranger or someone with whom we expect no contact—our overall evaluation of a person may give his perceived positive and negative aspects equal weight. As in the research done by Anderson (described in

Chapter 3), we may simply average the person's assets and liabilities in our determination of his or her likableness. But Anderson's weighted average model was built on studies in which subjects were judging a hypothetical stranger. Psychological distance was at a maximum. What happens when the stimulus is psychologically close? Extrapolating from Miller's research, as we get closer, the perceived negative aspects of the person should assume greater weight, eliciting implicit avoidance responses. Such response tendencies are represented cognitively as "bad." In other words, a perceiver attaches greater significance to perceived negative characteristics than to perceived positive characteristics when forming an overall evaluation of someone who is psychologically close.

Consider your reactions to a stranger you meet on a bus and to someone you have been dating for six months. Assume that both have three desirable qualities (good looks, sincerity, intelligence) and one not-so-desirable quality (a proclivity for punning). Your initial reaction to the stranger would probably be quite positive; the three positive traits outweigh the one negative. But over time, the steady date's punning may become a major irritant to you; the person's rewarding looks, intelligence, and sincerity are outweighed as the punning becomes punishment. At a distance, then, tolerance for a person's drawbacks comes easy. Close up, the same faults are intolerable. This increased importance of negative aspects at close distances is reflected in the adage, "The grass is always greener on the other side of the fence."

Research also supports the idea that "One bad apple spoils the barrel." In a variety of experiments (see Kanouse and Hanson, 1971, for a review), it has been demonstrated that observers place greater weight on negative characteristics than on positive ones when they form an evaluation of a person. This *negativity effect* means that negative qualities are more likely to function as central traits in the individual's implicit personality theory. Moreover, as pointed out by Kanouse (1971), the negative aspects of a person can interfere with the positive aspects, but the reverse is less often the case—positive aspects do not cancel the negative aspects. Finding out that someone you like and respect once spied on his mother for the CIA is likely to shatter your illusion about the person. However, discovering that a thoroughly dishonest person is highly intelligent, witty, and sociable is not sufficient to make you seek him out as a friend. This follows nicely from the distinction between approach and avoidance gradients.

There are at least two plausible explanations for the negativity effect. While neither is incompatible with the approach-avoidance reasoning, each examines the phenomenon from a slightly different perspective. Because they shed light on the nature of evaluation, we shall examine these two alternative (but not mutually exclusive) interpretations of negativity—*figure-ground* and *vigilance*.

A basic assumption of the figure-ground explanation is that people generally perceive most of the things that happen to them as good rather than bad. In the course of a normal day, for example, the majority of our interactions with others are marked by cordiality, if not friendliness. If the typical person sees the world as a predominantly positive place, a negative event or characteristic should stand out as the "figure" and be more readily noticed against the background of pleasant occurrences. From a slightly different perspective, if most personality characteristics are positive, it is easier to make discriminations on the basis of a few negative ones. If you have to choose between two people, both of whom have twenty positive traits and two negative ones, it is more economical to base your decision on the importance of their negative qualities. A choice between two attractive political candidates is often made in this fashion: "Fodsworth and Jones both have impressive records, but Jones once had an affair with a go-go dancer, so I'll vote for Fodsworth."

The attribution model outlined by Jones and Davis (1965) is also relevant to the figure-ground hypothesis. As discussed in Chapter 2, personal characteristics are attributed to an individual when his behavior violates norms or expectancies. Most norms and situations prescribe positive behavior. Thus, positive behavior is more appropriate and will less often be attributed to a personal quality of the individual than will negative behavior. In most situations, for instance, we expect people to behave in a more or less friendly fashion. Hence, information that Rita is behaving in a friendly way is not taken as evidence of what she is really like; the situational forces alone could account for her behavior. But unfriendliness is unexpected and thus constitutes an important piece of information in our evaluation of Rita. In short, because negative behaviors more often violate situational expectancies than do positive behaviors, they stand out and are given greater weight in the formation of an overall evaluation.

The second negativity explanation—vigilance—invokes concepts such as threat and survival. The underlying notion is that heightened sensitivity to negative events is adaptive and makes good evolutionary sense. The first prerequisite of survival is to avoid injury and death. An organism's primary concern, then, is with the threatening objects in its environment. Pleasant objects and events are like frosting on the cake; one can't be concerned with them until the dangers are eliminated. It is more important to know whether someone will hurt us than to know whether he or she will reward us. Hence, the individual is particularly sensitive to negative aspects of others since such vigilance may spare him unpleasant experiences. In this regard, it is worth noting that although most things that happen to a person are perceived to be good, extreme negative events are probably more common than extreme positive events. For most people, the likelihood of a severe accident or the loss of a loved one is greater than the likelihood of winning a million-dollar lottery or a Nobel prize. And it is difficult to imagine a positive counterpart to the most negative, yet most certain outcome of all—death. Adaptation to a potentially threatening environment requires a heightened awareness of negative events.

In summary, there is evidence that the implicit psychologist attaches greater weight to negative aspects of a person than to positive aspects when he attempts to form an overall evaluation. In part, this phenomenon reflects the fact that approach behavior (response to positive stimuli) and avoidance behavior (response to negative stimuli) follow different gradients; as the psychological distance between the perceiver and the stimulus decreases, avoidance tendencies increase more sharply than do approach tendencies. In addition, the negativity effect may be partially attributable to two other factors. First, because they are expected to occur with less frequency than positive characteristics, negative characteristics are more noticeable when they do occur. Second, negative characteristics are attended to because they signify potential threat.

Good and Bad Persons
Although evaluation can be specific, limited to one characteristic of a person, this is not often the case. An observer does not stop thinking about an actor once the actor's observed behavior is explained. Instead, as we pointed out in Chapter 3, the individual uses his implicit theory of personality to flesh out his impression of the actor, inferring additional unobserved qualities. Since implicit personality theories are characterized by evaluative consistency, when a good characteristic is attributed to an actor, it is likely that other positive traits will be inferred. Conversely, if the original attribution is negative, the total impression will probably consist of many negative traits.

The impressions of good and bad persons differ not only in their evaluations, but in another important way. Because bad traits are typically more important or central to the observer than good traits, more additional traits are inferred for a bad actor than for a good actor. As the vigilance hypothesis suggests, the observer is more concerned with a threatening person than with a rewarding person, and therefore has a more differentiated cognitive representation of the former than of the latter. To illustrate, consider the following exchange:

Peter: "What do you think of Fred?"

Paul: "Great guy—we're best friends. He likes to do the same things I do."

Peter: "What do you think of Raymond?"

Paul: "That creep! He's stupid, dishonest, self-centered, phony, boring, foulmouthed, and disgusting."

Paul is doing more than simply telling Peter that Raymond is bad; in effect, he is warning Peter about the variety of ways in which Raymond could provide unpleasant experiences for Peter. No such warning is necessary in Fred's case; he is not threatening, so less need be said about him.

In part, the enhanced differentiation of disliked others could simply reflect greater emotionality in the descriptions of enemies. When angry, we can list one unflattering adjective after another to show our contempt for someone. But this is not the full story. Irwin, Tripodi, and Bieri (1967) controlled for the "list of adjectives" effect and still found support for the vigilance hypothesis. In their study, subjects described several liked and disliked others along fifteen rating scales such as honest-dishonest, energetic-lazy, and sociable-unsociable. For each subject, a measure of differentiation (in this case, a combination of articulation and dimensionality) was calculated separately for the liked persons and for the disliked persons. These investigators found that there was greater differentiation among conceptions of disliked persons for most of the subjects. On the fifteen rating dimensions, subjects made clearer distinctions be-

tween disliked persons than they did between the liked persons.
A somewhat similar finding has been reported by Carr (1969).
People differentiate more among negative figures in their social
environment in order to identify and isolate potentially dangerous individuals.

At the same time, it seems likely that the greatest differentiation occurs when *neutral* figures are being judged. A lack of
involvement—pleasant or unpleasant—allows us to see many
aspects of a person, not just the ones that have personal relevance for us. Psychological distance encourages a more differentiated and less evaluative view of others. Keep in mind, however, that a detached perspective is not necessarily an accurate
perspective. As noted in Chapter 2, the readiness with which an
observer attributes traits to an actor often reflects a *lack* of information rather than an abundance. The question of accuracy—specifically, the relationship between the observer's
perspective and accuracy—will be discussed in more detail in
Chapter 7.

Judging Good and Bad: Sources of Evaluative Information

Any judgment involves the selection
and processing of relevant information.
In the case of evaluative judgments,
"relevant information" more often than
not boils down to rewards and punishments. At the most general level, we
like and think favorably of those who provide rewards for us,
dislike and think poorly of those who provide punishment, and
ignore those who provide neither. There are a variety of ways,
however, in which others can make us feel rewarded or
punished, pleasant or distressed. In this section, we shall discuss what the implicit psychologist considers to be "relevant information" and how he uses such information to make overall
evaluations of others.

Personal Characteristics

We mentioned one basis for evaluation in our discussion of good and bad characteristics. To review briefly, the individual may simply average what he considers to be the good and bad points of a person, giving extra weight to the bad points if the person has significance for him. This simple little model may well predict evaluations under certain circumstances. Detailed historical or literary accounts of persons, for instance, present us with considerable trait information. As we read about the person, we form an impression that probably reflects a rational processing of this information. Similarly, because of the mass media we can observe public figures—politicians, entertainers, athletes, and suspected felons—from a detached perspective and over a considerable period of time. This vantage point allows us to process many pieces of information before forming an overall evaluation.

When there is social interaction between the observer and the person he is observing, evaluation may proceed in a different way. As noted in Chapter 2, internal attributions are usually made when the actor's behavior has hedonic relevance—that is, when it is rewarding or punishing to the observer. This is often the case in social interaction; encounters between people are often exchanges of various rewards and punishments. If the person makes us feel pleasant, we attribute a good quality; if unpleasant, a bad quality. And once the internal attribution is made, the observer uses his implicit personality theory to complete his impression, inferring additional attributes of the person that are consistent with the original trait. Even a brief encounter is thus sufficient to generate a full-blown evaluation of a person. In situations characterized by hedonic relevance, then, there is no pretense of sampling a person's various traits before characterizing him as good or bad. Rather, it is *after* an initial evaluation is made that many traits are perceived in a person; these traits reflect not the person so much as the evaluator's concern for evaluative consistency.

This is not to suggest that the perceived personal characteristics of a person do not affect our evaluation of him. It is just that in many situations only a very few traits are noted before an evaluation is made. If someone were to punch you in the nose, for instance, it is unlikely that you would withhold judgment of him until you had found out whether he was smart, humorous, or sincere. Instead, because his behavior is punishing, a negative trait that corresponds to his act (aggressiveness, perhaps) would be attributed to him. And even if the person did have desirable qualities, as judged by other people, you would not see it that way. Global evaluations are often made quite confidently on the basis of limited trait information.

Often, in fact, only one trait need be noted for general assessment to begin—the person's physical attractiveness. Most people do not like to admit it, but physical attractiveness operates as a very central trait in our implicit theories of personality. Despite the lip service given to the adage, "Beauty is only skin deep," the individual seems to live by the notion, "What is beautiful is good." In recent years, the role of physical attractiveness in determining interpersonal evaluations has received much research attention, most notably in studies by Ellen Berscheid, Elaine Walster, and Karen Dion. When college students are asked what qualities they consider desirable in someone of the opposite sex, both males and females put such "inner" qualities as intelligence and sincerity at the top of the list, far ahead of such "superficial" attributes as attractiveness. However, these investigators suggest that good looks may be the single most important factor in determining popularity among college students.

In one experiment, for example, Dion, Berscheid, and Walster (1972) asked college students to estimate the personal characteristics of other students on the basis of facial photographs. Each photo had been judged earlier by another group of students to be either attractive or unattractive. Not surprisingly, students felt the attractive persons were more sexually responsive than the unattractive persons. More interestingly, both male and female subjects estimated the good-looking persons, males and females alike, to be more interesting, sociable, exciting, kind, sensitive, strong, and even more modest, than the not-so-good-looking persons. Thus, physical attractiveness is associated with many other positive traits in the individual's implicit personality theory.

The centrality of physical appearance in evaluation is not limited to college students. Even the perception of young children by adults is heavily influenced by the child's beauty or lack thereof. Dion (1972) presented reports of disturbances caused by second-grade children to adult females. Along with a description of the incident was the name and age of the transgressor, as well as a photograph of a boy or girl that another group of adults had judged to be either attractive or unattractive. After reading the report, the women were asked to comment on the incident and the child. Dion found that the women interpreted the same incident differently depending on whether the transgressor was attractive or not. Particularly when the misconduct was rather extreme—throwing rocks at a sleeping dog, for example—negative qualities were more likely to be attributed to an unattractive child than to an attractive one. The good-looking child was seen as having a more well-adjusted personality, to be better behaved, more honest, and less likely to transgress in the future. This finding is somewhat unsettling. Naughty behavior by a plain or homely child is attributed to the child's bad character; an identical act by a handsome boy or pretty girl is attributed to external or variable causes like "a bad day." Starting early in life, good-looking people are perceived more favorably and judged more compassionately than their less physically appealing counterparts.

We have emphasized physical attractiveness to the exclusion of other personal characteristics because it, more than others, allows us to predict in advance how someone will be evaluated. Obviously, other personal characteristics of a person can influence our evaluation of him or her. But while most people agree about who is good-looking and who is not, this is not the case for the majority of other traits. As pointed out earlier, different observers are likely to attribute different traits to the same person (recall also the study by Dornbusch and his colleagues, described in Chapter 3). The good and bad characteristics of a person are thus difficult to specify; it depends on the perceiver as much as the perceived. So unless the evaluator is given information about someone's traits in advance—for example, a detailed historical or literary account—it is hard to tell ahead of time whether the evaluator's judgment will be favorable or unfavorable. Of course, some persons are evaluated in the same way by different observers. Someone who routinely robs from the poor, for example, or who tries to wear his pants as shirts, is not going to win many popularity contests. But within the more mundane realm of everyday behavior, there is little consensus regarding who is good and who is bad. Attractiveness, on the other hand, can be specified more or less independently of the perceiver. Thus, knowing how attractive someone is allows us to predict how he or she will be evaluated by most people.

Similarity-difference
One of the more obvious facts of social life is that we like those who share similar attitudes with us and dislike those who don't. Not surprisingly, then, numerous studies have shown similarity in attitudes and beliefs to be a potent and consistent determinant of interpersonal attraction. The similarity-liking relationship has been documented convincingly in real-life settings (for example, Newcomb, 1961) as well as demonstrated in many laboratory experiments (Berscheid and Walster, 1969;

Byrne, 1971). As we pointed out in Chapter 1, assumed dissimilarity in attitudes may be the psychological mechanism underlying antagonism toward members of different racial and ethnic groups. The individual implicitly evaluates others according to the adage "difference is deviance." In short, judgments of good and bad are often based on the most subjective and self-centered standard possible—similarity or dissimilarity to the evaluator.

In part, we dislike those who hold different attitudes because their disagreement suggests they may have bad characteristics, like stupidity or insensitivity. Someone who shares our views, meanwhile, is assumed to be as perceptive, bright, and well-informed as we are. From this perspective, it is not similarity or dissimilarity per se that causes liking or disliking; rather, it is the characteristics perceived or inferred to be associated with similarity and dissimilarity that determine attraction. There is more to it than that, however. Dissimilar others are not disliked simply because they are assumed to have inferior qualities. In fact, dissimilar others who are bright and powerful are often disliked *more* than dissimilar others who are dull and insignificant. There is a very good reason for this. Quite often, our attitudes are based on ambiguous or conflicting evidence. On almost any issue, there is a surplus of "facts" supporting conflicting positions. Ambiguity and uncertainty, however, are psychologically uncomfortable; the individual desires unequivocal evidence regarding the correctness or validity of his opinions. Because the validity of one's opinions often cannot be unequivocally assessed with objective evidence, the individual must judge the correctness of his attitudes by comparing them with the attitudes of others. The evidence regarding one's attitudes, in other words, is largely social. Hence anyone who expresses an opinion contrary to that of the individual is in effect providing him with contradictory evidence. People with dissimilar attitudes thus pose a threat to the validity of our thoughts and feelings. This potential for threat is particularly strong if the dissimilar person is perceived to be competent and influential. We aren't too ruffled when someone who is notoriously slow, and who cannot even influence his pet puppy to wag his tail, suggests that everything we know is wrong. Conversely, agreement by someone—particularly a bright and powerful person—increases our confidence in the correctness of our attitudes. All in all, we prefer support for our beliefs rather than threats. We therefore like people with attitudes like ours and consider them good and dislike people with attitudes unlike our own and consider them bad.

So far we have discussed similarity only with regard to attitudes. People can also be similar or dissimilar to one another in personality, or at least *perceive* themselves to be similar or dissimilar. Is this type of similarity related to evaluation? Do similar people like each other more than dissimilar others, or do opposites attract? As it turns out, the perception of personality similarity is related to interpersonal evaluations, but not in a simple or obvious manner; perceived similarity sometimes leads to positive evaluations, sometimes to negative evaluations.

To understand how perceived similarity relates to evaluation, it is helpful to introduce the notion of *social comparison* (Festinger, 1954). All of us have a desire to assess our personal worth. When we lack objective standards for self-assessment, we compare ourselves with other people. Our choice of others is not indiscriminate, however. To provide meaningful and precise comparisons, we seek out others whom we perceive to be similar. Consider, for example, a young woman who started playing tennis recently and who wants to assess her skill level. It would be silly and not very informative for her to judge herself against a tennis star like Arthur Ashe. Instead, someone like herself— the same age and sex, the same degree of athletic ability, and the same degree of tennis experience—provides a more meaningful comparison.

Because similar others are meaningful objects for personal

comparison, their behavior is highly salient, receiving our attention and evaluation. In some situations, the behavior of someone perceived to be similar could be highly distressing, more so than identical behavior on the part of a dissimilar person. It would be embarrassing, for example, to see one's twin brother or sister break into uncontrollable sneezing during a concert. Observing a stranger or dissimilar other making a fool of himself is not nearly so distressing; it would not reflect on one's own qualities so painfully. Because the behavior of someone perceived to be similar has greater personal relevance than the behavior of a dissimilar other, the similar person's behavior is likely to receive closer scrutiny and be subject to more extreme evaluation. In some situations this evaluation will be highly positive; in others, highly negative.

A demonstration of this point is provided in a study by Taylor and Mettee (1971). Female undergraduates were recruited for a study of "impression formation." Each subject was informed that she would be paired with another female, and that the two of them were to form impressions of each other. Half the subjects were told that the other female was highly similar to them in personality, as assessed by a "valid personality inventory." The remaining subjects were told that the other female was not at all similar to them in personality. While the experiment was being introduced to the subject and her partner, a telephone in an adjoining room conveniently rang and the experimenter went to answer it. While she was gone, the subject's partner—an accomplice of the experimenter—behaved in either a pleasant way or an obnoxious way to the subject. In the pleasant condition, she smiled a lot, agreed with the opinions of the subject, and expressed interest in the subject's academic major, career plans, and so forth. In contrast, the obnoxious partner bragged about herself and by implication insulted the subject.

After a few minutes, the experimenter returned, and again explained that the study was concerned with impression formation. To assess their impressions of each other "before the experiment begins," she asked each woman to complete a questionnaire. One of the key items on this instrument was, "How much do you feel you like your partner at this moment?" A fifteen-point scale was provided for the subject's response. The results, portrayed in Figure 4.2, showed that the subject's attraction for the similar partner tended to be extreme: if the partner behaved pleasantly, she was liked a great deal; if she behaved obnoxiously, she was judged very negatively. Liking for the dissimilar partner, however, was not significantly affected by the pleasantness or obnoxiousness of her behavior; she was judged rather neutrally in both conditions. In short, if the indi-

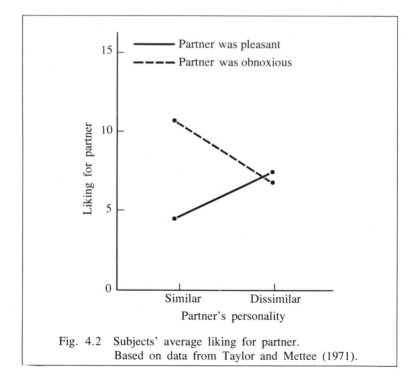

Fig. 4.2   Subjects' average liking for partner.
Based on data from Taylor and Mettee (1971).

vidual perceives someone to be similar to himself in personality, it matters a great deal how that person behaves. The behavior of someone with whom the individual does not identify, meanwhile, is far less salient, since it does not reflect on the individual's own qualities.

To summarize briefly, it appears that similarity is strongly implicated in our judgments of good and bad. Similarity in attitudes, first of all, is directly related to evaluation. Those with similar attitudes are seen positively because their agreement provides supporting evidence for the individual's opinions and feelings. Persons with dissimilar attitudes, on the other hand, tend to viewed negatively since they threaten the individual with contradictory evidence for his beliefs. The relationship between perceived personality similarity and evaluation is somewhat different. Because a person perceived to have the same characteristics is a meaningful object for personal comparison, the behavior of such a person is highly salient and subject to intense evaluation. Whether this evaluation will be positive or negative, however, depends on the similar person's behavior.

Difference in Fate: The "Just-World" Assumption
It is a fact of life that some people experience more tragedy and suffering than others. It is also apparent that some individuals receive more than their share of good fortunc, enjoying unexpected rewards denied to those around them. What may be less obvious is that such differences in fate are often the basis for interpersonal evaluations. According to Melvin Lerner (Lerner, Miller, and Holmes, 1976), the individual has a need to believe in a "just world," one in which people obtain the outcomes they deserve. Belief in a just world gives the individual a sense of security. If the individual did *not* believe that people get what they deserve, then he would have to acknowledge the possibility that terrible, undeserved things could happen to him. Assuming that the world is basically just reduces the threat of unwarranted misfortune.

Although this belief serves an important psychological function, it can sometimes lead to unjust evaluations of others. Suppose that someone has suffered an extreme misfortune—has been robbed and beaten on a city street, for example. Rational as well as compassionate considerations should lead one to blame the perpetrator of the act, the situation in which it occurred (an unsafe part of town) or possibly bad luck or chance (it could happen to anyone). According to the just-world notion, however, the victim will be seen as at least partially responsible for his fate. The observer may come to feel either that the victim in some way provoked the act (wearing expensive clothes in a poor neighborhood, for example) or that some personal quality of the victim made him a more deserving target than someone else (he cheats on his taxes or exploits others in business transactions). In other words, people tend to make internal attributions for others' misfortunes; if luck or outside forces were solely responsible, it could happen to us.

To demonstrate the just-world belief in action, Lerner and Simmons (1966) conducted an interesting laboratory experiment. Female undergraduates volunteered for a study allegedly concerned with the perception of emotional arousal in others. Over closed-circuit TV, subjects saw another female—actually, an accomplice of the experimenter—trying to learn the correct pairing of certain nonsense syllables (for example, *xif* paired with *anw*). By prearrangement, she occasionally made mistakes, incorrectly pairing two nonsense syllables. To "promote learning," each mistake appeared to be punished with a severe electric shock. The accomplice's feigned reaction to each shock was decidedly unpleasant; she would clench her fists, grit her teeth, and otherwise give evidence of anguish and suffering. Subjects were instructed to observe her reactions to the shocks carefully, since they would later report their perceptions of her arousal.

There were several conditions in this experiment. In the

"midpoint" condition, subjects had a brief intermission after observing the victim suffer for ten minutes. Before again observing the learning trials, and hence the suffering of the victim, subjects were given an opportunity to indicate their evaluation of the victim on a variety of dimensions (likableness, maturity, etc.). In the "endpoint" condition, after viewing the victim's plight for ten minutes, subjects believed that the experiment was over and hence that she would suffer no more. Again, subjects were asked to evaluate the victim on a variety of dimensions. In another important condition, the victim at first refused to take part in an experiment where she would receive electric shocks. But when the experimenter pointed out that none of the observers (subjects) would be able to receive reimbursement for their participation if "she loused up the experiment," she reluctantly agreed to participate. This "martyr" condition resembled the endpoint condition in that after ten minutes of observing the victim's suffering, the subjects believed the experiment to be over. As in the other conditions, subjects evaluated the victim at this point.

Lerner and Simmons reasoned as follows. If an observer believes that the victim's suffering has ended and no permanent harm has been done, there should be little need to derogate her in order to maintain belief in deservingness and justice. Her fate is not bad enough to require lowered evaluation of her personal characteristics. However, if faced with the prospect of seeing an innocent victim continue to suffer, the observer might feel compelled to devalue the victim's characteristics. Hence, the victim in the midpoint condition was expected to be evaluated more harshly than the endpoint victim. The most negative evaluation of all, however, was expected in the martyr condition; the suffering of someone who is acting out of altruistic motives should be most threatening to belief in a just world. Their predictions were confirmed; the martyr was described more negatively than the midpoint victim, who in turn received a lower evaluation

than the endpoint victim. To make sense out of continued innocent suffering, especially altruistic suffering, the individual attributes negative qualities to the victim and thereby reduces the
perceived injustice.

Following the just-world logic one step further, consider how
an observer might react to the suffering of someone for whom
devaluation is more difficult. What if we learn that nasty things
have happened to someone who is highly regarded? Remember
that there are two ways in which a person might "deserve" to
suffer: his personal characteristics may be undesirable, or he in
some way may have acted to bring about his own fate. This
suggests that if something awful happens to someone, the victim
will be seen as more responsible for his suffering if he is good
and respectable than if he is bad and not respectable. In a just
world, disasters don't happen to good people—victims must be
partly responsible for their own fate.

A study designed to test this prediction demonstrates how unjust the just-world assumption can be. Jones and Aronson
(1973) presented college students with the details of an alleged
case of rape and asked them to make various judgments about it.
According to a written account of the incident, a young woman
had attended a night class at the university and was walking
across campus toward home when she was assaulted and raped
by the defendant. There was nothing in the description to
suggest that the woman had in any way enticed the man or
otherwise brought about her own fate, although too few details
were given to rule out this possibility entirely. The descriptions
varied in one important way: some subjects read that the victim
was a divorcee, others that she was a married woman, and a
third group that she was a virgin. In addition to indicating the
prison term they would recommend for the defendant, subjects
were asked, "how much do you consider the crime to be the
victim's fault?" Ratings were made on a twenty-one-point

scale, ranging from -10 (not at all her fault) to $+10$ (entirely her fault).

Again, there are two ways in which a person can maintain belief in a just world on hearing of someone's suffering. The person can assume either that the victim brought about her own fate (through enticement, for example, or simply by being in the wrong place at the wrong time) or that some personal characteristic of the victim made her a more deserving victim than someone else. Jones and Aronson provide evidence that, at least in our culture, married women and virgins are generally seen as having more social respectability than a divorcee. Thus, we are left with the rather curious prediction that, in order to salvage the belief in a just world, the married woman and the virgin should be seen as more responsible for their rape than the divorcee for her rape. Because of their greater respectability, the married woman and virgin did not deserve the rape as a function of their intrinsic characteristics; hence, they must have done something to cause it. As can be seen in Figure 4.3, this is what the results indicated.

In one sense, it is reassuring to find that people strive to maintain belief in a just world; according to Lerner, society could not function if this were not so. But this belief can have a distorting effect on our perceptions—it can lead to an unjust derogation of an innocent victim's personality as well as an unnecessarily skeptical interpretation of his or her behavior.

Labels

It is possible for an extreme evaluation to be made of someone without any knowledge of the person's personal characteristics, the degree to which he or she shares similar attitudes or a similar personality, or whether he or she has suffered particular misfortunes. It is not even necessary for any contact to have taken place between the evaluator and the evaluatee. This can happen when a person is identified by a label, particularly a label suggesting deviance or abnormality. Terms like "criminal," "pervert," "psychotic," "alcoholic," "prostitute," and "dope addict" generate vivid images of the person so labeled, even though the person has never been encountered by the imaginer. Of course, labels are useful, sometimes even necessary. Having to experience every object in one's environment directly in order to determine whether it is safe or dangerous, good or bad, is not only time-consuming, but potentially unpleasant or even dangerous. By summarizing many pieces of information with a handy word or phrase, the individual can respond more or less

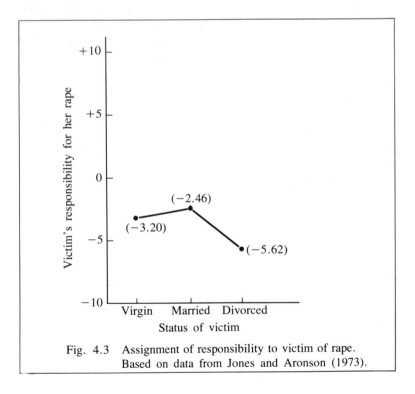

Fig. 4.3   Assignment of responsibility to victim of rape. Based on data from Jones and Aronson (1973).

appropriately to different stimuli. Labels tell us whom to approach and whom to avoid.

Most people assume, for example, that ex-convicts are not to be trusted and that former mental patients are unstable. Most people therefore would tend to avoid interaction with someone said to be an ex-convict or a former mental patient, even though they know nothing about the particular individual. But, of course, not all ex-convicts are untrustworthy or dangerous, nor are all former mental patients on the verge of bizarre behavior. There is thus a drawback to a reliance on labels for evaluative information: they can cause us unnecessarily to avoid or think ill of someone who may really be quite approachable and deserving of a good evaluation.

In addition to this obvious drawback, there are other consequences of labels that are somewhat more subtle and considerably more distressing. A study by Rosenthal and Jacobson (1968) illustrates one such effect—the "self-fulfilling prophecy." Children in an elementary school in San Francisco were given an intelligence test. Besides giving a measure of the child's IQ at the time, this test was said to predict "intellectual blooming," that is, whether the child would show significant gains in IQ over time. The teachers of these children were then given false information about the results of the test. They were told that some of the children had scored high on the "blooming" test and would therefore show significant gains in intellectual development during the next eight months. In reality, however, the children identified as bloomers (about 20 percent of the children in each classroom) were chosen completely at random. There was no difference between these children and their classmates except in the minds of the teachers.

Rosenthal and Jacobson were interested in whether this evaluative information—the bloomer label—would affect the teacher's treatment of these children and thus, perhaps, the actual performance of the children. To test this possibility, all the children were given the same IQ test at the end of the school year. The results were revealing: the children randomly designated as bloomers showed a significantly larger gain in IQ than did their "non-bloomer" classmates. Even more striking are the differences in personal evaluations of bloomers and non-bloomers given by the teachers. Compared with the non-bloomers, children in the bloomer group were described by their teachers as more interesting, more curious, and happier. They were also seen as better adjusted, more appealing, more affectionate, and as having less need for approval from others. Of course, some of the children in the non-bloomer group also demonstrated gains in IQ. But rather than perceiving these pupils positively, as they did the bloomers, the teachers reacted *negatively* to their unexpected improvement. The more a non-bloomer gained in IQ, the more he or she was seen as less well-adjusted, less interesting, and less affectionate.

If labels affect interpersonal behavior and perception in an academic setting, imagine the effect of a label that suggests not something positive like high IQ potential, but instead something "abnormal" like mental illness. Such a label may generate a strong expectation for certain behaviors. This expectation, in turn, may function as a self-fulfilling prophecy. Suppose you are "warned" ahead of time that someone you are about to meet is in therapy with a clinical psychologist for emotional problems. Your notion of what "neurotics" are like may affect your behavior toward him, bringing about reactions on his part that confirm your expectations. Even a "sympathetic" approach on your part may bring out evidence of his presumed instability. You may talk slowly and in a measured, reassuring voice about such nonstressful topics as the weather, the use and abuse of light bulbs, and the meaning of lunch. Such an approach would probably be interpreted by the person as either evidence of your dim-wittedness or as condescension. If the former, the person might well adopt a similar orientation toward you ("Yes, the trees are pretty and the birdies are nice . . ."), thus confirming your expectation of weird conversation with him; or he might become impatient, thereby demonstrating his instability. If he interprets your behavior as condescension, he may become insulted and angry and begin to behave very much as you think a "neurotic" should.

Even if a labeled person is not influenced by our expectation, we may still *think* that he or she is behaving as anticipated. Remember that attribution involves complex information processing. The number and variety of "facts" surrounding a person's behavior is enormous, often rendering the meaning of a given act somewhat ambiguous and open to different interpretations. An act as simple as a smile, for example, may represent warmth and affection or sarcasm and condescension. Because social reality is often ambiguous, a perceiver's expectations can yield an explanation for someone's behavior that is consistent with his preconceptions. One of the rules of attribution, in fact, is that stable internal attributions tend to stick. Once someone has been labeled, all his subsequent behaviors, even inconsequential ones, are interpreted in terms of that label. A laughing fit by someone considered "normal" is not interpreted in the same way as a similar laughing fit by someone labeled "mentally ill." The former represents heightened appreciation of a funny event; the latter suggests heightened deterioration of a funny mind.

Earlier we pointed out that the perception of difference can lead to a negative evaluation of someone. The reverse is also true: a negative evaluation engendered by a label like "mental illness" can lead to the perception of difference. Mental illness is more threatening than physical illness. A person recovers from a broken arm and perhaps can even be cured of cancer. But mental illness is perceived to be a stable, internal quality, something that never really goes away. The possibility that one may harbor the seeds of mental illness is therefore highly distressing.

Not surprisingly, then, the individual attempts to place as much psychological distance as possible between himself and anyone labeled as "crazy" or "disturbed." To demonstrate the threatening quality of mental illness, Novak and Lerner (1968) led college students to believe that they were either similar or dissimilar in some essential ways to a former mental patient. They found that the mental patient was avoided more if he was believed to be similar than if he was believed to be dissimilar. The belief that one is similar to a mentally ill person is very threatening; it implies the possibility that one may also have the potential for "craziness."

Many people, not just those in therapy, experience difficulty in adjusting to the demands of daily living. As an implicit psychologist, the individual is rarely at a loss to characterize someone's "problem." Over the years, jargon from clinical psychology has become commonplace in everyday language. At one time or another, each of us has diagnosed an acquaintance as "paranoid," "compulsive," or "defensive." Labels such as these give the illusion of explanation since they predict the person's behavior in a wide variety of settings. Suppose you infer that someone is paranoid, for example. Not only can you guess his reaction to hordes of people whispering behind his back, you can confidently estimate his interpretation of a wrong-number telephone call ("Burglars are checking to see if I'm home") or his reaction to an accidental collision in a hallway ("Where's my wallet?").

In sum, labels are powerful sources of evaluative information, and have important consequences for one's perception and treatment of others. First of all, by attending to the label, not the person, we may unnecessarily avoid contact with people whom we might otherwise like. Perhaps more importantly, labels can function as self-fulfilling prophecies: when we expect a person to act a certain way, we sometimes behave in a manner that brings about the expected behavior. In addition, labels, especially those suggesting abnormality, represent stable, internal attributions; a person's behavior is interpreted in a way that is consistent with his or her label. And because of their threatening connotation, labels indicating abnormality can lead to the perception of exaggerated difference between oneself and the labeled person. Finally, most of us have been influenced by theories of abnormal psychology, and are quite adept at assigning clinical labels to others.

Implicit Abnormal Psychology and Clinical Psychology

Experimental psychology does not attempt to identify who the good and bad people really are. To the experimental psychologist, particular individuals are neither good nor bad; they are objects to be investigated, not evaluated. From this perspective, a person's attitudes, personal characteristics, and outcomes simply represent data points. Not all psychologists are detached experimentalists, however. In fact, a sizable percentage of psychologists—known as clinical psychologists—are professionally concerned with identifying those individuals who are deviant, abnormal, disturbed, or who generally perceive themselves to be less than OK. Having identified those with problems, clinical psychologists attempt to help such individuals become healthy and happy people. Because of the nature of their profession, clinical psychologists have standards for judging and evaluating others. They also have explicit theories about how healthy and unhealthy people got to be the way they are. It is of interest, then, to compare the implicit psychologist's notions of good and bad with the more explicit notions of good (desirable functioning) and bad (undesirable functioning) held by the clinical psychologist.

Similarities

There is much in common between implicit psychology and clinical psychology. First of all, in both cases there is a pronounced tendency to assign traits to people. Like the layman, but unlike most experimental psychologists, the clinician readily infers inner dispositions that cause a person to behave in certain ways across many different situations. Of course, the clinician has fancier terms at his disposal than the layman. Clinicians do not use terms like "crazy," "loony," or "bananas" to characterize disturbed individuals. Instead, words like "schizophrenia," "personality disorder," and "manic-depressive psychosis" are employed when someone who seems very disturbed is diagnosed. Similarly, what the layman would call "nervousness" or "insecurity" might be labeled "manifest anxiety" and "chronic need for approval," respectively, by a clinician.

The clinician's use of traits to explain behavior may reflect, in part, the same factors that lead the layman to make internal attributions. Like the lay observer, the clinical psychologist observes the actor in very few settings. And these settings are hardly typical; most people, even neurotics, feel and act differently in a therapist's office than they do in their living room. Of course, the client in therapy reports how he behaves in everyday settings, but his selection of events to report is probably based on their significance rather than their representativeness. Hence, lacking distinctiveness information (information about how the person behaves in different situations) the clinician must rely on consensus and consistency information. As noted in Chapter 2, inadequate distinctiveness information is one of the reasons the individual tends to make internal rather than external attributions.

It should be kept in mind, though, that clinicians are not exactly dealing with a random segment of the population. The people who seek or require professional help for emotional and behavioral problems are generally those who feel atypical, different from others, and perhaps innappropriate in their responses to various stresses, demands, and expectations. Unlike the typical actor who feels that his behavior "depends on the situation," the disturbed individual is likely to ascribe dispositions such as anxiety and depression to himself. Even in a nonstressful situation, for example, such a person may experience considerable anxiety. Because individuals with psychological problems demonstrate greater trans-situational consistency than do "normal" individuals (Campus, 1974; Snyder and Monson, 1975), the clinician may be justified in assigning broad dispositions to explain their behavior. That is, if such a person's behavior does not vary from situation to situation, there must be something about the person that causes him or her to act that way.

Implicit and clinical psychology are similar in another respect. We have argued that evaluations of others depend to a large extent on the perceiver; an individual considered good by one perceiver often seems undesirable to another. Clinical judgments, too, often depend on the clinician. It has been shown, for example, that two clinicians are likely to disagree in their trait judgments about the same person (Goldberg and Werts, 1966). There is evidence, moreover, that the problems attributed to clients by therapists often reflect areas in which the therapists themselves have problems (Weingarten, 1949). A therapist concerned with his inability to express anger may see evidence of "repressed feelings" in many of his clients. Thus, just as the individual consistently selects certain information about others, the clinician looks for the same sorts of problems in a wide variety of clients. Clinicians also differ in their conceptions of health and normality. A bias of many psychologists in the Western world is to consider individuality healthy; conformity and dependence on others, by contrast, are undesirable. But clinicians in the People's Republic of China and other Eastern countries are more likely to consider individuality to be deviant, potentially threatening to their political system, and hence bad. Even within our own country, clinicians disagree about which characteristics are desirable and which are not. Someone who spends much of his time alone, engaged in artistic endeavors, and unconcerned about mundane earthly matters would be considered a "self-actualizer" by many clinicians. Others, however, might consider such a person to be arrogant, self-indulgent, and lacking in social sensitivity. Just as two observers often differ in their evaluation of the same person, two clinicians may disagree in their diagnosis of a given client.

There is yet another similarity between implicit and clinical psychology that deserves mention. As discussed earlier, labels play a significant role in our evaluations of others. We noted, among other things, that the behavior of a labeled person is often interpreted in a way that is consistent with the label. This is particularly true for clinical labels, since they are assumed to be scientific and authoritative. And it appears that clinical psychologists are similarly impressed by these labels; an unusual experiment by Rosenhan (1973) demonstrates that mental health experts, like implicit psychologists, often see what they want to see. To discover how it feels to be a mental patient, eight well-adjusted individuals attempted to have themselves admitted to a mental hospital. In addition to Rosenhan, the volunteers included two other psychologists, a psychiatrist, a pediatrician, a psychology graduate student, a painter, and a housewife. Five of the volunteers were men, three were women. Each attempted to gain admission to a different hospital in a different part of the country.

At the admissions office, the "pseudopatient" complained that he or she had been hearing voices. The voices seemed to be saying words like "empty," "hollow," and "thud." Aside from giving the symptoms and a false name and occupation, no further deceptions were committed by the pseudopatient. When asked about his or her life history, the pseudopatient reported as accurately as possible his or her relationships with parents and siblings, with spouse and children, and with acquaintances and co-workers. Apparently, hearing voices is enough to get oneself labeled "insane"—all the pseudopatients but one were diagnosed as schizophrenic and admitted to the psychiatric ward.

After being admitted, the pseudopatients immediately ceased to display any evidence of abnormality. Their task was to act perfectly normal, convince the staff that they were "sane," and thereby gain their release. This turned out to be difficult; despite their outward signs of normality, *none* of the pseudopatients were detected by the staff. Interestingly, some of the *patients* in these hospitals did suspect the pseudopatient's "sanity." Occasionally, for example, a patient would approach a pseudopatient and ask if he or she were really a professor "checking up on this place." All were eventually discharged, of course, but not as "cured" or "normal"; instead, they were discharged with a diagnosis of "schizophrenia in remission." The average length of hospitalization was nineteen days, although it took one unfortunate volunteer fifty-two days to be discharged.

This study demonstrates the "stickiness" of diagnostic labels. Once the pseudopatient was labeled as schizophrenic, all of his or her behaviors were perceived accordingly. Many normal behaviors were either ignored or given abnormal interpretations. And normal reactions to the institutional setting were often attributed by the staff to the pseudopatient's pathology. For example, pacing the long hospital corridor out of boredom was interpreted as chronic tension. Expressing resentment when mistreated by an attendant—not an uncommon experience— was considered evidence of the pseudopatient's instability. The staff expected pathology; if obvious pathology was not forthcoming, more mundane behavior was interpreted to fit the expectation.

To summarize, there are three noteworthy similarities between implicit evaluations and clinical diagnoses. First, both the layman and the clinician are trait psychologists; dispositions are attributed to people to explain their behavior. Secondly, diagnosis, like evaluation, depends to an important extent on the perceiver; it is not unusual for two clinicians to disagree in their judgment of someone's health or adjustment. And third, if a person is identified by a diagnostic label, both the layman and the clinician judge the person's behavior in accordance with that label.

Differences

At the same time, there are some important differences between implicit abnormal psychology and clinical psychology. To begin with, clinical psychologists are more sensitive to the fact that "causes have causes." Unlike the layman, the professional typically investigates *causal chains*—the sequence of causes leading up to the present—before forming a detailed impression of someone. Under certain circumstances, for example, both the layman and the psychologist might attribute a bad act to an internal quality of the actor. The psychologist would want to know *why* the actor has that particular quality—what forces in the actor's past caused his present trait. Only after attributing the causes of the actor's attributes does the clinician feel comfortable in generating a characterization of him or her. The layman, on the other hand, ends his causal analysis once a trait has been attributed to the actor. There is less of an explicit concern with remote causes. All that really matters is what caused the act, not what caused the cause. Deducing a characteristic of the actor makes him or her fair game for evaluation.

Let's say that both a clinician and a layman have learned of an incident in which a man with a record of assault attacked and injured another man at a bar. It is clear to both the layman and the psychologist that the man has a tendency toward aggression that, with minimal provocation, causes him to attack others. Once the immediate cause of the act has been established, the layman wastes little time in evaluating the person—anyone who beats up another person without provocation is bad. In contrast, the clinical psychologist would be reluctant to render a final judgment, arguing that much more needs to be determined before the man can be accurately characterized. The psychologist is aware that there are a number of possible reasons why the man is predisposed to behave in this fashion. It may be, for example, that during the past year he has suffered a number of frustrating and unfair setbacks, such as being swindled, having his car stolen, and losing his home and possessions. These experiences have made him somewhat irritable, even touchy. Unable to tolerate even minor frustrations any more, he reacts violently to the slightest provocation by anyone. On the other hand, the cause of the man's aggressiveness may be much more remote, stemming back to his relations with his parents during childhood. They may have treated him harshly or, perhaps worse, ignored him most of the time. Clinical psychologists are keenly aware that childhood experiences, particularly those involving one's parents, are crucial in determining one's behavioral tendencies, even in adulthood.

Vastly different characterizations of the man follow from these possible explanations of his aggressiveness. If the psychologist feels that the man is responding to a series of recent setbacks, the cause of the man's aggressiveness will be perceived to be internal but variable—his aggressive tendency may dissipate if his misfortunes cease. But if his aggressiveness stems from parental mistreatment, an internal and *stable* attribution will be made—the man is doomed to be aggressive. In one case, the person's deviance is temporary; in the other, it is a basic and undesirable part of his personality. In short, the clinician ponders missing links in the chain of causation before judging an actor. The layman, meanwhile, is concerned only with immediate causes. That the layman often does not fully consider remote causes before passing judgment on someone has been demonstrated in research on attribution (Brickman, Ryan, and Wortman, 1975).

A second difference between the clinician and the layman follows from the first. Because the clinical psychologist is sensitive to remote causes, he is likely to stress the similarities rather than the differences between normal, well-adjusted individuals and those who experience emotional and behavioral difficulties. A well-adjusted person is simply someone who has experienced fewer causes of maladjustment during his lifetime than a troubled person. And anyone, no matter how well-adjusted, is capable of emotional crisis and bizarre behavior if the right forces impinge upon him. Thus, to the clinical psychologist, normality and abnormality are represented along a continuum; everyone has certain problems and undesirable tendencies. This attitude is in contrast to the implicit psychologist's perspective. As we pointed out earlier, the belief that one is similar to a disturbed person is threatening. The individual would rather believe that disturbed people are a unique species, qualitatively different from himself. Moreover, the tendency toward cognitive consistency makes it unlikely that the individual will see health and abnormality together in the same person. Thus, the implicit psychologist emphasizes the differences rather than the similarities between normal, well-adjusted, desirable people and those whom he considers to be abnormal, deviant, and undesirable.

The implicit psychologist and the clinical psychologist also differ in the means by which they validate their notions of good and bad. When the psychologist infers that someone has a problem, he attempts to test his inference objectively. Most often, validation consists of psychological testing. Numerous tests have been developed over the years; some of them are fairly good predictors of various emotional and behavioral problems, although many are not. Occasionally, the astute professional will look for other sources of evidence. He may, for example, interview the family and acquaintances of the problem person, or seek out the opinions of other mental health experts. Unfortunately, quite often the psychologist's evidence, even the evidence from psychological tests, is not reliably objective; in fact, it can be quite insubstantial (see Chapman and Chapman, 1969).

But at least the professional makes an attempt at objective validation.

The layman, on the other hand, makes little pretense of obtaining unbiased evidence and objectively testing his evaluation of someone. If outside evidence is sought at all, it is the opinions held by friends—those with similar attitudes. This concern with consensual validation is strongest when the individual is uncertain of his views. Suppose a young woman, Mary, has a negative impression of a recent acquaintance, Phyllis. If she is convinced that Phyllis is a terrible, nasty person—perhaps because Phyllis disagrees with Mary on topics ranging from women's rights to the need for microwave ovens—then there is little need for Mary to find out how her friends evaluate Phyllis. In fact, if she discovered that her friends *liked* Phyllis, Mary's evaluation of *them* might go sour—after all, they hold a dissimilar attitude. However, if Mary is uncertain of her evaluation of Phyllis, she is likely to seek out her friends to see how they feel about Phyllis. If they dislike Phyllis, this would confirm Mary's suspicion about Phyllis's unworthiness; if they like Phyllis, Mary might change her opinion and try to find Phyllis's good points. Compared with the clinician, then, the layman is relatively unconcerned with objective evidence regarding the soundness of a person's character. Implicit judgments of good and bad have no necessary relation to objective reality.

Finally, the individual and the clinician sometimes have different notions about what characteristics of a person are desirable and healthy and what characteristics are bad or indicative of pathology. Consider, for example, a man who is dissatisfied with his job and tormented by his in-laws, but maintains his job because of the security it provides his family, and inhibits his anger towards his in-laws to avoid putting his wife in an uncomfortable situation. His acquantances may see him as highly mature and responsible since he places the financial security of his family above his own personal needs. His wife will no doubt appreciate his tactfulness and consideration, attributing qualities such as tolerance and strength to him. In short, he is seen as a good fellow.

In contrast, a clinical psychologist might see this man as unhealthy psychologically. His commitment to a rotten job is the mark of a man who has given up hope of finding fulfillment in his career; a defeated man is not a healthy man. As for his tactful dealings with his tormenting in-laws, the clinician might label such behavior as "repressive" rather than considerate. Many psychologists feel that it is unhealthy to hold back anger and resentment. Repression of negative feelings and impulses, no matter how pragmatic, is like a central trait to many clinicians; a repressed person is in psychological trouble. Not only is repression a sign of a wounded psyche, it is implicated in bodily malfunctions such as ulcers, asthma, and arthritis as well. To take another example, a woman who agrees with her husband on every single issue may be seen by him—and his male friends—as a "fine wife." But a clinician—as well as her liberated acquaintances—might judge her to be insecure, afraid to express her own ideas, and high in need for approval. Thus, the same behavior on someone's part can lead to vastly different evaluations of the actor, depending on whether the evaluator is an amateur or a professional.

In sum, there are important differences between implicit abnormal psychology and the orientation shared by many clinical psychologists. Clinicians, first of all, are more likely to take into account an individual's personal history before making judgments of him or her. Second, the clinician stresses the relativity of concepts like normality and mental health, while the layman emphasizes the discontinuity between desirable and undesirable people. Third, the clinical psychologist attempts to support or refute his diagnosis with objective evidence; the layman relies on consensual validation, using the opinions of like-minded others to support his own subjective impressions of someone.

And fourth, the professional and the implicit psychologist sometimes have different evaluations of the same behavior.

The processes of evaluation discussed **the implicit** above apply more or less to everyone. Whether we like to admit it or not, **psychologist** all of us judge people against subjective standards. However, this does not mean that evaluation is a simple-minded affair. Although deciding whether someone is good or bad is hardly a detached and objective undertaking, it does involve observation, information processing, and deduction—in short, thinking. Adult thinking is different from childhood thinking; it is reasonable, therefore, that certain aspects of evaluation should show developmental changes. Moreover, because adults differ from one another in how they think, there should be individual differences in how others are evaluated. In this section, we will discuss some of the ways in which evaluation changes during the course of development, as well as differences in evaluation tendencies among adults.

Developmental   According to Jean Piaget, there are sev-
Changes   eral important ways in which thought
                     changes from infancy through adulthood.
In Chapter 2, we discussed one of these developmental progressions, namely, the change from a damage-based to an intention-based assessment of good and bad behaviors. The very young child judges the goodness or badness of an act in accordance with the consequences of the act: if good things happen, the act as well as the actor are good; if bad things happen, the act and actor are bad. At a later age, the child considers the intention of the actor when he evaluates the actor and his deeds. Thus, even if someone has caused considerable damage, that person may be judged favorably by the older child if the per-

son's intentions are perceived to have been good. Conversely, the perception of a bad intention condemns the person to a negative evaluation, even if the outcomes of the person's acts are desirable.

Perhaps this is why it is easier to ingratiate a six-year-old than a twelve-year-old. To make friends with the younger child, all that is usually required is providing him with nice consequences, such as giving him a piece of candy or making a funny face. Bribery, flattery, or other forms of ingratiation are less likely to succeed with the older child. Of course, he or she may readily accept any goodies that are offered, but this is not enough to win a positive evaluation if the child sees the gift-giving as an attempt to manipulate him or her. After consuming his seventh candy bar, the child may anticipate and reject a forthcoming request, pointing out that "you're only being nice because you want me to clean the chimney again."

Actually, the shift from a concern with consequences to a concern with intentions reflects a more general developmental progression. As the child matures, his thinking becomes less *concrete* and more *abstract*. The very young child often can give detailed accounts of specific events or describe the physical features of objects, but is unable to specify the underlying similarities and differences among the various events or objects. The ability to abstract features of one's environment is not really developed until about twelve years of age. This age-related difference is apparent also in the child's characterizations of other people. Concrete characterizations involve references to specific observable features, such as "red hair," or to specific events, such as "she eats big lunches." Abstract characterizations refer to inferred inner qualities of the person that transcend specific features or behaviors. While the younger child might describe someone in terms of specific overt acts ("he hits me a lot"), the more mature child attributes a disposition to the person that can account for a number of specific acts ("he's aggressive"). Since the mature thinker is more concerned with inner qualities than is the immature thinker, the former is somewhat less likely to judge someone on the basis of personal habits, mannerisms, or other "superficial" behaviors. A six-year-old, Trixie, might be troubled by Rudy's penchant for running in circles at inopportune times and decide not to associate with him for that reason. But an adolescent, Irma, might overlook similar habits by Ricky, and even feel attracted toward him if she considered him to be kindly, warm, and witty.

Another developmental change in thought is the transition from *egocentric* thinking to *non-egocentric* thinking. The child whose thinking is egocentric knows and understands things only in relation to himself. The notion that people, objects, and events can have value apart from his relation to them is not understood by the very young child. When asked to describe her best friend, for example, six-year-old Sarah might say, "She gave me her nicest doll and she lets me lick her ice cream cones." At a later age, the child begins to realize that people exist as separate entities apart from their relation to him. With the ability to see things from a more detached, less egocentric vantage point, the child begins to judge others on their own merits. Thus, ten-year-old Tim might consider Tom a good fellow because Tom "wears neat cowboy shirts and can run real fast." Note that the egocentric–non-egocentric dimension is different from the concrete-abstract dimension. Concrete characterizations are often egocentric ("she gave me her nicest doll") but can be non-egocentric as well ("he wears neat cowboy shirts"). Abstract characterizations, however, are typically non-egocentric; the inner qualities of a person are judged to exist independently of the person's relation with the observer. Although the concrete-abstract and egocentric–non-egocentric dimensions are independent of each other, research has shown that the progression from concrete to abstract characterizations roughly parallels the transition from egocentric to non-egocentric evaluations (see, for example, Bigner, 1974; Scarlett, Press, and Crockett, 1971).

Another developmental change in evaluation has to do with differentiation. The more mentally mature a child is, and the more interpersonal experiences he has had, the greater his ability to distinguish among people in his social environment. One way in which differentiation is accomplished is through the judgment of others in terms of many independent dimensions. According to Olshan (1974), the increase in differentiation with development reflects the decomposition or "breaking up" of a global evaluative dimension into more specific dimensions. The immature child makes only one evaluative distinction among people; the world is divided into those who are good and those who are bad. With development, the child begins to distinguish between two types of good and bad—social good-bad and intellectual good-bad. Attributes like warmth, friendliness, and sincerity characterize the socially desirable person, while intellectual desirability is reflected in such traits as intelligence, energy, and creativity. It is thus possible for the more mature child to see someone as bad in one of these ways but good in another. With increasing maturity, the individual recognizes that many traits are relevant to both social adjustment and competence, and that these traits may be independent of one another. Thus, by adulthood the individual acknowledges that a person can be friendly but insincere or smart but not particularly creative. Of course, acknowledging the possibility is one thing and perceiving someone in this manner is another. As stressed earlier, implicit personality theories are characterized by evaluative consistency; even the mature adult tends to make fairly global evaluations of others. But because of his potential for seeing others in a differentiated way, the tendency toward evaluative consistency can be counteracted if the individual perceives evidence in support of an evaluatively differentiated impression of someone. Typically, the better we know someone, the more we realize that he or she is not all good or all bad; instead, we perceive the person to have a particular combination of assets and liabilities.

In short, although evaluation is inherently a subjective, self-serving process, the child demonstrates increasing maturity in his evaluations as he gets older. Compared with the cognitively immature person, the more mature person judges others on the basis of perceived intentions and dispositions rather than simply on their overt behavior. Moreover, the mature individual is better able to recognize that people exist and can be good or bad apart from their relation to him. Finally, the mature individual is able—though not always willing—to see someone as good in some ways and bad in others.

Individual Differences   Quite often evaluation depends as much on the observer as on the object of evaluation. A person who seems bright and lovable to one observer may appear dim and despicable to another. This does not mean, however, that evaluation is entirely idiosyncratic; some individuals are highly similar to one another in their evaluation tendencies. Whether two individuals share various evaluation tendencies depends in part on their personalities. Individuals who are similar to one another with regard to certain attributes tend to approach the evaluation of others in much the same way. We will consider two such personality variables that are relevant to individual differences and similarities in evaluation: self-esteem and dogmatism.

Self-esteem

People differ in how they feel about themselves. Some people, those said to have high self-esteem, think quite highly of themselves. In contrast, those with low self-esteem have serious doubts about their personal worth. This self-evaluation tendency is related to the way one typically evaluates others. In general, a person who likes himself evaluates others more positively than does a person who does not like himself. If a person has low self-esteem, he is obsessed with his own flaws and shortcomings, and tends to notice similar liabilities in others. A person with a positive self-concept, on the other hand, is ready to perceive positive qualities in others and can confidently approach others without fear of rejection.

The close relationship between self-acceptance and acceptance of others has been noted quite frequently by both personality theorists and clinical psychologists (see, for example, Maslow, 1954; Rogers, 1951). The reason behind this relationship lies in the different world-views held by high and low self-esteem persons. Earlier, we pointed out that people tend to attach greater weight to negative information than to positive information when forming an evaluation of someone. In part, this tendency reflects the individual's concern with threat; it is more important to know what is dangerous than what is pleasant. This tendency, however, is stronger for those with low self-esteem than for those with a more positive self-concept. A person with high self-esteem has a subjective sense of power to control his outcomes, expects success rather than failure, and is more concerned with potential rewards in his environment than with likely costs. This reward orientation allows the high self-esteem person to encounter others without fear of rejection or humiliation. In marked contrast, the low self-esteem individual expects things to go wrong and thus is more likely to be cost-oriented. Other people are likely to be seen as potentially threatening rather than as potentially rewarding. An individual with low self-esteem, in other words, is especially sensitive to the negative rather than the positive aspects of other people. This enhanced vigilance makes it difficult for such an individual to form positive impressions of others. Only when it is made abundantly clear that a person poses no threat will a low self-esteem person form a favorable evaluation and approach him or her.

Self-esteem also affects the relationship between attitude similarity and evaluation. Recall that people usually are more attracted to others with similar attitudes than to those with dissimilar attitudes. It appears, however, that this relationship does not hold for people who have negative views of themselves. A study by Leonard (1975) demonstrates that people with positive self-concepts typically think favorably of those with attitudes like their own—although they do not necessarily reject or judge harshly those with dissimilar attitudes. On the other hand, people with low self-esteem are no more attracted to those with similar attitudes than to those with dissimilar attitudes. For the person who is dissatisfied with himself, agreement is not an important basis for evaluation—why should you like someone who thinks as you do if you are not pleased with yourself? Still, because most people have at least a moderately positive attitude toward themselves, the relationship between similarity and evaluation appears to be quite general. Self-esteem obviously is an important topic; we shall discuss it in greater detail in Chapter 6.

Dogmatism

Some people are especially intolerant of different points of view. People who are closed-minded in this way are called *dogmatic*. According to Milton Rokeach (1960), the social psychologist who first identified dogmatism as an individual difference variable, the dogmatic person has a very rigid set of beliefs about reality and is unwilling to accept, or even tolerate, information or ideas that conflict with those beliefs. In addition, dogmatic individuals are characterized by an almost blind adherence to authority and rules; ideas and behaviors are good or bad because people with established power decree that they are good or bad.

Dogmatism has obvious implications for the way in which others are evaluated. Because of their closed-mindedness, dogmatic persons attach considerable weight to attitude similarity-dissimilarity when judging someone. They are highly intolerant of difference, rejecting those with incompatible ideas as "deviant" and hence bad. A nondogmatic person might not exactly jump for joy when he encounters someone with a different point of view, but he is more open-minded about such differences and can tolerate disagreement to a far greater degree.

The dogmatic person's adherence to authority also has implications for evaluation. For one thing, compared with highly dogmatic persons, those who are less dogmatic perceive authority figures in a more balanced fashion, reporting their negative as well as their positive characteristics (Kemp, 1963). Dogmatic persons are likely to consider policemen, military officers, and their own parents as admirable, fault-free exemplars of mankind. Similarly, it might prove difficult for a dogmatic person to acknowledge evidence of wrongdoing by someone in a position of power, particularly if the powerful person is of his own political persuasion. No doubt dogmatic Republicans experienced an unusually high number of headaches during the Watergate period. Finally, with their positive attitude toward authority and rules, dogmatic individuals are especially likely to condemn anyone who expresses opinions contrary to the views held by those in power. In the 1960's, for example, the dogmatic person—like Archie Bunker of TV's "All in the Family"—had no use for those who criticized American involvement in the Vietnam war (Karabenick and Wilson, 1969).

In summary, there are reliable differences between individuals in evaluation tendencies. Differences in self-esteem affect the relative weight given to positive and negative characteristics of others; the lower the evaluator's self-esteem, the greater his sensitivity to potentially threatening aspects of a person. This enhanced vigilance means that very few people—only those who clearly pose no threat to the evaluator—will be reacted to positively. In contrast, persons with favorable self-concepts are less threatened by others and tend to perceive people in a more positive fashion. In addition, self-esteem affects the similarity-evaluation relationship; unlike high-self-esteem persons, those with low self-esteem do not seek out those with similar attitudes. Individual differences in dogmatism also moderate the importance attached to attitude similarity in the formation of judgments, but in a different way. While high-self-esteem people like similar others, they do not actively reject dissimilar people. Dogmatic individuals, however, are highly sensitive to differences of opinion and think ill of those who express "deviant" attitudes. And because of their concern for law and order, dogmatic persons are intolerant of those who do not conform to the attitudes expressed by legitimate authority.

Summary   The individual attempts to evaluate others, not merely to understand them. This is because the individual is an applied psychologist; the theories formed about others serve as a basis of action toward them. Lacking the detachment of the experimental psychologist, the implicit psychologist exhibits certain biases in his processing of information about others. First, because he is concerned with self-protection, he gives the negative aspects of a person greater weight than the positive aspects when he forms an overall evaluation. Second, because other people cannot be both approached and avoided at the same time, the individual shows a strong concern with evaluative consistency: he tends to see other people as all good or all bad.

Several sources of information are attended to when another person is evaluated. Physical attractiveness is a superficial attribute but nonetheless operates as a very central trait; good-looking people are judged as having better characteristics and abilities than their less physically appealing counterparts. Other traits are also central (warmth, for example), but often there is little consensus among observers about whether an actor has the trait in question. Similarity in attitudes is another source of evaluative information: similar others are liked because they provide support for the individual's construction of reality. The perception of personality similarity relates to evaluation in a different way. Someone thought to have similar characteristics provides a meaningful standard for judging oneself. Such a person therefore is subject to close scrutiny and intense evaluation; compared with a dissimilar person, the similar person will be liked or disliked a great deal.

Evaluation not only is highly subjective, it can be unjust as well. Sometimes an innocent victim of misfortune is evaluated negatively; this follows from the tendency to believe in a just world. Identifying someone with a label also can produce an unwarranted evaluation of him or her. Labels can generate expectations that, in turn, can influence how one interprets and evaluates even the most normal or mundane behavior on the part of the labeled person.

Evaluation by the implicit psychologist is in some ways analogous to diagnosis by the clinical psychologist. However, despite some similarities, there also are some important differences. Unlike the layperson, the clinician examines causal chains before commiting himself to a diagnosis. This perspective sensitizes the clinician to the similarities rather than to the differences between adjusted and maladjusted persons. And, in contrast to the layperson, the clinician conducts tests of his inferences to see if they are valid.

Though evaluation is subjective, there are developmental progressions. Young children judge others egocentrically, are concerned with concrete rather than abstract characteristics, and fail to recognize that a person can be good in one way but bad in another. Although adults are capable of making evaluatively differentiated judgments, they rarely do so since evaluation is a basis of action toward others.

Differences among adults in evaluation tendencies often can be traced to two personality variables, self-esteem and dogmatism. Compared with high self-esteem people, those with low self-esteem tend to be cost-oriented and thus likely to not a person's bad (potentially threatening) characteristics. The hig self-esteem person, meanwhile, is more likely than the low self-esteem person to employ attitude similarity as evaluative information. Dogmatic individuals also judge others according to similarity in attitudes. Unlike high self-esteem persons, however, they are intolerant of difference, actively rejecting those with "deviant" beliefs and opinions.

chapter five

We will begin this chapter by conducting a brief demonstration. All we ask is that you sit quietly and read while we introduce a group of people to you. Pretend you are reading a cheap novel. First, we have Roy. He and his wife Greta have been head-over-heels in love for over 23 years. That is why he lives in Dallas, she in Seattle. Then, we have Mary Ann and Polly. They get along very well together, but only when Mary Ann insults and criticizes Polly's children. Alice, the neighbor down the block, hen-pecks and dominates her husband, Rudy. He, of course, also dominates her. Dennis, on the other hand, loves and cherishes his family very deeply. Thus, he goes out of his way to avoid them at all times.

The depiction of these social relationships, while perhaps resembling a cheaper novel than you may have thought we had in mind, illustrates a basic point—that you have expectancies about the relationships among people. The network of relations described above tends to clash with those expectancies. Fritz Heider (1958) was one of the first psychologists to describe the structure of our expectancies for interpersonal relations. He recognized that some types of relationships do not seem to "add up"; they appear confused or imbalanced. Such unlikely and conflict-filled social relations often form the basis for both comedy and tragedy. When a person says "I like to be with my loved ones," for example, everyone yawns and looks at his buttons; the statement seems drab and almost tautological because it fits our expectancies. But when Oscar Wilde wrote "Yet each man kills the thing he loves," critics and audiences sat up and took notice.

implicit social relations theory

Balance and Group Organization

That we do have expectancies about relationships among people and that these expectancies guide the formation and change of actual relations among people is the theme of this chapter. Just as the social psychologist is interested in interpersonal activities and small group interaction, so also is the implicit psychologist attentive to the matrix of relations among persons. Our strategy in delineating the nature of this particular implicit theory is to describe first the building blocks—the primary kinds of relationships that are perceived as linking people together. In a sense, the perception of social relations is similar to the perception of persons; in both cases, the complexity of everyday life is reduced to a few manageable dimensions. In later sections of the chapter, we will turn to three of these basic relations—belonging, liking, and dominance—and show how certain combinations are seen as balanced and harmonious, others as chaotic and conflicting.

Social Relations

To determine the basic relations perceived among people, we must first recognize that the possibilities are endless. Heider, followed by other theorists such as Abelson and Rosenberg (1958) and Gollob (1974), noted that the possible relations among people and between people and objects correspond to a large proportion of the verbs in any language. Given the general statement, "subject-verb-object," we can define a social relation as any such statement that makes sense when either "subject" is a person, "object" is a person, or both are persons. Statements in which "subject" and "object" are not persons (as in "the dog sat on the air hose") are excluded from consideration. This is not exclusive enough, however, because we could still sit down with a dictionary and spout relations all day—Aaron helped Bill, Celia jilted Donald, Earl talks to woodland creatures, geese confuse Fred, and so on. Although each of these relations is of some interest, it is much easier to consider them as specific examples of more general types of relations.

Basic Relations

Many theorists, Heider included, have speculated on the nature of the basic relations that are perceived among people. Their speculations have been substantiated in recent research by Wish, Deutsch, and Kaplan (1976). These researchers asked a large group of people to make ratings of a variety of different dyadic (two-person) relationships. These included, for example, relations "between close friends," "between husband and wife," "between guard and prisoner," "between mother-in-law and son-in-law," and so on. Ratings of these and other relations were made on fourteen bipolar scales such as "very relaxed versus very tense," "always harmonious versus always clashing," "exactly equal versus extremely unequal power," and so forth. On the basis of these ratings, Myron Wish and his colleagues developed a measure of the perceived similarity of each type of relationship to each other type of relationship; when a pair of relations was rated very similarly on all the scales, the pair was considered similar. These similarity values were then subjected to multidimensional scaling, the mathematical technique (discussed in Chapter 3) that develops a spatial representation of similarities and differences. Recall that similar stimuli (in this case, interpersonal relationships) are near one another on such a representation, whereas different stimuli are more distant from each other.

Wish and his co-workers found that four dimensions accounted quite well for the perceived similarities and differences among relationships. These cannot all be shown at once on a two-dimensional page; thus two dimensions are shown in Figure 5.1 and two are shown in Figure 5.2. Wish named these dimensions *competitive and hostile* versus *cooperative and friendly, equal* versus *unequal* (both in Figure 5.1), *superficial* versus *intense,* and *socioemotional and informal* versus *task-oriented and formal* (Figure 5.2). When we inspect the relationships corresponding to each dimension, the nature of the dimensions becomes clear. It seems, for example, that the first dimension is an evaluative one; whether a relationship is competitive and hostile or cooperative and friendly depends entirely on whether the pair of persons dislike each other or like each other. The second di-

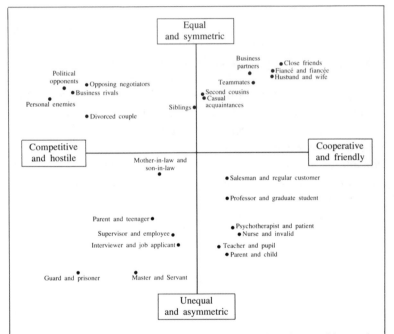

Fig. 5.1   Major dimensions of social relations: liking (competitive and hostile versus cooperative and friendly) and dominance (equal and symmetric versus unequal and asymmetric). Adapted from Wish, Deutsch, and Kaplan (1976). Copyright 1976 by the American Psychological Association. Reprinted by permission.

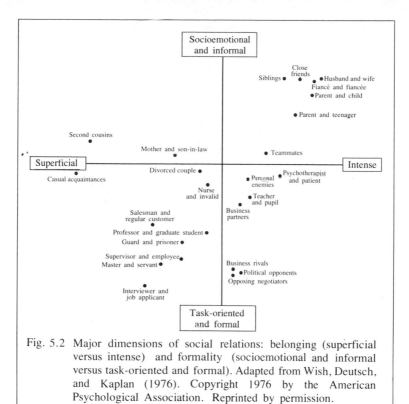

Fig. 5.2 Major dimensions of social relations: belonging (superficial versus intense) and formality (socioemotional and informal versus task-oriented and formal). Adapted from Wish, Deutsch, and Kaplan (1976). Copyright 1976 by the American Psychological Association. Reprinted by permission.

mension, equal versus unequal, reflects the perceiver's concern with dominance. "Master and servant" and "guard and prisoner," pairs that appear very close to the unequal end of the dimension, are relationships in which one person is clearly running the show. "Business partners" and "political opponents," near the other end of the dimension, are relations in which neither member of the dyad is clearly in power. These first two dimensions define *liking* and *dominance* as important perceived interpersonal relations.

Dimensions three and four also make intuitive sense. Superficial versus intense, the third dimension, is a statement of the feelings of the people involved in a relationship, and also refers to the frequency with which they interact. Superficial relationships such as those between second cousins or casual acquaintances are marked by little real togetherness, while intense relations such as those between parent and child or husband and wife are characterized by much greater frequency of interaction. For this reason, we prefer to call this dimension one of *belonging*; superficial relations are those in which the persons do not really belong together, whereas intense relations are those in which the persons involved are seen as a group. The fourth dimension, socioemotional and informal versus task-oriented and formal, depicts the difference between groups that form just to be together (socioemotional) and groups that form for the purpose of doing a job (task-oriented). In other words, certain people are seen as related because of a mutual concern with some object, idea, or event (task-oriented), while other people are linked because of their feelings toward each other (socioemotional). In this chapter, we are concerned with only one end of this dimension—the perception of informal relations among people. We will discuss these complex kinds of relationships in terms of the first three basic relations—liking, dominance, and belonging.

Each of the three basic relations summarizes a wide variety of specific "subject-verb-object" relations. *Liking* summarizes relations such as "Kenny loves Rhoda," "Gail dislikes her boss," and "Aston hates Martin." *Dominance* represents relations such as "Trudy pushes Fred around," "Cecil knuckles under to his mom," and "Bob never tells Ray what to do." *Belonging*, in turn, reflects specific relations such as "Uri lives with Betty," "Feodor has never met Harry," and "Howard seems to be involved with his secretary." In each case, we can let a general

relation stand for a more specific relation. Although the complexity and the wealth of imagery inherent in specific relational
statements is obscured through this summary, the basic meaning
of each specific relation is not lost.

Social Schemas

To depict relations between people, it is often necessary to consider combinations of relational statements. This is true even in
the most basic of groups, the dyad. Consider "liking" relations,
for example. It may be the case that one person likes the other
but the other does not like him in return. To specify the state of a
dyad with regard to liking, we must make two statements—one
telling whether Person A likes Person B, and another telling
whether Person B likes Person A. But when we start to combine
statements in this way, it becomes evident that certain combinations are more preferred than others. In this case of liking between two people, for example, both outside observers and the
people themselves would prefer to see the relationship as recip-
rocal. It feels funny to like someone who dislikes you, and also
seems strange when someone you dislike acts as though they
like you. In each case, the lack of concordance between the two
relations makes both observers and actors uncomfortable.

A *social schema* is the particular combination of relationships
in a group that a perceiver thinks ought to occur. The individual
has social schemas for the combination of relations of one basic
type (such as the two liking relations in the dyad) and also has
schemas for the combination of different basic relations (such as
liking and belonging). If you are very pleased with your new
album by Bob Marley and the Wailers, for instance, it is unlikely that you will try to use it as a Frisbee. Liking implies belonging. This is why the statement "Yet each man kills the thing
he loves" seems so inside-out and wrong. Social schemas have
a powerful influence on our perceptions of social relations.

In the past, there has been some argument among theorists about where social schemas come from. How do these expectancies develop? Appealing to Gestalt psychology, Heider and others have suggested that social schemas are "perceptual good figures." Just as a person tends to see a circle with a small segment missing as a circle nonetheless, he sees groups in particular ways because they look better, more complete, and less confusing. This sort of explanation of social schemas is not popular among psychologists these days. It is much like saying that firemen wear red suspenders because they are prettier than blue suspenders. We all know they wear suspenders in the first place to keep their pants up. The individual sees social relationships in certain ways for similar functional reasons. When groups actually do conform to implicit psychological rules, they function more smoothly. For this reason, the individual comes to expect that groups should behave in particular patterns.

In summary, our discussion of social relations has centered on the definition of three basic relations—belonging, liking, and dominance—and on the preferred combinations of these relations—social schemas. As we now move on to consider the particular social schemas that characterize the individual's perceptions of groups, we will build our discussion around the schemas involving each of the basic relations.

Belonging Schemas   We pointed out in Chapter 1 that one of the major ways in which the person cognitively structures his or her experiences is by grouping them. The individual stimuli that impinge on the person are not reacted to one by one, but rather are conceptualized on the basis of their membership in groups. Belonging schemas are, in this sense, the implicit psychologist's recognition that people also come in groups. It is simply easier to think about people when we combine them, on the basis of belonging schemas, into what

Heider called "perceptual units." Not only are belonging relations the most basic relations, they are also the most general relations. Since a statement of most any social relation means that "subject" and "object" are linked in some way, most relational statements presume that a positive belonging relation exists. Relations such as "Barney dominates Clarence" and "Doris dislikes Evelyn" are possible only if a belonging relation is perceived for each of these dyads.

Whether we do see people or things as belonging together in groups or as separate, ungrouped entities depends on three factors—*similarity, causality,* and *proximity.* Heider (1958) has commented on these factors and has provided a number of examples of how they operate. In this line of characters, for example, we see the two stars as belonging together because of their similarity:

!!!**!!!

By the same token, we tend to see similar people as belonging together. We expect that two Brownie Scouts are more likely to belong together than a Brownie and a plumber. Grouping by similarity is achieved through the identification of common attributes of things or people; we see the Brownies together because they are both young girls, they both wear brown uniforms and brown hats, they both went on a tour of a dairy farm, and they both made puppets for a show last Halloween. The plumber has none of these attributes; he is thus seen as dissimilar and as not belonging with the Brownies.

We usually see cause and effect as a unit. A cause (such as a slap in the face) may be very similar to its effect (a returned slap), or may be quite unlike its effect (a subpoena), but in either case we see them as a unit. If a person causes an event (Miss Muffet spills her curds, for example), we are likely to see the person and the event as a unit. And if a person causes something to happen to another person, we are likely to see them as belonging together. Suppose, for example, that a plump little man made his way across a crowded restaurant to your table and tweaked your mom on the nose. Everyone in the place— including you—would wonder what was going on between them.

Proximity is the third important unit-forming factor. People close together in space are assumed to be close together in general. In the following set of stars, for example, you tend to see groups of two:

* * * * * *

Simple proximity in space defines units that belong together. It is interesting also that the effect of proximity is relative. The two middle stars in the following set are the same distance apart as those in the previous set, but are seen as members of different groups:

*** ***

Thus the *relative* closeness of stars (or people) determines just how much belonging is perceived. This means that at a party you can sit as close as you like to your best friend's date, as long as you are sitting even closer to your best friend.

Belonging and Spacing

Some of the most inventive research on belonging schemas has focused on the proximity factor. This type of research, in general, is based on the realization that spatial relationships among people are often symbolic of deeper, "psychological" meanings. Negotiators at the Paris peace talks, for example, illustrated the importance of spatial relations in interpersonal transactions when they spent nearly as much time deciding on the shape and position of the negotiating table as they did deciding on the eventual fate of Vietnam. The idea that we have very definite expectancies about our spatial relations with others and that these expectancies are closely entwined with our belonging schemas was first investigated in depth by Kuethe (1962, 1964). In his experiments, he set up a large felt board in his lab and asked people to arrange felt-backed figures of people and objects on the board. He found that the subjects typically placed a man and a woman near each other, that little felt "families" were formed with figures of a woman, a man, and children, and that people were grouped in such spatially close configurations much more often than were objects. Following a similar line of inquiry, Little (1965) found that figures labeled as "friends" or as "acquaintances" were placed closer together than were those termed "strangers." The degree of belonging between the felt figures figured into the observers' estimation of the distance between them.

Our expectancies about proximity—called *spatial schemas*—are closely related to our belonging schemas. Evidence for this proposition comes not only from these felt board studies, but also from studies using people and dummies. Ford, Cramer, and Knight (1977), for instance, asked subjects to walk up very close to a styrofoam dummy and then to approach another dummy and try to replicate the distance they had been from the first. In general, subjects were successful at this task, making very few errors in approximating the first distance. This was also true for subjects asked first to walk up near their own spouse, and then to walk up to the same distance from the dummy. But when subjects first walked up to a stranger and stood close to him, and then attempted to replicate that distance with the dummy, they made frequent errors. As a rule, they stood much closer to the dummy. With a stranger, they found themselves too close for comfort and therefore believed that their distance from him was smaller than it actually was.

Belonging relations affect not only our expectancies and perceptions of spatial relations, but also our *actual* spatial relations. Many studies of interpersonal distance, especially those by Edward T. Hall (1959) and Robert Sommer (1969), have shown that people do space themselves at certain distances from others and that violations of this distance (which tend to indicate greater or less belonging than is expected) are stressful or tension-provoking. Of course, the distance we place between ourselves and others is dependent on other factors as well. It would be a considerable strain on the vocal apparatus to carry on a conversation at a hundred meters, and a similar strain on the eyes if we were to converse at two centimeters. But between these extremes, the various distances at which people interact seem to be determined, in large part, by the amount of belonging they perceive.

The spatial proximity of two persons, however, is not always mutually decided. Many times, especially when people are just becoming acquainted, space may be used by one person to communicate belonging expectancies to the other. Rosenfeld (1965) found that subjects instructed to "seek the approval" of a person placed their chairs about 1½ meters from him during the interaction, but that those instructed to "avoid winning the approval" of a person placed their chairs well over 2 meters from the person. Spatial closeness was used as a tactic in the attempt to establish a friendly relationship. You will note, however, that the subject trying to win approval did not sit touching knees with the person, or worse yet, fog the person's glasses with his breath. Such "intimate" distances, as attempts to create a sense of togetherness, are likely to backfire. The person whose space is invaded in this way may take the closeness as a threat because it violates his spatial schema so dramatically. After all, close distances are useful not only for hugging and fondling, but also for hitting and poking. Studies by Sommer (1969) and others have repeatedly shown that the most common reaction to extreme, unexpected closeness is *flight;* when a stranger comes too near, we try to escape. Thus, the potential friend-maker might keep in mind that there is a fine line between the distance appropriate for a stranger trying to make friends and the distance at which a stranger has the same effect as a ticking package.

Until now, we have been discussing the relationship between

belonging and spacing as it occurs in specific incidents—brief episodes in which spacing suggests a certain amount of belonging or in which belonging suggests the appropriate spacing. But these episodes are only glimpses of the more profound and general correspondence between belonging and spacing. The people who are close to us in space over long periods of time are ultimately those with whom we form relationships. And spatial separation, in turn, has broken off more than one wedding plan and has ended more than one feud. In short, simple proximity is a major basis on which interpersonal relations are built; the lack of proximity leads to their downfall. A recent experiment (Segal, 1974) has made the point well. Forty-four Maryland State Police trainees were questioned about the friendships they formed during their first six weeks of training. As is common in police training, the trainees were assigned to classroom seats and to living quarters according to the alphabetical order of their last names. Thus, the individuals near one another in the alphabet were also near one another in space throughout training. The results of the study showed that proximity in the alphabet (and hence in space) was closely related to friendship choice. By the time training was over, the Andersons and Bakers preferred each other to the Youngs and Zimmermans.

Belonging and Liking
It is interesting that the police trainees did not just develop into groups on the basis of alphabetical order—they ended up *liking* and choosing as friends the trainees near them in the alphabet. Spatial proximity brought about a certain level of belonging and togetherness, and this relation in turn engendered liking. As a general rule, belonging and liking relations are closely associated. As we noted earlier in this chapter, people seldom dispose of their liked possessions or dislike the possessions they have. Similarly, they usually like the people they see themselves as belonging with and try to get together with the people

they like. But while these observations tend to indicate that belonging and liking are highly interdependent, the fact that counter-examples pop up from time to time suggests that belonging and liking must still be counted as separate types of relations. A husband and wife, for instance, may hate each other and still live under the same roof. You probably own and therefore "belong with" certain articles of clothing, household appliances, books, and other paraphernalia that you dislike intensely. And unfortunately, there are many objects you like that you will never possess and many people you like who will never even know your name. That liking and belonging frequently (and tragically) fail to correspond is the lesson to be drawn from these examples.

Liking and disliking relations, as we have emphasized previously (especially in Chapter 4), are implicit approach and implicit avoidance tendencies. They are the individual's anticipated responses to objects or to persons. As such, liking and disliking relations imply a change in circumstances that the individual intends to bring about. If you like Ginger, for example, and see her at the other end of a long hallway, you will probably wave and then walk down the hall to meet her, provided other things do not get in the way. In other words, belonging together is the goal of a liking relation. If you dislike Ginger, and find that the forces of evil have arranged for the two of you to be together (sitting in a dentist's waiting room, for instance), you will try to get away from her as soon as you can, and may even find the dentist's drill a welcome relief. Disliking relations have not-belonging (separation) as their goal. Thus, while belonging and not-belonging are *static*—end states or final circumstances that are not being changed—liking and disliking are *dynamic*—expressions of change toward an end state.

Heider recognized this important distinction between belonging and liking, and went on to point out that *combinations* of these relations could similarly be either static or dynamic. When liking occurs with belonging, or when disliking occurs with separation, there is no pressure toward change because the dynamic liking relations are "satisfied." These combinations, according to Heider, are static and *balanced*. When liking is combined with separation, or when disliking is combined with belonging, however, there is pressure toward a change in the system—the liking and disliking relations are not combined with their goals. So in these cases, the entire system of relations is dynamic and *imbalanced*. This idea is the starting point of *balance theory,* one of Heider's many contributions to our understanding of implicit psychology. As we now move on to discuss liking relations and balance theory in more depth, keep in mind that the relative balance or imbalance of any set of relations is simply a measure of their tendency to change.

Liking
Schemas
After spending a considerable amount of time differentiating between liking and belonging relations, Heider proceeded to lump them together, calling liking and belonging both *positive* relations and disliking and not belonging both *negative* relations. This seems to have been a mistake. Other theorists commenting on this combination have generally concluded that liking and belonging should be analyzed separately (see, for example, Zajonc, 1968; Wyer, 1974). One reason for keeping this distinction is that belonging relations are *symmetrical,* while liking relations need not be. In other words, when we say A belongs with B, it is also true that B belongs with A. But when we say that A likes B, it is still very possible that B may not like A. Belonging relations are strictly symmetrical in a logical sense, whereas liking relations only have a tendency toward symmetry.

Another reason for retaining the distinction between liking and belonging is that the nature of *not-belonging* is somewhat obscure. When we speak of liking relations, we can distinguish between liking (approach), disliking (avoidance), and indifference (no movement). But when we consider belonging relations, we can speak only of belonging and of not belonging. There is no "middle ground" as there is with liking. Thus, the *not-belonging* relation can be taken either as a simple lack of contact, or as the result of active avoidance. Balance theory cleverly surmounted these conceptual difficulties by ignoring them; they didn't belong and they were avoided. Instead, attention has been directed primarily to liking relations and their combinations. Although this may seem to limit the scope of balance theory, there is still a wealth of theory and research to consider.

Balance

The notion of balance, while rather mundane when we are considering combinations of liking and belonging in the dyad, becomes much more complex and intriguing when we investigate combinations of liking relations in larger groups. Before we make this jump, however, we should note that balance between liking relations in the dyad occurs when the relations are symmetrical; imbalance is the result of asymmetry. To simplify matters with regard to larger groups, let's assume that all dyadic relations within a large group are symmetrical (and hence balanced). We can thus consider each possible dyadic relation as either positive (mutual liking), negative (mutual disliking), or neutral. Even though the dyadic relations in a large group may be balanced, certain combinations of positive and negative relations may produce imbalance in the group as a whole. Heider focused much attention on this type of balance problem in the *triad*—the three-person group. In particular, he was concerned with balance and imbalance in the liking relations that occur when two people express their liking or disliking for each other and for another person (or object). He maintained that balance occurs in such three-entity groups when all three dyadic relations are positive, or when two of the relations are negative and one is positive. Imbalance occurs when two relations are positive and one is negative, or when all three relations are negative.

Let us consider an example to clarify these rules of balance. Once upon a time, there were two knights, Sir Rupert and Sir Bart, both of whom were liked and trusted by the King. The knights were best of friends and spent almost every day together either strumming lutes in the castle gardens, plundering neighboring kingdoms, or lifting mugs of ale to hail the King. All was happy in the court because the triad of King, Sir Rupert, and Sir Bart was balanced. All three relations were positive (see Figure 5.3). But dark and sinister forces were churning in the kingdom. One day early in autumn, the King heard word of a dragon nesting on a nearby mountain and forthwith sent Sir Bart and Sir Rupert to slay the beast. After riding for days through shadowed forests and barren moors, they suddenly came on the creature. Sir Rupert charged and thrust his sacred sword deep into the dragon's heart as Sir Bart knelt quaking behind a haycart. Soon news of Sir Rupert's conquest and Sir Bart's cowardice came to the King, and the King was both pleased and deeply grieved. As the winter slowly passed, word crossed and criss-crossed the kingdom that Sir Bart had fallen into disfavor with the crown. These were times of chaos and wailing in the kingdom, for the triad was imbalanced. The King liked Sir Rupert; Sir Rupert liked Sir Bart; but, the King thought Sir Bart a fool and coward and did not like him. Two positive relations and one negative relation are imbalanced (see Figure 5.3).

What could become of the kingdom with all this befuddlement and perplexity? The King was walking the palace rooms at night, muttering, cursing, and stroking his chin. Sir Rupert still idled in the gardens and on the jousting fields, but with a heavy heart, for he was torn between his loyalty to the King and his love for dear Sir Bart. Sir Bart, besotted each evening with ale at the inn, was cheered only by the lasting trust of Sir Rupert and by the yards of mead he drank. And too, he had begun to

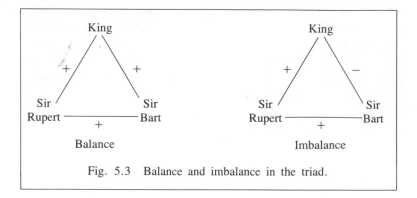

Fig. 5.3   Balance and imbalance in the triad.

fear for his life. The King's court, his jesters, and the peasants in the fields alike were raising eyebrows and questions about the strife in the castle. On every street corner could be heard the cry, "Things sure are imbalanced up there!"

At long last, the King summoned a wise man. The wise man said, "You have four choices. The first is to forgive Sir Bart. This would make all three relations positive and would balance the triad."

"I cannot," said the King. "'Twould spread cowardice through all the kingdom."

"The second choice, then, is that you make Sir Bart and Sir Rupert dislike one another. Perhaps a joust. This would make two negative relations and one positive relation and would balance the triad. You and Sir Rupert liking each other and both hating Sir Bart would be OK."

"No. No persuasion, royal or heavenly, could turn the two against each other."

"Your third choice, Sire, is to turn against Sir Rupert. Declare him a scoundrel for liking a coward like Sir Bart. This would balance the triad by creating two negative relations and one positive relation. They might like each other until death, but their foolishness and fearfulness would never tarnish the crown."

The King reflected a moment and said, " 'Tis also impossible. I cannot spurn my last brave and valiant knight. Sir Rupert must remain at my side. What then is my final choice?"

"This imbalance came to be, My Lord, because you are a group of three. If you behead Sir Bart, 'twill be only a group of two. You and Sir Rupert may go on liking each other as a balanced dyad."

"It is so easy?" The King turned to the wise man and stared into his old and wrinkled visage. "I fear you are not as wise as you seem. Beheading Sir Bart would anger Sir Rupert, perhaps to the point of treason against the crown. Such a relationship, were I to remain positive toward him, would be imbalanced by reason of asymmetry." The wise man edged backward and the King spoke again. "Do you like your head?"

"Oh yes, Sire."

"But imbalance seems to suit you, dear fellow. Methinks separation is in order."

Of the variety of different morals that could be drawn from this story, we would like to point out two in particular. First, imbalance in liking relations brings about a stress toward change. Second, this stress can be resolved in a number of different ways. Balance theory as formulated by Heider does not predict what action the King will take or what change in liking relations might be initiated by Sir Bart or Sir Rupert. It simply says that two positives and one negative in a triad yield an imbalanced situation, and that this imbalance will tend to change toward balance through some change in liking relations.

More precise predictions can be made from balance theory when the relations in a group are just beginning to form. If the liking relations in a group are incomplete, then balance principles can be used to generate specific predictions about relations that will form in the group. Suppose, for instance, that P likes O

and O likes Q, but that P and Q have never met and have therefore never formed a positive or a negative relation. For the triad
of P, O, and Q to be balanced, a positive relation between P and
Q is necessary; if they disliked one another, the two positive relations that were already present would combine with the newly
formed negative to produce imbalance. Thus, if P and Q were to
meet and become acquainted, we would predict that they would
like each other.

The use of balance principles in predicting the formation of
specific relations was illustrated nicely in an experiment conducted by Aronson and Cope (1968). These researchers were interested in testing the balance theory prediction that "your
enemy's enemy is your friend." In balance theory terms, two
negative relations that exist in a triad (you dislike your enemy;
your enemy dislikes his enemy) can be balanced by the formation of a positive relation (you like your enemy's enemy). To
examine this idea, Aronson and Cope arranged for some of the
subjects entering their lab to make an enemy—the experimenter. Each subject came to the lab and was asked to write
some creative stories..For half of the subjects, the experimenter
was pleasant and gentle as he told the subject that the stories
were not quite up to snuff. The other half of the subjects were
also told that their stories were lackluster and uncreative, but
were given the information harshly and somewhat brutally. The
experimenter seemed to enjoy making the negative statements.

Near the end of the session, the experimenter's supervisor
dropped in and asked the experimenter to step out into the hall
for a moment. Within earshot of the subject, the supervisor then
proceeded to evaluate the experimenter. Some subjects overheard the supervisor compliment the experimenter on a report he
had written; the supervisor even said that he was going to try to
arrange for the experimenter to get a raise in pay. Other subjects
overheard the supervisor tell the experimenter that the report he
had written was virtually worthless, sloppy, and somewhat

stupid, and that he was going to see about getting a replacement for the experimenter. In short, it was arranged for subjects in the experiment to have either a positive or a negative relation with the experimenter, and for the subjects to perceive that the experimenter had either a positive or a negative relation with the supervisor.

The question of interest, then, was whether the subject liked or disliked the supervisor. To find out how the subjects felt about him, after the experiment was over, each subject was asked (by someone other than the experimenter) if he or she would be willing to help the supervisor on a project by making some phone calls for him. The average number of phone calls that subjects in each of the groups volunteered to make is shown in Figure 5.4. The balance theory predictions were substantiated. Subjects liked the supervisor (and hence made more calls for him) when he was negative to the experimenter who had been negative to them; the subject saw his enemy's enemy as his friend. Subjects also liked the supervisor when he was positive to the experimenter who had been positive to them; the subject saw his friend's friend as a friend. In each case, the two relations that were already present in the triad suggested what the third relation would be. The two other combinations shown in

		Relation between supervisor and experimenter	
		Positive	Negative
Relation between experimenter and subject	Positive	13.5	6.3
	Negative	6.2	12.1

Fig. 5.4   Average number of phone calls subjects volunteered to make for supervisor. Data from Aronson and Cope (1968).

Figure 5.4—the supervisor is a friend's enemy or the supervisor is an enemy's friend—resulted in much less liking. This is also congruent with balance principles. When the initial relations in a triad consist of one positive and one negative, the triad can be balanced with the addition of another negative.

Let us summarize what we have said about balance. A good way to start would be to state a handy rule for determining when a small group is balanced. Here it is: Both dyads and triads are balanced when the number of negative relations is even; they are imbalanced when the number is odd. In the dyad, balance occurs when relations are symmetric. Thus, the number of negative relations is either zero (because both relations are positive) or two (because both relations are negative). In the triad, it is assumed that all dyadic relations are symmetric. Balance exists in the triad when the number of negative dyadic relations is zero (because all three dyadic relations are positive) or two (because one relation is positive and two are negative). These rules of balance are helpful in predicting when the liking relations in a small group will be stable and when they will be unstable. Balance implies stability while imbalance implies change. But balance theory cannot predict exactly which particular relation in a group will be changed to reduce imbalance. Rather, balance theory predicts the *formation* of specific relations in a group when all the other relations have already been formed.

Alternatives to Balance
Heider saw balance as simple common sense. He developed his theory by observing people, by studying philosophy and literature, and by paying careful attention to common-sense ideas about people. In recent years, a number of psychologists have examined these ideas to find out if they do correspond to the conceptions of interpersonal relations held by most persons. Do people actually see balanced sets of relations as more pleasant,

stable, and sensible than imbalanced sets? Is Heider's description of common sense all that sensible? As it turns out, research has demonstrated some important exceptions to Heider's rules, although many of his basic ideas have been supported.

Research testing balance theory has taken a very direct approach. Usually, subjects are asked to consider various hypothetical relationships and to judge whether they would be pleasant or unpleasant, stable or unstable, and so on. In such a study you might read something like this: "Suppose that you *like* Bill, that you *like* Roy, and that Bill *dislikes* Roy." Then, you would be asked to rate, perhaps, the pleasantness of this situation. On turning to the next hypothetical situation, you would find a different combination of liking and disliking relations and would be asked again to rate the situation. Researchers using this method to study perceptions of liking relations have people rate every possible combination of liking and disliking in the triad. As you can see in Figure 5.5, there are eight possible combinations that could occur among a perceiver (P) and two other persons (O and Q). The top four combinations in the figure are balanced; the bottom four are imbalanced (according to Heider's rules).

People rating situations in this manner typically do see balanced situations are more *stable* (unlikely to change over time) and *consistent* (logical and sensible) than imbalanced situations (Crano and Cooper, 1973; Gutman and Knox, 1972). However, they do not always see balanced situations as more *pleasant*. Apparently, balance is not a sign of pleasantness or comfort in a social situation—it is a sign of stability. When people rate the pleasantness of situations, their ratings are influenced by factors other than balance. In particular, people tend to judge as more pleasant the situations in which there are a greater number of positive (liking) relations; this is called the *positivity bias*. In addition, people tend to rate as more pleasant the situations in

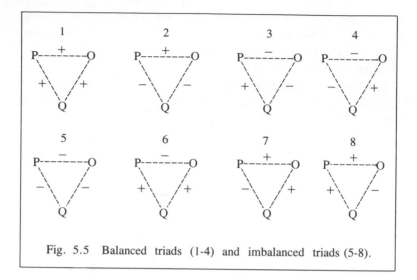

Fig. 5.5   Balanced triads (1-4) and imbalanced triads (5-8).

which two persons (P and O) agree in their evaluation of Q; this is called the *agreement bias*. Research summarized by Robert Zajonc (1968) and by Robert Wyer (1974) indicates that these two factors are often more important than balance when it comes to a person's perceptions of pleasantness.

The positivity bias is not especially surprising. Liking and being liked—both positive relations—are by their nature almost synonymous with pleasantness. Thus, while one positive relation in a triad is somewhat pleasant, and a triad with two positive relations is very pleasant, a triad with three positive relations is downright hunky-dory. This seems like a very simple principle of social perception, and it is. Moreover, the positivity bias can be traced to a central foundation of balance that we explored earlier in this chapter—the correspondence between belonging and liking relations. In other words, people in groups should like each other. The positivity bias, then, is the perception of balance between belonging and liking relations. We might predict a *negativity* bias under certain circumstances. If, for example, P lived in Tampa, O was on a plane bound for Mexico City, and Q was stowed away in the hold of a ship steaming toward the Canary Islands, negative relations would probably be more pleasant than positive relations. For there to be a correspondence between belonging and liking relations, members of a group that is disintegrating (changing from belonging to not-belonging relations) should dislike one another (have negative relations).

The agreement bias is also important in determining the perceived pleasantness of a social situation. People tend to prefer and rate as more pleasant the triads in which P and O agree in their evaluation of Q—either they both like Q or they both dislike Q. Balance theory would say that agreement is pleasant when the two individuals like each other, and that disagreement is more pleasant when the two dislike each other. But people see disagreement—even among enemies—as less pleasant than agreement. This challenge to Heider's theory has led a number of theorists to reconsider the rules of balance. A slightly different version of balance theory has been devised, for example, by Theodore Newcomb (1968). He suggests that situations in which the relation between P and O is negative (triads 3, 4, 5, and 6 in Figure 5.5) be called *nonbalanced*. This suggestion is based on the idea that the balance of a triad does not matter to P, the perceiver, if he does not like O. Why should he care whether O likes or dislikes Q when he does not even like O in the first place?

This conception of balance incorporates the agreement bias as a principle of balance. It says that when P and O like each other, the balance or imbalance of the situation is determined by their agreement. If P and O dislike each other, then agreement is unimportant because the rules of balance do not apply. In essence, this view of interpersonal relations suggests that we are quite involved with and care very much about our friends' likes and dislikes; it hurts to find out that a good friend of ours admires one of our enemies. But we are much less concerned about the likes and dislikes of our enemies; it simply does not matter to us what they think. This view does seem to coincide with common sense, and in addition, has been supported by research (Crano and Cooper, 1973).

The revisions of Heider's balance theory that we have discussed help to enrich our understanding of the individual's perception of liking relations. We have pointed out that while balanced structures are usually seen as more consistent and stable than imbalanced structures, balance is not the only indication of the perceived pleasantness of a social structure. Instead, it seems that the pleasantness of combinations of liking relations is determined also by the number of positive relations and by the amount of agreement. The impact of agreement is especially great when people in the triad like each other and is only of marginal importance when they dislike each other.

Jealousy, Envy, and Rivalry

There are a number of possible combinations of belonging and liking relations in groups that, at first glance, do not seem to fit the principles of balance. Suppose, for example, that a married couple, Theo and Kate, are sitting in their living room one evening, and Kate has invited a good friend of hers from medical school, Lucy, to drop by for a while. Now, since there is a strong belonging relation between Theo and Kate, and since Kate and Lucy are linked by a liking relation, a direct application of balance rules implies that Theo and Lucy should also engage in a liking relation. What? Does balance theory say that the threesome would be most stable if Theo snuggled up with his wife's best friend? It seems more likely that such an activity would produce a quick exit for Lucy and a long evening for Theo. In this case and a variety of others, the rules of balance do not apply because of the presence of a particular type of belonging relation—the *exclusive* belonging relation.

Some belonging relations are open to intrusion; others are not. You may belong to clubs or organizations, for example, that are continually on the lookout for new members; all sorts of new people might form belonging relations with the club and you would never be concerned. If you are a member of a married couple, however, or are in a belonging relation with an automobile (because you own it), you would be understandably concerned if two or three people expressed interest in having your spouse or your car belong to them. These exclusive belonging relations differ from nonexclusive relations in two major ways. First, as Heider has pointed out, exclusive belonging relations always link a person and a *specific* object or person. Thus, while you don't want to give a friend *your* Chevy (a specific object), you would not mind and might even be pleased if he bought his own Chevy. Nonexclusive belonging relations occur between a person and a *class* of objects (Chevies) or persons (club members). The second distinctive feature of exclusive belonging relations derives from the first. Since an exclusive relation is a link to a specific object or person, there are *limited rewards* that can be obtained. The rewards you may receive from owning an object such as a bicycle, for example, would be considerably reduced if someone else also owned it. Each time you wanted to go for a ride, you would have to contend with the possibility that the other person was already pedaling around on it. For certain types of activities, the rewards we can obtain from another person are also limited; if the person is rewarding someone else, he or she can't simultaneously be rewarding us. Thus, we may strive to enter an exclusive belonging relation with such a person in an effort to keep all the enjoyment for ourselves.

Rules of balance for combinations of liking relations and exclusive belonging relations are quite unlike the rules for combinations of liking and nonexclusive belonging relations. If we consider a case in which persons P and Q both desire an exclusive belonging relation with person O, the reason for this difference becomes clear. The statement "P likes O" has the goal of "P belongs with O." But with exclusive belonging, this goal is incompatible with "Q belongs with O" and also with "Q likes O." Thus, any liking or belonging relation between P and O would conflict with any liking or belonging relation between Q and O. In a triad containing an exclusive belonging relation between two members, imbalance occurs when any liking or belonging relation links either of the two members to the third member of the triad.

The imbalance that occurs in the presence of exclusive belonging relations is often the cause of interpersonal conflict, and is also a source of much inner turmoil for the persons involved. To clarify the balance rule stated above, let us consider one such sticky situation—the love life of a young couple, Dot and Willy. From Willy's point of view, he and Dot are members of an exclusive belonging relation. This blissful relationship can hit the skids very quickly, however, if one of two events occurs. First, it is possible that Leo, an acquaintance of Willy's, might express his appreciation of Dot's many outstanding features. This might make Willy uneasy and a tiny bit jealous. Second, it is possible that Dot might like Leo. This would probably make Willy feel very jealous, and might over time lead to the end of the relationship between Dot and Willy. Jealousy, therefore, is a form of imbalance. It occurs when an exclusive belonging relation is threatened by the formation of an incompatible liking relation.

Envy is another possible imbalanced state. From Leo's point of view in this threesome, his goal of an exclusive belonging relation with Dot is blocked by the exclusive relation she has with Willy. Until things change in some way—Leo forgets Dot, or Dot and Willy separate—Leo will remain envious because of imbalance in the triad. Envy and jealousy are complementary emotions felt by two individuals competing for an exclusive belonging relation. The person who is currently in the relation feels jealous, while the person who wants to be in the relation feels envious. If neither person has a firm grasp on the desired object or person, then a rivalry exists. This, too, is an imbalanced state.

Dominance Schemas   The dominance relation is structurally different from both liking and belonging relations. The most obvious difference is that, unlike belonging and liking, the dominance relation is *asymmetric*. The statement that "A dominates B" is logically inconsistent with the statement that "B dominates A." So, while liking and belonging relations merely suggest that A and B form a *group*, the dominance realtion specifies an *order* of persons or entities in the group. Dominance relations share this property of "ordering" with a number of other relations. Questions of "Which building is taller?" and "Who is the better cook?" and "Is there more water in this glass or in that glass?" all have in common the ordering of entities along some dimension. In a series of studies, Clinton DeSoto and his colleagues (1960, 1968) have examined the properties of combinations of such asymmetric relations. In discussing the dominance schemas that characterize an individual's perceptions of groups, we will draw heavily on DeSoto's theory.

Grouping and Ordering

In essence, DeSoto says that people do not stop analyzing social situations when they have divided people into groups. The balance principles proposed by Heider suggest that observers do prefer to see people as members of homogeneous groups; balance is obtained when all the liking relations *within* a group are positive and those *between* groups are negative. But groups do have leaders. They also have unpopular members. They may even have gods. The question of who is on top may come up frequently. Thus, it seems that the individual does not just think about people in terms of groups or categories. Although Elks and Blacks and Presbyterians and Democrats, and even that clique that hangs around the Coke machine during lunch, are all perceived as groups, the individual differentiates within each group by determining the ordering of group members.

There is evidence from a number of different sources that indicates that the individual does use two kinds of organizational tactics in forming cognitive representations of objects and persons—*grouping schemas* and *ordering schemas*. This distinction is similar to the distinction between categorical and dimensional attributes made in Chapter 3. In short, it seems that people have names for classes or categories of objects or people, and that they also make some distinctions among the members of each class or category. In fact, some recent research by Rosch (1973) has shown that there may be no such thing as a true "category." She asked people to rate a variety of dogs on their membership in the "dog" category and found that not all dogs were seen as equally "doggy." Some dogs, such as Irish Setters and beagles, were seen as good examples of a dog; others, such as Chihuahuas and Pomeranians, were seen as only marginally "doggy." Of course, they were not then classified as chickens. Both Chihuahuas and Pomeranians were seen as members of the dog category, but as low in "dogginess" next to other dogs.

According to DeSoto, once the individual has conceived of a group of objects or people (through perceptions of similarity, causality, or proximity), he is then likely to search for order within that group. Such an ordering follows principles that are distinct from the principles governing grouping and balance. In particular, orderings are usually perceived to be linear, single, and end-anchored. A *linear* ordering is transitive (if A bears a relation to B and B bears a relation to C, then A bears the relation to C) and complete (all elements in the group are included in the ordering). Linearity, therefore, refers to an arrangement of group members in a line such that each member has a place in line. Linear ordering can be contrasted with nonlinear orderings such as the branching, multiple ordering in a family tree.

DeSoto's suggestion that people also have a propensity to perceive a *single order* among the members of a particular group means that it is difficult to keep more than one order in mind at the same time. When we note that a certain set of buildings is ordered with respect to height, for example, we usually go on to assume that the tallest one has the most rooms, the fastest elevators, and the largest number of windows, even though this may not be true. Finally, the idea that orderings are *end-anchored* means that we almost always identify the best, the biggest, and the strongest; we also note the worse, the smallest, and the weakest. An ordering in which each element has "more" of something than the previous element always has one element that has the "most" and one that has the "least." These end-anchors are the elements of the group to which we pay the most attention. In summary, DeSoto's principles of ordering schemas say that the individual perceives a single linear order among the members of a group, and that he is most attentive to the top and bottom of this order.

Dominance and Order

For most social groups perceived by the individual, there are two possible bases for ordering group members. One is the set of attributes that characterize members of the group; members may be ordered on the basis of the number of attributes they hold in common with the group (Rosch, 1973). In such an order, the top members are those who are most similar to the ideal or average member of the group. Another basis for ordering in social groups is dominance. Since dominance was the only asymmetric relation identified as a basic relation by Wish and his colleagues (1976, noted earlier in the chapter), we can be fairly certain that some large proportion of the social orderings perceived by the individual are orderings based on dominance. When are orderings based on an "ideal" and when are they based on dominance? Although there is no experimental evidence on this question, we can propose that "ideal" orderings are perceived when the ideal group member is very different from the average member of the population. When the individual considers the members of some very unusual group, he is likely to order them according to their unusualness; the best example of the group is seen as the top of the order. We tend not to think about leaders or dominance in a group of clowns, bigots, or fat people. Rather, we concern ourselves with identifying the funniest, the most prejudiced, and the plumpest. If a group is not very different from the general population, however, we pay greater attention to dominance in our ordering. We speak quite often of the President of our country, the leader of a union, or the dean of a university because these individuals are dominant in their groups, not because they are the best examples of the group. It should be noted, however, that the propensity toward single orders may lead us to confuse these two dimensions; we see the most dominant member of the group as the ideal member of the group.

Research on dominance relations indicates that small groups of people are more likely to develop linear orders than are small groups of animals (DeSoto and Albrecht, 1968). Among goats, for instance, there is little relationship between dominance (which goat wins ramming contests) and leadership (which goat decides where the group should go). Among birds, intransitive pecking orders are quite common. Bird A pecks bird B, and B may peck C, but C then pecks A. Among dogs, the "leader of the pack" is often seen assuming a submissive posture (on its back) in the presence of "lower" members of the hierarchy. Among people, however, there is a pervasive tendency for the dominance relations in small groups to take on linear orders. Usually, the members of such a group show a great deal of consensus in judging which individuals are the highest and lowest members of the ordering. And while there may be some confusion in determining the exact order of members in the middle, people nevertheless insist that such an ordering is present.

A tendency to perceive single linear orderings also extends to perceptions of larger groups. Many theories of social structure and many social ideologies claim that a dominance order exists in every society. Marx argued that such a dominance order was inevitably based upon wealth; Aristotle saw the order as a consequence of perfection; Darwin's theory suggested that dominance was based upon fitness for survival. But all of these arguments are based on the assumption that a single linear ordering of dominance exists in a society. Although, as suggested above, linear ordering often characterizes small groups, this may not be the case for a large-scale social system. Society is much more complex than that. While it is possible to isolate a few "dominant" members in any social system and to isolate a complementary group of "dominated" members, the single linear order is undoubtedly an oversimplification of the real state of affairs. A person who enjoys status in one area may be unrecognized and powerless in another area. The perception of social relations is guided by social schemas—such as an expectation for a single linear order—and may not accurately reflect reality.

Dominance and Liking

For many philosophers, psychologists, and other commentators on the human condition, liking and dominance are opposing forces. One the one hand, we have individuals concerned with dominance: for them, progress equals more competition, greater conquests, bigger deals, more weapons, and, in the end, being on top. On the other hand, some individuals are more concerned with liking: for them, progress consists of greater cooperation, less oppression, more sharing, and less conflict. To some extent, this stark dichotomy is a realistic characterization of some of the grand struggles of human life. But from another perspective—the perspective of the individual attempting to understand social relations within groups—liking and dominance are not simple opposites. Rather, they are perceived as highly interdependent. Perceptions of dominance relations are based upon perceptions of liking relations; the reverse is also true.

Often, of course, the perception of dominance is a trivial exercise. If we see that A is standing on B's chest, or know that A owns the mortgage on B's condominium, it is relatively clear who is in command. But in other instances, we have little or no basis for determining dominance other than the liking relations in a group. What combinations of liking relations lead to perceptions of dominance? Research by Thompson and Phillips (1977) indicates that in dyads we infer a dominance relation when liking is imbalanced (asymmetric). If A likes B while B dislikes A, we infer that B dominates A. In many different settings, this principle seems to hold. The member of a married couple who initiates the divorce proceedings is seen as dominant; the woman who turns down a date with an admirer is seen as dominant; the employer who fires an employee is seen as dominant. In each case, an imbalanced combination of liking relations in the dyad leads to perceptions of dominance. Given no other information, we assume that people in balanced dyads— who like each other or who dislike each other—are equal in power. At the same time, however, we assume that people in an imbalanced dyad are unequal in power; the liked person dominates the disliked person.

A similar principle can be derived for the perception of dominance in a larger group. In general, it seems that the individual perceived as dominant is the one who is a member in the most liking relations. In balanced groups, there is never a single person who is engaged in more liking relations than any other person (you might prove this to yourself by inspecting the triads in Figure 5.5). In imbalanced groups, however, there is often a person who is "most liked" in the group. Under these conditions, the perception of dominance is likely. In a sense, we are suggesting that the dominant person in a group is the one who can provide the most rewards for all group members. In imbalanced groups, such "focal" individuals exist and are seen as responsible for holding the group together; in balanced groups, there is no stress toward change, and no one person is seen as the source of the group's rewards. This analysis reinforces once again the importance of the *single linear order* in the individual's perceptions of groups. Asymmetry or imbalance in liking relations leads to perceptions of the asymmetric dominance relation. Individuals have a tendency to see only one order among members of a group, and therefore infer dominance on the basis of imbalanced liking.

In summary, our comments on dominance schemas have centered on the difference between grouping schemas and ordering schemas, the perceived ordering of dominance in a group, and the way in which dominance can be inferred from liking. In general, it seems that the individual expects to find a single linear order of group members; in many particular cases, this order is based on the dominance relation. All group members are seen as ordered from most dominant to least dominant; each member has a specific place in line; and no other orders are perceived. Finally, we have indicated that dominance and liking are not "opposites," but rather are complementary perceptions of social relations. We perceive dominance most often when liking relations are imbalanced.

the implicit psychologist

An understanding of interpersonal relations is not something one comes by in an afternoon. The cognitive structures we have catalogued in this chapter are, needless to say, quite complicated. The way in which a person conceptualizes interpersonal relations and their combinations seems every bit as intricate and complex as some of the most baffling mathematical equations and logical proofs. It is no wonder, then, that the ability to conceptualize single and multiple relations among people is an ability that is acquired with growth and is an ability that differs among adults. In this section of the chapter, we will examine these differences among individuals by inspecting research on a particular topic—the understanding of balance.

Developmental Changes

In a systematic study of children aged five to twelve, Atwood (1969) investigated changes in the understanding of balance that accompany intellectual development. First, he classified the children according to their level of intellectual development by testing their ability to perform a number of intellectual tasks (for example, placing sticks of different lengths in order on the table, judging the volume of a piece of clay molded into various shapes, and so on). On the basis of their performance, children were categorized as *preoperational, concrete operational,* or *formal operational.* These three broad categories were originally identified by Piaget as stages of intellectual growth. According to his studies of development, children are initially unable to understand logical operations (such as "and," "or," and "greater than"). As they develop, however, they achieve an understanding of these operations in an orderly sequence. *Preoperational* children (usually younger than seven or so) are unable to conceptualize many simple operations. This is the stage (mentioned in Chapter 1) in which the child believes that pouring water from a short wide glass into a tall narrow glass changes the amount of water. *Concrete operational* children (from about age seven to age nine or ten) can understand such elementary operations, but are not able to perform more abstract operations. Thus, when the concrete operational child is told that "Joe is taller than Bob and Joe is shorter than Tom," he finds it difficult to determine who is tallest and who is shortest. He can order concrete entities like sticks according to height but cannot deal with ordering in verbally presented problems. *Formal operational* children (from about age twelve on up) are capable of dealing with such abstract verbal operations.

Atwood presented children in each of these stages with a set of stories about social relations. In each story, a triad with two existing relations (both liking, both disliking, or one liking and one disliking) was given; the child was asked to predict the third. In one story, for example, Butch, the captain of a baseball team, turned down the requests of two children who wanted to play. He insulted them in the process, even telling one child he "couldn't hit a baseball in a million years." Atwood quizzed each subject to make sure he had understood the story, and then asked whether the two children disliked by Butch would like each other or dislike each other. According to balance, the children should like each other. But preoperational children missed this point entirely. As a group, they did not consistently predict liking or disliking. And, when asked *why* a certain relation should form between the two bench-warmers, these preoperational subjects never referred to the other liking relations in the triad. Instead, they picked out details of the situation as reasons for their judgments (for example, "They should dislike each other because they are bad baseball players," or, "They should like each other because they have pretty good faces").

Concrete operational children, in contrast, *always* made their predictions on the basis of balance. In the story about Butch, they decided the two nonplayers would like each other. In fact, when asked if it would be possible for the boys to dislike each other, a number of the concrete operational children said it would be impossible. They seemed to believe that the rules of balance were absolute and unchangeable, somewhat akin to logical deductions. A few of the children at this stage did agree that the two children *could* dislike each other, but then explained that this would occur only if one of them liked Butch. These children rearranged the relations in the story in order to create a new balanced system.

Formal operational children saw balance not as a logical necessity but as a likely occurrence. They predicted balanced sets of relations in every story, but when asked whether imbalanced combinations could occur, were willing to allow the possibility. Most often, they saw the relations becoming imbalanced through additional events happening at a later time. The two boys in the Butch story, for instance, might remain friends at a later date even though one of them was invited to join the team. This recognition of balance without strict adherence at all times is probably similar to the conception of balance held by most adults.

The conclusion we can reach from this study is this: Balance among liking relations is not an "innate" cognitive tendency. Rather, the individual develops an understanding of balance by observing his or her social world. When the individual's intellectual capacity is sufficient to allow for a workable understanding of such social complexities, balance rules are followed consistently. When the individual develops an even greater understanding of social relations, the flexibility and sometimes haphazard organization of interpersonal relations become apparent. At this point, balance principles serve as expectations, not as laws.

Individual Differences The perception of social relations is guided by general principles (such as balance and linear ordering) rather than determined by invariant rules. For this reason, adults differ from one another in the way they see social relations and combinations of social relations. There are two ways of looking at such differences. First, it is likely that people differ in the importance they attach to particular types of social relations. Some people may be highly concerned with dominance, for example, while others may see relations mainly in terms of liking and disliking. Secondly, people may differ in their reliance on social schemas for perceiving social relations. To some people, perhaps, social reality would be uninterpretable without a set of organizing principles. Others, meanwhile, may understand certain relationships even if they violate expectations for balance. Research has examined both realms of individual differences.

We can examine the different amounts of emphasis that people place on different social relations by finding out how they classify the relations in which they are engaged. Does a person see his relation with his brother as one of loving, friendly equality (a liking relation) or as one of competitive, unfriendly inequality (a dominance relation)? This is exactly the type of analysis that Wish and his colleagues performed on the maps of basic relations we discussed earlier in the chapter (Figures 5.1 and 5.2). They found, for example, that males were more likely than females to emphasize dominance relations; males more often saw dominance as the major difference between each pair of relations they rated. Females, in turn, placed greater weight on the belonging relations; they more frequently differentiated among relations in terms of their closeness. Since Wish also found that many other characteristics—from social class to religious persuasion to political leanings—were indicative of different emphases on social relations, we must conclude that not everyone sees interpersonal relations in the same way. What one person takes as a dominance relation another may take as a negative belonging relation. No doubt, these differences arise from differences in the experiences people have in relations with others.

Adults also appear to differ in their dependence on social schemas for understanding interpersonal relations. For some adults, organizing rules such as balance and linear ordering have powerful effects on everyday perceptions of social groups; for others, these schemas have only little influence. Research conducted by William Scott (1969, 1974) has verified that individuals do differ in their reliance on social schemas. Some people, for example, tend to see liked persons as a group and disliked persons as a separate group. This tendency, which Scott identified as a personality variable, is called *affective balance*. Scott's research further demonstrated that this tendency is related to differentiation in person perception (see Chapter 3). Compared with people high on affective balance, those who showed less of this tendency demonstrated greater dimensionality in their perception of other people. Thus, a concern with balanced social relations is associated with a rather undifferentiated way of thinking about people.

But affective balance does have some benefits as well. Recall that ambivalence (discussed in Chapter 3), the tendency to describe people in terms of both good and bad qualities, was found to be indicative of maladjustment; the person who is ambivalent toward others and toward himself does not get along very well with people. Scott has also found that individuals high in affective balance are likely to be low in ambivalence. Apparently, an ability to balance our conceptions of social relations, while leading us to simpler, less differentiated cognitions, also insulates us from the confusion and inaction that can result from conceptions too complex to be acted upon.

Summary   The individual's implicit social relations theory is his cognitive structure for understanding the patterns of relationships among people. Every statement of "subject-verb-object" in which subject or object or both are persons is a social relation. Of the various social relations perceived among people, liking, dominance, and belonging are the most basic. Social schemas are the individual's expectations about how such social relations are combined.

Belonging relations exist when persons or objects are seen as belonging together; they are perceived on the basis of similarity, causality, and proximity. Belonging schemas are closely related to spatial schemas; the amount of belonging provides a cue for the appropriate interpersonal distance, and distance, in turn, provides information about belonging. In addition, belonging schemas are closely linked to liking schemas. The most elementary definition of balance is the congruence between belonging and liking in the dyad.

Balance among liking relations in the triad occurs when all dyadic relations are symmetrical and when there are an even number of negative relations. When balance is not apparent, the individual feels that the group is unstable and logically inconsistent; his liking schema is disconfirmed. Balance principles are useful, therefore, in predicting both when a group will change and what particular relations will form in a group when relations are incomplete. The research on liking schemas has shown that individuals are influenced not only by principles of balance, but also by a preference for positive relations (the positivity bias) and by a preference for agreement (the agreement bias). In a revision of Heider's balance theory, Newcomb has suggested that when people dislike each other, the rules of balance become unimportant. One final aspect of balance theory involves the exclusive liking relation; individuals vying over such a relation may become jealous, envious, or rivalrous.

Dominance relations, unlike belonging and liking relations, are naturally asymmetric. Thus, while both belonging and liking relations are perceived as grouping people together, dominance relations are seen as ordering the persons in a group. Most commonly, the individuals in a group are seen in terms of a single linear order that is end-anchored, transitive, and complete. Such a dominance schema permeates the individual's perception of both small and large groups. Perceivers also tend to infer a dominance relation when liking relations are asymmetric or imbalanced.

The development of social schemas is closely related to the development of intellect. The very young (pre-operational) child does not use balance schemas in predicting social relations; the older (concrete operational) child adheres quite strongly to balance principles; the still older (formal operational) child recognizes balance principles as general guides. Adults also differ in their implicit theories of social relations. There are differences in how particular relations are perceived (as liking or dominance, for example), and differences in the use of social schemas to organize thoughts about people. Some individuals adhere to social schemas quite closely; others are more flexible in their expectations.

chapter six

Social reality would be incomplete without a construction of the self. The individual, after all, is the center of his implicitly constructed world; questions that are of interest about others are of crucial importance when asked of oneself. We are all concerned, for example, with our personalities ("What am I like?"), with predicting our future ("Will I succeed or fail?"), and even with our own thought processes ("Why am I asking myself questions?"). But the construction of a firm conception of oneself is not an easy task. An individual may spend a lifetime trying to answer some of these basic questions. This may seem ironic. We are in constant contact with ourselves, and thus have a wealth of information available with which to construct a detailed theory. Friends, lovers, and assorted antagonists may come and go, yet we always have ourselves to think about. But while we often form firm impressions of total strangers within minutes of meeting them, our conceptions of ourselves are often equivocal and unstable.

It is probably *because* of our special relationship with ourselves that self-construction is never really completed. We can form rather "final" impressions of others with great ease. If we dislike someone, for example, all we have to do is avoid contact with him or her, and we will never encounter a bit of disconfirming evidence. If we like someone, on the other hand, we can structure our interactions with the person in such a way that potential problem areas are avoided. But every person, whether he likes it or not, is in constant contact with himself. He can't ask his secretary to tell himself he is not in today. He can't see himself at a distance and duck into a broom closet. He can't avoid thinking about those events in his past that made him look foolish. Inevitably, the special relationship a person has with himself

implicit
self-theory
Self-Perception

gives rise to special problems in theory construction.

In many respects, self-perception is different from person perception. The self, after all, is not only an object of thought, but also a process. William James (1890), the eminent philosopher and psychologist, distinguished between the self as the "knower" and the self as the "known." He believed that the individual's "stream of consciousness," his active process of experiencing, was quite different from his "concept of self," the accumulated knowledge about the self's actions, abilities, and desires. Alfred Schutz (1932), C. H. Cooley (1902), and George Herbert Mead (1934), all astute philosophers of the mind, have elaborated similar theories about the self. In each case, it has been recognized that the self is not only an object of thought—it is also the thinker. Although we can view other people as objects of thought, we can not enter their streams of consciousness or experience their subjective realities. In this respect, self-perception is never the same as the perception of others.

The *theories* we build about ourselves, however, may be remarkably similar to our theories of others (Epstein, 1973). When we consider ourselves as "objects in the world," entities that can be observed, then we are the same as other people. Just as we explain the actions of others ("He's wearing the lampshade because he is drunk"), so also must we explain our own actions ("I'm wearing the lampshade because the drapery was too bulky"). We estimate the abilities of others ("He'll probably pass the exam"), and in the same way, we estimate our own abilities ("I'll probably pass away during the exam"). Our constructions of others' likes and dislikes ("She does not enjoy warm milk or beer") are similar to our constructions of our own preferences ("I do not enjoy warm milk mixed with beer").

The construction of implicit self-theory proceeds through the same processes as the construction of implicit theories about others. In this chapter, we will discuss each of the major processes of implicit psychology (as presented in Chapter 3)—selecting information, generating information, organizing information, and combining information. First, information about oneself must be selected: the individual attends to specific sources of information in attempting to answer such questions as "What am I like?" Second, the individual generates information: on the basis of selected information, the individual makes inferences about other aspects of himself and predictions of his future behavior. Third, the individual organizes his selected and generated information into a total theory of self; difficulties inherent in this process make salient the question of identity—"Who am I?" Fourth, the individual must deal with new information that conflicts with his self-theory; such combination often is quite anxiety-producing because it threatens the validity of the theory. In the final section of the chapter, we will consider an important issue raised by recent research—when does the individual see himself in terms of his theory? There appear to be some rather intriguing behavioral changes that occur when the individual sees himself as an "object." We will consider these changes when we discuss the effects of self-awareness.

Selecting Information

In large part, the individual's self-theory is derived from information obtained from others. Each of us attends to the opinions, abilities, and behaviors of various people in an attempt to find out about ourselves. Depending on how this information is processed, we learn one of two things: how we are perceived by others (this is *social feedback*) or how we compare with others (this is *social comparison*). Not all the data for an implicit self-theory is social in origin, however, because we may sometimes observe our own behavior without reference to others. To make sense of these observations, we may attribute a characteristic to ourselves (this is *self-attribution*). In this section of the chapter, we will introduce each of these sources of information.

Social Feedback

This is perhaps the first source of information about himself to which the individual attends. The very young child's first glimpse of what he is like comes through feedback from others. In fact, Cooley (1902) and Mead (1934) have argued that social feedback is necessary for the original development of a self-theory. The child only begins to view himself as an object in the world when he finds that others sometimes have views of *him*, and that these views can help him predict and understand their behaviors toward him. Thus, the young child begins to take the perspective of other persons toward himself, and, in so doing, becomes capable of conceptualizing himself.

Social feedback is a powerful determinant of self-perception in the young child. If people praise him, he feels good about himself; if they condemn him, he shares their apparent repulsion. Although other sources of self-information develop over time, we never really lose our initial concern with the appraisals of ourselves made by others. Unfortunately, as we grow up, this source of information becomes more and more ambiguous and elusive. Occasionally, people tell us directly what they think of us—praising, for example, our ability to arrange such an appealing display of our lunch on our clothing. But direct and honest feedback is very rare. Simple courtesy (as well as cowardice) can inhibit others from speaking bluntly. Thus, quite often a person's true opinion must be inferred from his or her nonverbal behavior—facial expression, tone of voice, spatial distance, and so on. Adults become quite adept at transmitting and receiving social feedback in these "disguised" forms and can interpret many subtle evaluative cues communicated by others. You probably are not fooled by someone's verbal praise if, at the same time, he or she is snarling, hissing, and crouching behind the sofa.

The opinions of some people carry more informational value

than do the opinions of others. During childhood, special weight is given to the appraisals made by "significant others"— parents, other family members, and perhaps one's teachers (Mead, 1934). Later in development, of course, feedback from a variety of other people is encountered and receives attention. The significance that is attached to any one person's opinions depends in part on the perceived distinctiveness of the person's comments. Hearing "You're great!" from someone who says the same thing about everyone does not do much for us. But even faint praise from someone who is hard to please is taken to heart.

The impact of information gained from others' opinions of us also depends on our relationship with them. An appraisal from someone tends to be discounted if the nature of the relationship suggests that such an appraisal is necessary and expected. For instance, it has been shown that favorable feedback from a friend has less impact on one's self-evaluation than does similar feedback from a stranger (Harvey, 1962). Since we expect to hear nice things from a friend, unless the friend is unusually sincere and convincing, we attribute the positive comments to the friendship and fail to consider them as features of ourselves. But friendship does not usually produce negative appraisals. Hence, a critical comment from a friend is more devastating than criticism from a stranger (Harvey, Kelley, and Shapiro, 1957). It might be noted that these findings follow nicely from the discussion of social and situational expectancies in Chapter 2.

Social Comparison

As pointed out in Chapter 3, the individual develops a set of general attributes as he matures. General attributes provide the potential for a differentiated view of social reality, since they allow the individual to compare and contrast people with regard to common criteria. One of the people the individual judges in this fashion is himself. If intelligence is one of Betty's general attributes, for example, she not only judges the relative intelligence of all her acquaintances, she also notes how *she* rates in comparison with them. If she happens to be surrounded by dim-witted people, she may decide that she is a rather bright person. Note that self-assessments made in this way are based upon relative—not absolute—information. Thus, if Betty discovered her friends received especially high grades, social comparison might bring about a drastic drop in her self-assessed intelligence, even though her actual IQ score was unchanged.

Social comparison often provides more solid and believable information than social feedback. Consider a young man, Calhoun, who wants to know if he is romantically desirable. He could obtain social feedback directly by asking his female acquaintances for their opinions. Sally might say he was cute; Judy might say he was a nice person; Lucy might say she had never even thought about it. But Calhoun's approach is awkward and is unlikely to net him much in the way of accurate or trustworthy information. Even if the women had designs on him, his forward manner might dampen their enthusiasm. Of course, by noting subtleties in their behavior toward him, he could infer their uncensored opinions. This inferred feedback, while certainly informative in its own right, would take on added meaning if it were examined in a *comparative* manner. Thus, Calhoun might compare the reactions he elicits from his female friends with the reactions he perceives other males receiving. A smile and hello from Sally become especially meaningful when she says nothing at all to Calhoun's friend, Bert. A brief dance with Judy takes on new significance when she turns down Mort, Vince, and Donald. And, a snub from Lucy becomes humiliating if she is friendly to every other man in sight.

Social comparison thus provides information about one's strengths and one's weaknesses. At the same time, a study by Morse and Gergen (1970) demonstrates that comparison processes are also useful in making global ("I'm a good person" versus "I'm a bad person") self-assessments. For this research, male undergraduates were recruited for a part-time job in the University's research institute, and were asked to fill out some self-rating forms. One of these was a test of general self-evaluation (self-esteem)—how positively or negatively a person feels about himself. While they were filling out these forms, another student (actually an accomplice of Morse and Gergen) entered the room and began to fill out the same forms. For half the subjects, this other person appeared to be quite an admirable fellow. He was good-looking, well-dressed and groomed, and sported an attaché case that he opened briefly, conspicuously revealing books ranging in subject matter from philosophy to statistics. Morse and Gergen referred to him as "Mr. Clean." The other subjects were exposed to someone who was far less appealing. This individual (who was also an accomplice) was outfitted in ragged clothes, was strikingly unkempt, and looked as though playing with his buttons without falling down posed a real challenge for him. After shuffling in and depositing himself in a chair, he pulled out a well-perused copy of a trashy novel. He was "Mr. Dirty."

Morse and Gergen wanted to see if the presence of Mr. Clean or Mr. Dirty would have an effect on the subjects' self-evaluations. In comparison with Mr. Clean, a subject might feel somewhat inferior; hence, his self-evaluation might drop temporarily. But compared with Mr. Dirty, subjects should feel quite satisfied with themselves, and possibly superior to him; their self-evaluation thus should show a temporary increase. Morse and Gergen scored the subjects' tests of self-evaluation in two parts, the section they filled out before either Mr. Clean or Mr. Dirty arrived in the room, and the section they filled out after he was present. As can be seen in Figure 6.1, the social comparison hypotheses were confirmed; subjects exposed to Mr. Clean showed a decrease in self-evaluation from the first part to the second part of the test, while those exposed to Mr. Dirty showed an increase.

It should be noted, though, that the choice of comparison

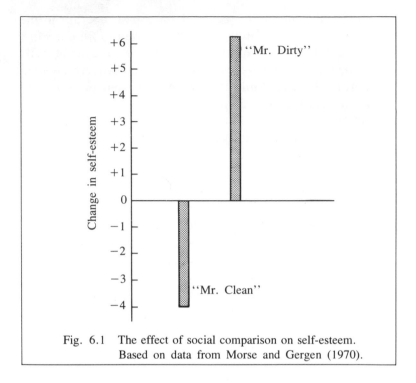

Fig. 6.1   The effect of social comparison on self-esteem.
Based on data from Morse and Gergen (1970).

others is not always "forced" on people like this. As pointed out in Chapter 4, others who are perceived to be similar in some relevant way are often sought out by the individual because they provide more meaningful standards for comparison. Presumably, if the subjects in the Morse and Gergen experiment had been exposed to someone other than a fellow student—for example, six-year-old versions of Mr. Clean and Mr. Dirty— less information about themselves would have been conveyed. Their levels of self-evaluation might not have changed at all.

Self-attribution

In our discussion of attribution (Chapter 2), we noted that a person typically attributes his behavior to external factors such as situational demands or the possibility of reward or punishment. What happens, though, when the external forces are very subtle and seemingly insufficient to account for your behavior? According to Daryl Bem's (1967, 1972) theory of self-perception, when forces in the situation appear to be weak, the person attributes internal states to himself that correspond to his behavior. Self-perception, in other words, is very much like person perception. Individuals come to know their internal states —feelings, attitudes, and even dispositions—by inferring them from observations of their behavior and the circumstances surrounding their behavior.

This analysis might sound a little backward; we normally assume that attitudes cause behavior, not that behavior causes attitudes. Whether you approach or avoid something, for example, would seem to depend on your attitudes toward that object. However, the influences on our actions are often difficult to perceive. Sometimes our behavior is caused by factors of which we are unaware. In these cases, we are in the same position as an outside observer of our behavior, and therefore make internal attributions for our acts. When behavior does not seem to be caused by noticeable external forces, we infer internal forces (our own attitudes) as a means of explaining our behavior.

To appreciate the self-attribution reasoning, consider a classic study conducted by Festinger and Carlsmith (1959). As part of a psychology experiment, male undergraduates spent an hour and a half performing rather dull tasks—putting pegs in holes, stacking spools in a tray, and so on. Upon completion of the tasks, each subject was asked to describe the experiment to the next subject (who was a female accomplice of Festinger and Carlsmith). They were told that the person who usually did this job was not around, and that they were to convince the next subject how "interesting and enjoyable" the tasks had been. Some of the subjects were promised twenty dollars to do this, while others were promised only one dollar. All of them agreed to do it. After talking to the female accomplice and advocating participation in the experimental tasks, subjects completed a questionnaire that assessed their feelings about the task. Subjects who were promised *one* dollar indicated that they enjoyed the "pegs and spools" task very *much,* while those promised *twenty* dollars indicated much *less* enjoyment. We commonly assume that greater rewards are associated with greater satisfaction with an activity. But the subjects in this experiment exhibited what is called a *reverse incentive* effect; the more money they were offered, the *less* they expressed liking for the tasks. This finding follows nicely from attribution principles. While twenty dollars is more than enough reason to tell someone a task is enjoyable, one dollar is not at all a good reason. Thus, the subjects offered one dollar inferred an internal cause for their behavior. They decided that they must have liked the task.

It could be argued that the one-dollar subjects in this study initially had an unfavorable attitude toward the task (because it was boring), and that they changed this attitude when they agreed to tell someone that the task was interesting. After all, arguing in favor of something you dislike is rather inconsistent (Festinger, 1957) and potentially embarrassing (M. J. Rosenberg, 1965), especially if you do it for a paltry one dollar. To do so for twenty dollars is not quite so bad; who wouldn't tell a white lie for that much money? This, in fact, was similar to the explanation offered by Festinger and Carlsmith. They argued that the subjects in the one-dollar condition experienced *cognitive dissonance*—and thus felt the tension that might accompany inconsistent or dissonant thoughts. The discomfort and tension caused them to change their attitudes as a means of reducing the conflict. Although there is a large amount of convincing experimental evidence in support of this view, Bem (1967) has conducted an experiment that suggests that the *self-attribution* explanation is equally appealing.

Bem asked subjects to observe (by listening to a detailed tape recording) a typical subject in the Festinger and Carlsmith experiment. Bem argued that if self-attribution was really the principle underlying the findings of the study, then outside observers simply listening to the sequence of events experienced by a subject should make attributions to the subject that would agree with the subject's self-attributions. Person perception (by the observer-subjects) should be the same as self-perception (by the original subjects). He played the observers a tape recording of the experimental procedure. Half the observers listened as the subject, "Bob Downing," was offered one dollar for convincing the next subject that the "spool and peg" task was enjoyable. The other half of the observers heard the condition in which Bob was promised twenty dollars for advocating the task. Both sets of observers then heard Bob enthusiastically endorse the tasks in his conversation with the next subject. The observers were then asked to estimate how Bob really felt about the tasks. As Bem predicted, Bob was judged to have a more favorable attitude toward the tasks when he was offered one dollar to endorse them than when he was offered twenty dollars to endorse them. Thus, the attributions made by outside observers matched the self-attributed attitudes expressed by the actors in the original study.

This experiment is not the only evidence in support of self-attribution. In several different studies, it has been demonstrated that individuals infer their attitudes, emotions, and motives from observation of their behavior and the circumstances in which it occurs. Consider, for example, a study by Lepper, Greene, and Nisbett (1973). This research suggests that children may not develop intrinsic interest in an activity if they expect to be rewarded for engaging in it. Nursery school boys and girls were invited to play with a magic marker, an activity that would seem to be of intrinsic interest to a young child. Some of the children were promised a reward (a bright gold star and red ribbon) for playing with the marker. Other children were not led to expect a prize, but received one anyway when the activity period was over. A third group of children neither expected nor received a prize for playing with the marker. After toying with the marker for several minutes, children in all three groups were given a free-play period during which they could choose among a number of activities—including the magic marker. No reward was offered for any of the activities during this period. It was observed that children who had been in the expected-reward condition played with the marker significantly *less* than did children in the no-reward and unexpected-reward conditions.

These results are consistent with attribution notions. Children who had been in the expected-reward condition apparently attributed their initial performance with the magic marker to the reward ("I did it for the star and the ribbon"); thus, when no reward was offered during the free-play period they were not motivated to continue playing with the marker. Children who unexpectedly received a reward after the magic marker period could not reasonably attribute their initial performance to the reward. Instead, they attributed their magic-marking to a personal liking for the activity and therefore persisted in that activity during the free-play period. The no-reward children, too, had no good reason for playing with the marker besides their own liking for it; during the free-play period, they played freely with the marker. A number of other studies have converged on the idea that, for children and adults alike, personal motives and interests are acquired in a manner that follows from the principles of attribution (see, for example, the reviews by Deci, 1975; Kruglanski, 1975).

To summarize, both social and attributional sources of information serve as input to the individual's self-theory. Social feedback allows the person to see himself as others do; this provides information concerning his good and bad points. However, this information is often inconsistent (because different people evaluate the individual differently) and insincere (because ulterior motives may underlie the feedback that is received). To obtain less equivocal information, the individual actively compares himself with other people, especially with those he perceives as similar to himself. While social feedback and social comparison provide information about the self's qualities and abilities, they do not help the individual define his attitudes and values. To identify such internal states, the individual relies on attributional processes. By observing his behavior in light of the possible internal and external causes, the individual comes to understand his opinions, interests, and desires.

Generating Information   In the course of a normal day, each of us has to make many decisions. Some of these are consequential ("Should I look for a better job?"), others are not ("Should I have beverage with my tuna?"). Making a good decision requires a degree of self-insight. The decision to look for a better job, for example, is based on a perception of one's capacity to achieve and maintain such a job. But we often lack the information necessary to choose the right course of action. When this is the case, our decision must be based on *inferences* about ourselves—estimates generated from the information we have already selected. In deciding about the job, a person might have to estimate his competence at a number of skills he has never tried ("Can I lift up chickens and snatch their eggs? Can I make cows hold still? Will I know what to do with silage when I have some?"). No matter what the job, no matter what the new experience, the individual must extrapolate from his current information to future possibilities. As we shall see, information about oneself is generated in much the same manner that it is generated about others.

Self-esteem: Predicting One's Competence
Inferences about people reflect a concern for evaluative consistency—the "halo effect" mentioned in Chapter 3. If a piece of negative information is selected about someone, there is a

tendency to form an impression of the person that consists of many negative characteristics. Positive information, in turn, produces a favorable impression of the person. In a similar way, inferences about oneself are evaluatively consistent with one's selected information. If social feedback you have received since the age of five has convinced you that you are about as exciting as good penmanship, you might feel somewhat negative about your personality in general. On the other hand, if you have noted that you receive more attention from members of the opposite sex than do any six of your friends, you might infer other positive qualities about yourself, many of which could be completely unrelated to sex appeal. One tends, then, to develop an overall evaluation of oneself, just as one tends to form global evaluations of others. Global self-evaluation is commonly referred to as *self-esteem* by psychologists.

It seems that most individuals do hold themselves in at least moderate esteem. The average person considers himself slightly more desirable than the next person. In general, then, people make inferences about themselves that are slightly more positive than might be expected. These inferences extend to both the past and the future. Looking to the past, the individual typically explains his successes by inferring that his own ability and effort were important causes; he explains his failures by inferring that external causes were at work. In looking toward the future, people usually anticipate success rather than failure. They believe that since they intend to succeed, future success will be forthcoming. These principles can be summarized in terms of the general process of *egotistic attribution* (Miller and Ross, 1975; Snyder, Stephan, and Rosenfield, 1976). By and large, the inferences people make on the basis of their implicit self-theories tend to be moderately positive. People aspire to be better than they are, and in addition, interpret the causes of their behavior in a similar positive way.

Inferences about oneself frequently take the form of predictions of ability—will I be able to do this? Of course, for such a prediction to be confirmed or disconfirmed, it must be tested. We noted in Chapter 1, however, that certain predictions are unlikely to be tested by even the most detached scientists. For similar reasons, certain inferences about the self are unlikely to be examined for their validity. This would seem to be the case in particular for individuals with negative self-evaluations—that is, with low self-esteem. A person who feels socially inadequate, for example, may avoid meeting new people—an experience that would provide a test of his self-inference—for fear of being rejected. Such a person thus becomes a victim of his own self-fulfilling prophecy. Low self-esteem can have a paralyzing effect on one's behavior.

People with high self-esteem are less afraid to test the validity of their self-inferences. Because the outcomes they predict for themselves are positive rather than negative, they are less inhibited in their actions than are individuals with low self-esteem. This suggests an important difference between the self-theories of high- and low-self-esteem people. A theory that is tested repeatedly grows through internal refinement (see Chapter 1); a theory that is not tested fails to develop at all. Thus, an average- or high-self-esteem person is more likely to have a realistic assessment of his assets and liabilities than is a person with low self-esteem. The ability to find out about the self depends on the ability to test self-inferences. There is evidence suggesting that the high-self-esteem person is more likely to be certain of his self-theory, while the low-self-esteem person is more likely to hold his self-theory in doubt (Vallacher, 1975). Because his self-theory often goes untested, the low-self-esteem person is never really convinced of his own self-assessment.

Self-esteem: Interpreting One's Competence
Sometimes even the low-self-esteem person must test his inferences. Certain achievement and social situations are unavoid-

able; when a person encounters such situations, feedback regarding the validity of his self-inferences is automatically provided. This does not mean, however, that the high- and low-self-esteem person learn the same lesson from the same feedback. Even if a person's expectations are not confirmed, the person may *think* that they are. Much of the time, the outcomes of achievement and social situations are ambiguous and hence open to alternative interpretations. Thus if a person expects to succeed, he may interpret ambiguous feedback in a positive way; if he expects to fail, he interprets the same feedback negatively.

A study by Shrauger (1972) indicates that the role played by the perceiver in judging his own success or failure can be quite striking under certain circumstances. Female undergraduates were first given a test of self-esteem. Next, they worked on an involved conceptual task under one of two conditions: alone or in the presence of an audience. In the audience condition, two visitors sat behind the subject during her performance, occasionally whispering and shifting their chairs to remind her that she was being observed. All this was arranged to make the subject feel self-conscious. Shrauger argued that when attention is drawn to oneself, one's characteristic mode of self-evaluation should affect the way success and failure are interpreted. Thus, in the audience condition, low-self-esteem subjects were expected to have a lower estimate of their performance than high-self-esteem subjects. This difference in performance evaluation was not expected in the alone condition since attention was not focused on the self. As can be seen in Figure 6.2, Shrauger's predictions were confirmed. In the audience condition, high- and low-self-esteem subjects differed in their perceptions of their task performance. This is particularly noteworthy, since the *actual* performance of the groups did not differ. It appears, then, that people interpret their behavior in a way that reinforces their characteristic expectation—no matter what the outcomes really are. Since this tendency was only present when subjects were self-aware, however, it could be that inferences about the self are more consistent with implicit self-theory when the individual is paying attention to himself. We will discuss this possibility later in the chapter.

Self-esteem can not only bias perceptions of task success and failure, it can also influence estimates of social success and failure. Consider how two young men, one with high self-esteem (Vince), and the other with low self-esteem (Farfel), might interpret an ambiguous personal evaluation from an attractive female. Instead of providing clear acceptance ("I worship the ground you walk on") or clear rejection ("I bypass the ground

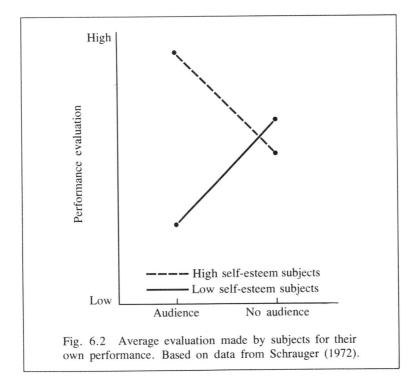

Fig. 6.2   Average evaluation made by subjects for their own performance. Based on data from Schrauger (1972).

you walk on"), she says something ambiguous like, "You may be an interesting person, but it's really hard to tell since I've just met you." The findings of Jacobs, Berscheid, and Walster (1971) suggest that Vince and Farfel would attach different meanings to such a comment. Because the high-self-esteem fellow, Vince, predicts success in his social relations, he interprets the message in a positive way ("She's mad about me"). In contrast, Farfel has low self-esteem and expects frequent social failures, so when feedback is ambiguous, he assumes the worst ("Another day, another rejection"). A similar conclusion was reached by Coopersmith (1967) in a study of self-esteem in preadolescent children. He found that although actual popularity was not related to self-esteem (children who liked themselves were no more often liked by others), the low-self-esteem children *felt* less able to make friends and to interact successfully with others.

Let us summarize the generation of information. To complete an impression of the self, the individual infers qualities that are evaluatively consistent with information selected earlier. In this way, the individual develops a particular level of self-esteem— perceived personal worth. Most individuals have a moderately positive self-image, and thus predict moderately positive outcomes for themselves; in addition, they explain their past successes and failures in a moderately positive light (this is egotistic attribution). But people tend to differ in their levels of self-esteem. The low-self-esteem person predicts negative outcomes and for that reason may avoid many potential areas of achievement. The self-theory of the low-self-esteem person is thus less clear and well-developed than the self-theory of the high-self-esteem person. Of course, the high-self-esteem person is also biased in his inferences and interpretations. But because he actively conducts many tests of his self-inferences rather than simply dealing with unavoidable feedback, he is more likely to develop a realistic sense of his assets and liabilities.

Organizing In the course of a lifetime, a person amasses
Information a huge amount of information about himself
and makes many inferences. But the implicit
psychologist does more than this; his self-theory would be chaotic if it were not organized in some way. One principle of organization was discussed above—evaluative consistency. But
there are a variety of other ways in which information is incorporated into the person's theory. In Chapter 1, we introduced
two basic organizational principles, differentiation and integration. As we shall see, these principles are quite useful in depict-
ing the organization of implicit self-theory.

Self-differentiation

The differentiation of self is somewhat analogous to differentiation in perceptions of others. A differentiated view of others
means that the individual distinguishes among people in a
number of different ways. A differentiated view of self means
that the individual perceives himself in a number of different
ways. In a sense, no person is always the same person. In different situations (such as restaurants, funerals, offices, or parties),
different roles (such as student, friend, worker, or lover), and
even at different times of the day (such as before breakfast or
after lunch), a person may behave and think quite differently.
The particular behaviors and abilities the person employs depend on the situation he is in. According to William Scott
(1969, 1974), the capacity to see the self as different (having
different qualities and different abilities) in these varied roles
and situations is a measure of self-differentiation. The person
whose self-theory is differentiated is able to view the self from
many different *perspectives*.

The capacity to take many different views of the self is, in
large part, the capacity to take the perspectives of other persons.
In many situations, our behavior depends on the expectations of
others. The husband behaves as he does, in part, because he can

take the perspective of his wife and thereby satisfy her expectations. To see himself in the role of husband, and to judge himself in terms of his "husbandly" qualities requires that he see himself through the eyes of his wife. He must construct a special self-theory to consider his actions from her point of view. Similarly, many other situations hold particular requirements and expectations that are best considered from the point of view of others. The more roles and situations the individual encounters, and the more varied they are, the more differentiated his self-theory must be.

Different perspectives on the self allow the individual to perceive and evaluate the self in different ways. The individual sees himself as having certain qualities and abilities from one perspective and other qualities and abilities from another. To illustrate this idea, let us consider the self-theory of a rather undifferentiated woman, Abby. Suppose that she considers herself in terms of two major qualities—talkativeness and assertiveness. In Figure 6.3, these qualities are presented as dimensions. Now suppose we asked Abby to rate herself on these qualities from a number of different perspectives—Abby as wife, as employee, as mother, as party-goer, as lover, and as student. What is she like in each of these roles? As we can see in Figure 6.3, she considers herself much the same from each of these perspectives; in each case, she believes she is talkative and unassertive.

Now consider the self-theory of a somewhat more differentiated person, Ann (see Figure 6.4). Ann, too, perceives herself in terms of the dimensions of talkativeness and assertiveness, but she perceives herself differently depending on the particular perspective she takes. In her role as lover, for example, she perceives that she is quiet and moderately assertive; in her role as mother, she sees herself as talkative and very assertive; in her role as employee, she believes that she is moderately talkative and moderately assertive. Her perception of herself depends on her perspective.

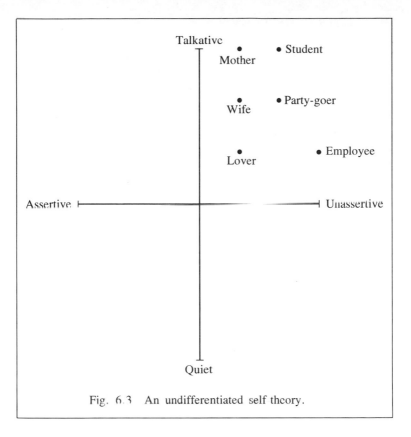

Fig. 6.3 An undifferentiated self theory.

The differentiation of the individual's self-theory takes place as the person encounters new situations and roles and takes the perspectives of others toward himself in each such encounter. Abby's implicit self-theory may be less differentiated than Ann's either because she has not experienced the particular roles and situations (she has never been gainfully employed, for example), or because she has failed to consider herself from each perspective. As might be expected, there are advantages to having a highly differentiated self-theory. For one thing, the self-esteem of a differentiated person is often less affected by failure than is the self-esteem of an undifferentiated person. A person whose identity is totally tied up with his role as student, for example, might be devastated by a single poor grade. Of course, such an experience would be distressing to most people, but it would reflect on only one of many aspects of a differentiated person. Seeing oneself from only one perspective means that a failure in that particular role or situation is a failure in all roles and situations; seeing oneself from many perspectives means that a failure from one point of view is compensated for by strengths from another. The failing student who has a dif-

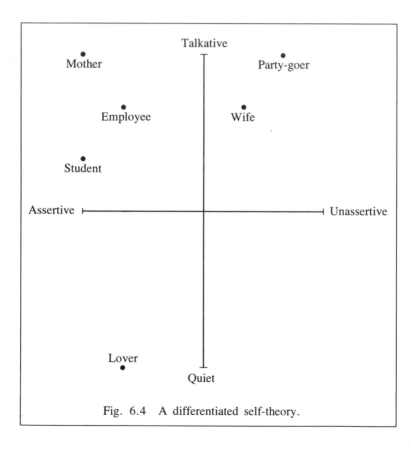

Fig. 6.4   A differentiated self-theory.

ferentiated self-theory can accept the poor grade and still congratulate himself on his performance in other classes and appreciate the successes he attains in other roles.

It is not surprising, then, that psychologists frequently consider a differentiated self-view to be a healthy self-view (Gergen, 1971; Kelly, 1955); the mentally healthy person is able to cope with the inevitable failures and disappointments he encounters in life. In this light, recall from Chapter 4 that poorly adjusted people behave more consistently in different situations than do well-adjusted people. Apparently, the ability to see the self as different in different situations allows a person to adjust to a wide range of demands and expectations. Seeing the self from different perspectives may well help the individual to behave in a less rigid and consistent manner. The differentiated individual is flexible in his approach to different roles and situations.

A highly differentiated conception of oneself is not without its drawbacks, however. A person who sees himself from many different perspectives faces the continuous problem of choice among perspectives, since it is not always immediately apparent which perspective might be appropriate in a given situation. Imagine, for instance, a person who, in his role as college instructor, sees himself as poised, solemn, and authoritative. But in his role as party-goer, he sees himself as carefree, silly, and rather mindless. How should he behave if he encounters one of his students at a party? Should he maintain the expectations of the student and behave in a reserved way, or should he maintain the expectations of the other party-goers and offer the student an exploding cigar? Psychologists have pointed out that conflicts arising from multiple perspectives on the self put a considerable strain on people and can even result in psychological problems. The individual who sees himself in many ways may find it difficult to isolate any common themes and may therefore have an incoherent self-theory. The question "Who am I?" may have too many different answers.

So, as we have said, a differentiated self-theory is a mixed blessing. It satisfies one requirement of a good theory—accommodation to a wide range of phenomena. The highly differentiated person can vary his perspective in accordance with the demands and expectations of a variety of interpersonal situations. At the same time, another feature of a good theory, coherence, is threatened by a high degree of differentiation. Thus, the person who feels overly differentiated may lack a sense of identity, a core self. In the next section, we shall see that the dilemma of coherence versus differentiation is not without a solution.

Self-integration

There are two possible solutions to the problem of over-differentiation. One is simply not to differentiate. By restricting the number of perspectives one has on oneself, one can maintain a coherent self-theory. The other solution makes for a more complex, and hence more interesting, self-theory. A theory can be highly differentiated and yet retain its coherence if it is *integrated*. As we noted in Chapter 1, cognitive integration is the process of combining thoughts or structures of thought. A number of researchers and theorists have considered the problem of self-integration in terms of *decisions among perspectives* (see, for example, Harvey, Hunt, and Schroder, 1961; Schroder, Driver, and Streufert, 1968). The individual who can exercise choice among his self-views, and who makes such choices on the basis of what have been called "higher-order decision rules," has an integrated theory of self. Self-integration, defined in this way, has two significant elements. First, the integrated individual has certain personal *decision rules* that enable him to choose which self-view to adopt in any situation. Second, this decision process gives the individual a feeling of *personal causation,* an awareness of himself as a causal agent.

The decision rules a person employs to generate different

perspectives on himself are essential to a stable and unified self-theory. You have no doubt met individuals who seem to have many different perspectives on themselves, but whose perspectives seem too changeable and chameleon-like. Sometimes their particular self-presentations are wholly inappropriate to the situation. With an employer, such a person may be humble and ingratiating all the time; with a parent, he may be similarly humble some of the time but stubborn and aloof at other times; with a professor, he may be studious and quiet in class but brash and overbearing elsewhere. In a sense, he is infinitely malleable, reflecting on some occasions the expectations of the situation and on other occasions a set of behaviors that are out of place. Schroder, Driver, and Streufert (1968) have suggested that such a person has a self-theory that is both differentiated and poorly integrated. Such a person may frequently seem negativistic, unpredictable, or inconsistent because he has a variety of self-views but no means of deciding among them.

Self-differentiation without integration is depicted schematically in Figure 6.5. At the top of the figure are two dimensions on which the self might be considered—humorous versus serious, and flattering versus critical. Suppose that a particular individual, the college professor–party-goer we discussed earlier, considered himself from each of these perspectives. From one point of view, he believes himself to be humorous and flattering; from the other point of view, he sees himself as serious and critical. Clearly, his self-view is dependent on the particular situation in which he finds himself—at a party or in class. Faced with the student at a party, he has no internal guidelines for deciding which self-view is appropriate. Thus, he may try to squirm out of the dilemma ("Excuse me, I have to go to Toledo"), or may behave in an anxious and uncertain manner, thereby failing to enact either role. In yet other situations, he may vacillate erratically between these views, never knowing which is appropriate.

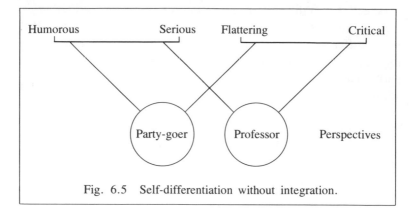

Fig. 6.5   Self-differentiation without integration.

Self-differentiation with integration is depicted in Figure 6.6. A new element in this conceptual system is a decision rule— "put people at ease." This decision rule is, in a sense, an expression of a *self-value*. Many psychologists argue that at the core of a person's identity is a set of basic notions about what is good and what is bad (see, for example, Rokeach, 1968). Certain values, such as the desirability of material gain, achievement, concern for others, and excitement, are common to many people. At the same time, each person's set of self-values is to some extent unique; this provides a sense of separate identity. If the "sometimes professor, sometimes party-goer" has the belief that "putting people at ease" is one of his central qualities as a person, then he can choose between his two perspectives on the basis of this rule. Meeting the student at the party, he would have an appropriate guideline for choosing his self-view and behaving accordingly. His concern for putting the student at ease might be translated into either self-view. He might concern himself with determining the student's expectation for his behavior, and then with putting the student at ease by fulfilling his expectations. An outgoing student might give the professor reason to put on his party-goer image. An insecure, reserved student might give the professor reason to become more "professorial," maintaining a serious and thoughtful attitude despite the plastic dart stuck to his forehead.

It is important to note that self-values, although they represent internal attributes, are not dispositions or traits. They do not require that the individual behave in any particular way, nor do they restrict his freedom to behave. Dispositions or traits suggest consistent behavior in most situations; the person is driven to behave in more or less the same way in all circumstances. Because self-values are abstract and general rather than concrete and specific, they can be implemented in a number of ways. Depending on the situation, for example, the professor's value of "putting others at ease" might translate into either of his self-views. The self-value is a higher-order decision rule that

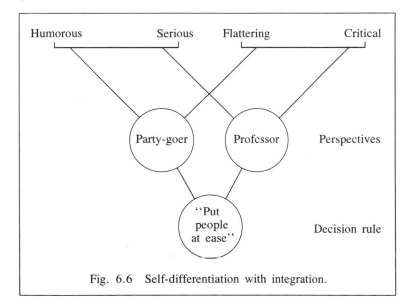

Fig. 6.6   Self-differentiation with integration.

allows the professor to express his sense of himself in diverse ways. Each of his self-views, rather than floating disembodied in his self-theory, is integrated into his whole self through basic values.

In their discussion of integration, Schroder, Driver, and Streufert (1968) argue that the integrated person has a sense of personal causation. Because he can choose among self-views, he is aware of himself as a causal agent in his environment. Rather than being buffeted about by the demands and expectations of external agents, the integrated person feels that he is actively deciding among perspectives and is therefore determining his own fate. It is often suggested that the human being's primary motivation is to have an effect on his personal environment (de Charms, 1968; Heider, 1958; Steiner, 1970; White, 1959). Psychologists have recognized that this form of motivation—the need to control—is both strong and pervasive. Indeed, people sometimes perceive internal causation in situations in which they actually have no capacity for control.

In a series of inventive experiments, Ellen Langer (1975) has shown that people experience an "illusion of control" in situations where their outcomes are determined by chance. One experiment involved a lottery in which some participants were given their choice of fifty-cent lottery tickets ("Pick any one you like"), while others were given no choice ("Here's your ticket"). Since choice is usually associated with personal control, Langer predicted that the subjects given a choice would perceive a higher probability of winning the lottery than would the no-choice subjects. To test this prediction, each subject was asked if he or she would be willing to sell the ticket, and if so, for how much. The average amount of money demanded by a no-choice subject was less than two dollars; in contrast, the subjects who had a choice of tickets held out for an average of almost nine dollars. Subjects apparently perceived personal causation in a situation completely determined by chance.

The perception of internal causation, then, is sometimes illusory. Indeed, it has been argued that the existence of personal causation *is* an illusion (B. F. Skinner, 1971). It could be that everyone's behavior is determined by his past experiences and present circumstances. The behavior of the self-integrated person might well be determined in this way, but his *perception* of personal causation raises him above the status of a simple automaton. In perceiving himself as an active causal agent, the integrated person is likely to make more concerted attempts to control his life. Indeed, the perception of personal causation appears basic to psychological health. The feeling that one cannot control one's environment is a major basis of chronic depression (Seligman, 1975). Even one's reactions to painful events depend on the self-perception of control. Noxious stimuli, for example, such as loud noises and painful shocks, usually produce physiological arousal and interfere with performance on tasks requiring clear thinking. However, Glass, Singer, and Friedman (1969) have shown that a person who believes he has some control over the occurrence of such noxious events is likely to be less aroused by them. In addition, his performance on a task is less likely to be disturbed when the event does occur. So, whether perceived personal control is an illusion or is real, it is indispensable to the health and well-being of the individual.

Self-differentiation and self-integration, in summary, are processes of psychological growth. Differentiation is the cognitive capacity to see the self from many different perspectives; integration is the ability to implement self-values in choosing among perspectives. The recognition of one's core values brings a feeling of personal causation. The integrated person feels free to choose among a variety of different selves, and through this process, to exert a causal influence on his world. For such a person, differentiation thus represents a well-stocked repertoire of strategies for the presentation of self.

Combining The individual is very protective of his con-
Information struction of social reality. Evidence that
threatens to invalidate even a trivial part of
that construction can be upsetting. As you might expect, this
concern with contradictory evidence is particularly strong in regard to the individual's construction of himself. We noted earlier that in generating predictions about himself, the individual
may come to interpret ambiguous information so that it is consistent with his self-theory. What happens, though, when the information is decidedly unambiguous? How does the individual
deal with information that clearly contradicts his self-theory?
Both negative and positive information can contradict one's
self-construction. Hearing that you were just named the person
"most likely to reflect poorly on the school" would be discon-
certing; hearing that you were just named the person "most
likely to succeed" also might be a burden. In this section of the
chapter, we will discuss the implicit psychologist's reaction to
both negative and positive information.

Negative Information
Imagine that someone walks up to you, takes you aside, and in a
sincere, concerned voice says that you have the intellect of a
turnip. Assuming your self-theory says otherwise—that you are
considerably brighter than the average vegetable—you might
find this remark unnerving. But because your critic made his
remark in a sincere voice, you cannot ascribe it to anger,
jealousy, or pettiness. How do you defend your self-theory
against this kind of information? For many years, psychologists
have been interested in the problem of self-defense. Long lists
of *defense mechanisms*—characteristic modes of dealing with
threatening perceptions and thoughts—have been put forth by
clinical psychologists and personality theorists. These psychologists have been mainly concerned with threatening thoughts
about the self that arise from internal sources—inner conflicts,

nasty impulses, and the like. Social psychologists, meanwhile, have focused more exclusively on the individual's defense against external threats, especially social feedback, social comparison, and experiences of failure.

Failure is an important kind of negative information about the self. A failure experience (failing to anticipate the end of a hallway, for example) is usually not incorporated into one's self-theory. This is especially true of persons with high self-esteem (Fitch, 1970). Instead of attributing failure to lack of ability—a self-attribution—people tend to blame other factors, even when consensus information would suggest otherwise. Thus, an individual may fail when all others succeed (a low consensus event), and yet attribute his failure to any number of obscure extraneous circumstances. It should be noted, though, that external attribution for failure may reflect more than egotistic attribution or simple self-defense. Miller and Ross (1975) have suggested that it is natural to attribute any unexpected event to chance or external factors. A failure is usually unexpected for most people; by and large, people set out to succeed. Even a detached observer is likely to attribute another's unexpected failure to external or variable factors (Jones, Rock, Shaver, Goethals, and Ward, 1968). Nevertheless, because his self-esteem is at stake, a person is usually ready to give himself the benefit of the doubt when he experiences a failure, and is usually more likely to do so than is an observer (Snyder, Stephan, and Rosenfield, 1976). Failure experiences, in short, are only infrequently included as part of the individual's self-theory.

Similarly, evidence of one's bad or immoral behavior is often attributed in the least self-damaging way. This is apparent when the actor's moral judgments are compared with those of an observer. As mature adults, actors and observers both tend to define personal responsibility in terms of intention rather than damage; thus a person is not blamed for an act that causes damage if he did not intend to cause the damage. However, when the damage caused by an act is *very* bad, the observer's moral perspective loses its sophistication. The actor is blamed even if he did not foresee or intentionally bring about the damage (Walster, 1966). In contrast, the actor's moral perspective may change in another way when his actions have very damaging consequences (Harvey, Harris, and Barnes, 1975). It is easy to take the blame for minor harm-doing, even if the act is unintentional. If you were to spill someone's coffee accidentally, for instance, you would no doubt apologize and offer to buy the person another cup. The blame would not be especially costly to you, nor would it reflect on your self-image. After all, everyone spills things once in a while. But what if you accidentally spilled the coffee into the person's lap, ruining his clothing and causing him to leap up and upset his food? You probably would be somewhat reluctant to take the blame—in part because restitution would be costly, and in part because it would lower your self-esteem ("I cause bad things to happen"). Instead, you might find fault with the other person ("What a stupid place to put a cup of coffee"). Research has demonstrated that when acceptance of responsibility for a harmful act would threaten a person's self-concept, or when restitution to a victim would be difficult, a harm-doer tends to justify his actions, often finding fault instead with the victim (Walster, Berscheid, and Walster, 1973).

Very frequently, the avoidance of negative information about oneself involves attribution of negative characteristics to others. This kind of defense has been called *projection* (Holmes, 1968). There are two ways in which the individual may "project" his own negative characteristics onto others. If a person finds out something unpleasant about himself, he may assume that other people are similar to him, and that they therefore have the same characteristic (Bramel, 1962). There is a certain amount of security in believing that one's own negative qualities are shared by others. Actors may therefore assume greater consensus for their negative behaviors than actually exists ("Just about every-body loses their temper once in a while"). The individual may also attribute a negative characteristic to another person as a means of justifying his own negative action. After delivering a painful electric shock to a subject in a psychology experiment, for example, the individual may come to believe that the subject deserved such shock. This kind of defense involves seeing nega-tive characteristics in others as the causes of one's own negative action.

Another way of dealing with negative information is simply to avoid it, or failing that, to deny its existence. This kind of defense is similar to the processes that often occur when we form impressions of others. As we noted in Chapter 3, the indi-vidual strives to form a consistent impression of another person, and, in so doing, may often discount information that conflicts with the total impression. For most people, negative informa-tion about themselves conflicts with their total self-theory. It may therefore simply be forgotten. In fact, although people with extremely high self-esteem are generally considered psycholog-ically healthy (Rogers, 1951), they may engage in more of this defensive forgetting and discounting than those with average or low self-esteem (Cohen, 1959; Bramel, 1962). Because nega-tive information is highly inconsistent with the self-theory of the high-self-esteem individual, he may actively pursue the seem-ingly "unhealthy" activity of avoiding, denying, or forgetting information about himself.

Positive Information
Why should anyone be concerned with avoiding positive infor-mation about himself? People seldom deny success ("I hope the professor changes my A to a C"); they seldom deny moral or heroic acts ("I couldn't help saving the child from the burning building—she was clinging to my leg"); indeed, they seldom deny fortunate events ("I'm planning on giving my winnings

back to the casino"). Why, then, might positive information be difficult to incorporate into one's self-theory?

Positive information can represent a threat to an individual's self-theory when his initial impression of himself is predominantly negative. For the person high in self-esteem, positive information has two properties—it is *consistent* with his self-theory, and it *enhances* his self-theory. For the person low in self-esteem, positive information may be enhancing, but it is inconsistent. This "consistency versus enhancement" issue has occupied the attention of psychologists for a number of years (see, for example, Jones, 1973; Shrauger, 1975). Many argue that consistency is more important to most people. From this perspective, evaluative feedback inconsistent with important elements in one's self-theory is likely to be distorted, considered less credible, or attributed to external or variable factors. This implies that the low-self-esteem person will tend to reject unexpected positive information; he is more concerned with validating his self-theory than with enhancing his self-esteem. The consistency point of view could explain why some people maintain, and even seek out, unpleasant relationships with others. Confirmation of one's self-theory—even if it entails little joy —is preferred over disconfirmation. Thus, the low self-esteem person may implicitly look for and unwittingly bring about behavior from others that supports his negative self-view.

Other psychologists, however, argue that self-enhancement is a more powerful motive than self-consistency. Central to this point of view is the assumption that people have a basic need to think favorably of themselves. If this need is not satisfied, its strength will increase in the same way that one's appetite increases when one is deprived of food. This implies that people who have low regard for themselves should have an especially *strong* desire for self-enhancement; they would like to follow the famine with a feast.

Self-consistency theory predicts that low-self-esteem people will react unfavorably to success; self-enhancement theory predicts that they will react favorably to success. Many studies have examined these competing predictions; some have confirmed consistency predictions, while others have confirmed enhancement predictions. The answer to this issue thus is complex; whether people are motivated by consistency or by enhancement depends on a number of factors. The *type* of reaction—cognitive vs. emotional—seems to make a difference (Shrauger, 1975). Sometimes it is important to distinguish between thoughts and feelings. On occasion, for instance, everyone has felt distressed (an emotional reaction) about information he believes to be true (a cognitive reaction). When a person's cognitive reactions are assessed, consistency seems to prevail. Individuals tend to remember consistent feedback better than inconsistent feedback and also judge consistent feedback as more believable. However, when emotional reactions are assessed, the results typically support enhancement theory. In some studies, for example, the subject's feeling about the person who provides evaluation is assessed. In this case, a low-self-esteem person tends to be more attracted to someone who provides positive feedback than to someone who provides negative feedback.

Another important factor is the nature of the task or activity confronted by the person. According to a study by Maracek and Mettee (1972), it matters a great deal whether success on a task is perceived to depend on skill or luck. If luck is perceived as the determinant, even a low-self-esteem person is motivated by enhancement—he prefers success to failure. In effect, a lucky success allows the low-self-esteem person to have his cake and eat it, too; he did not produce the success, so he can accept it without having to revise his self-estimate. When the task is perceived to depend on skill, however, consistency predictions are supported. To know that one has produced success when one expects failure is to learn that one's self-estimate is wrong.

Maracek and Mettee identified yet another factor, the person's degree of *certainty* regarding his tendency to fail. A person who is utterly convinced of his low self-estimate will actively resist disconfirming evidence, but a person who has not yet fully accepted his tendency to fail is open to new evidence that might lead him to revise his self-estimate in a positive direction. Thus, consistency predictions are supported for individuals who are certain of their self-theory, while enhancement predictions are supported for individuals who are uncertain.

In summary, it appears that self-defense takes on different forms depending on the individual's level of self-esteem. For the average person, and for those high in self-esteem, defense is rather straightforward—avoid, deny, or explain away unflattering pieces of information. In part, this defense reflects a desire to receive encouraging feedback. But it also reflects a basic attribution principle; namely, unexpected outcomes are attributed to external or variable causes, not to internal stable causes. In short, the natural processing of information is compatible with a desire for self-enhancement in the average- and high-self-esteem person. Things are not so simple for the low-self-esteem person. For him, the natural tendency to preserve his self-theory is at odds with the tendency to enhance the self. To attribute an unexpected success externally makes sense cognitively, but can be upsetting emotionally. One way out of this dilemma is to hope for success in endeavors where one's outcomes are determined by chance; in this way, positive information can be embraced without threatening the validity of one's self-theory.

The Relevance of Self-Theory

When does the individual's self-theory enter into the determination of his actions? We have argued that a person's conception of himself as a social object—his self-theory—has a pervasive influence on his behavior, his perceptions of himself, and his perceptions of others. He frequently behaves so as to remain consistent with his self-theory. However, as we noted at the beginning of the chapter, self-theory is not always the center of the individual's attention. People spend a great deal of time thinking about things and interacting with things in their environment—knitting, tinkering, reading, playing, and so on. Under these conditions, people seldom reflect on themselves. In recent years, the causes and consequences of such variations in self-awareness have received much attention from psychologists.

Self-awareness

Shelley Duval and Robert Wicklund (1972) have developed an enlightening new theory of self-awareness that has much in common with the traditional views of William James (1890), Alfred Schutz (1932), and George Herbert Mead (1934). Recall that James characterized the self as both the "knower" and the "known." As the knower, the individual considers his environment, manipulating and conceptualizing objects in his world. As the known, the individual focuses on himself, labeling and "objectifying" himself as something that can be known and understood. Duval and Wicklund have conceptualized these two "selves" in terms of *attention states*. The individual can focus his attention either on some object in the environment or on himself. An environmental focus is called *subjective self-awareness*, since the self is the subject or agent of perception. The other attentional state is called *objective self-awareness*; the self is the object rather than the subject of perception. Although the focus of attention may shift rapidly back and forth between the self and the environment, Duval and Wicklund maintain that a person cannot be in both states at one time.

In a state of subjective self-awareness, the person is focused on the external world of objects, people, and events. The individual constructs implicit theories about these things because he is focused on *them*. In a state of objective self-awareness, meanwhile, a person is specifically focused on himself as an object of attention. The individual considers his implicit self-theory at this time—it is his construction of himself as an object. However, even in a state of objective self-awareness, a person is not aware of all the elements of his implicit self-theory. Just as the individual focuses selectively on a few aspects of others at any one time, he focuses on just a few salient aspects of himself.

What conditions produce each of these two states? As we noted earlier in this chapter and also in Chapter 3, self-focused attention (objective self-awareness) can be the result of an audience or a camera. In such situations, we become highly aware of our appearance, our display of confidence, and even that trickle of perspiration over our eyes. In a sense, knowing that others are considering us as an object leads us to consider ourselves in the same way. Our focus of attention follows theirs, much as when we see a group of people looking at the sky and follow their gaze upward. Other stimuli in the environment may also produce objective self-awareness. Hearing one's tape-recorded voice, for example, generally causes self-consciousness, as does looking in a mirror. In fact, any stimulus that reminds the individual of his status as an object of attention or evaluation may produce objective self-awareness. The subjective state is produced, in turn, by stimuli that divert attention from a consideration of the self. Working on a task or being distracted by external stimuli, for example, is said to induce subjective self-awareness. Even attending closely to another person may, at times, induce the subjective state (Vallacher, 1976). When the individual manipulates and conceptualizes parts of the environment (even other people) that are unrelated to himself, an awareness of himself as object disappears.

Consequences of Self-awareness

Focus of attention has implications for self-perception. There are consequences, first of all, for self-evaluation—the most important aspect of the self-theory. Duval and Wicklund suggest that self-focused attention produces intense self-evaluation; and, more often than not, this evaluation tends to be unfavorable (Ickes, Wicklund, and Ferris, 1973). This makes good sense when you consider the logic behind the negativity effect in person perception, discussed in Chapter 4. We pointed out that when someone who is psychologically close is evaluated, greater weight is given to the perceived bad points than to the perceived good points of the person. You might say that psychological distance is at a minimum when the person being evaluated is oneself; hence, there is a negativity effect in self-evaluation. This is similar to the reasoning of Duval and Wicklund. They say that in a state of objective self-awareness, a person becomes aware of the inevitable discrepancies between the way he is and the way he would like to be. A perceived discrepancy between one's *actual* and *ideal* selves is a mark of low self-esteem (Wylie, 1961). Self-consciousness, therefore, draws attention to negative discrepancies. No doubt you can remember situations in which you felt painfully self-conscious. You probably were preoccupied with all sorts of personal shortcomings—physical imperfections, intellectual deficits, and various other insecurities—that you normally wouldn't think about at all.

Heightened self-esteem can also be the result of objective self-awareness. If a person has an experience of success, for example, or receives glowing feedback from a former critic, he may experience a *positive* discrepancy between his actual and ideal selves (Wicklund, 1975). In such cases—when he finds he is better than he expected to be—a person may seek out stimuli that increase his self-awareness. He may try to find an audience (people to tell), or even gloat in front of a mirror. However, there is a marked tendency for one's aspirations (the ideal self) to overtake one's real outcomes quite rapidly. Thus, if we experience a success, we don't gloat for long because we expect an even greater success in the future. "Rising expectations," in other words, can dissipate high self-esteem. So, in a self-focused state, the individual is more likely to experience negative than positive self-evaluation in the long run.

Objective self-awareness can also influence how a person perceives the causes of his behavior. Recall that in Chapter 2, we noted that attribution often follows an individual's focus of attention; we tend to find causes where we look for them. An actor tends to focus on the situation and to attribute his behavior to situational causes. The observer, in turn, makes internal attributions because he tends to focus on the actor. This reasoning implies that if the actor were induced to focus on himself, becoming a "self-observer," he would attribute causality to himself.

Duval and Wicklund (1973) conducted an experiment to test the hypothesis that self-focused attention leads the individual to attribute causality to self. They presented several hypothetical incidents to subjects in which the causal agent was not clearly specified. In one incident, for example, the subject was asked to imagine that he had jumped off a diving platform and landed on someone who came up from under water below. The subject was then asked to estimate the amount that he was at fault and the amount that the other individual was at fault. Half of the subjects completed this task under conditions designed to make them objectively self-aware—they were seated in front of a large mirror. The other half of the subjects were asked the same questions, but were not faced with their mirror image. As Duval and Wicklund predicted, the objectively self-aware subjects assigned greater responsibility to themselves for these incidents than did subjectively self-aware subjects.

Objective self-awareness thus instills in one a sense of personal responsibility for one's actions. This has important consequences for one's behavior, one's conceptions of self, and one's interactions with others. According to many psychologists (see Walster, Berscheid, and Walster, 1973), there are two basic reasons why people tend to treat each other fairly and make restitution for unjust behavior. First, we may fear retaliation from the victim if we fail to make restitution. Second, a failure to make restitution generates *self-concept distress*, the feeling that we are not living up to our ideal standards of morality and fair play. This second motive clearly is more significant when one is objectively self-aware than when one is focused on the environment. The self-focused person takes personal responsibility for his behavior, evaluating himself rather harshly when guilty of wrongdoing. Thus, when attention is drawn to a person, he will tend to treat others equitably and avoid exploiting or taking advantage of them.

Evidence in support of this reasoning is provided in studies of *deindividuation* (for example, Zimbardo, 1969). Deindividuation is the loss of personal or separate identity that can result from membership in large, unstructured groups. After all, when a person is part of a large audience, his attention is not focused on himself. The more people present and the more everyone dresses and looks alike, the greater the feeling of anonymity. Because attention is not focused on them, individuals in such groups are seldom objectively self-aware and thus do not feel personally responsible for their actions. As a result, they may engage in impulsive and even violent behaviors without ever feeling self-concept distress. The potential result, according to Zimbardo (1969), is mob violence, riots, lynchings, and looting. It appears, then, that self-focused attention is basic to morality.

The study of objective self-awareness has only begun in the last few years. At present, it seems clear that the focusing of a person's attention on himself has wide-ranging implications for his behavior. When a person considers himself as an object in the world, his self-theory becomes the outstanding content in his mind. Recent experimental evidence suggests that many of the aspects of self-theory discussed in this chapter may depend almost entirely on the individual's ability to focus attention on himself. It is possible to speculate that the process of self-attribution, as we have described it, takes place only when a person is objectively self-aware (Wegner and Finstuen, 1977); it is possible that self-consistency is only relevant to an individual's reactions to success and failure when he is objectively self-aware and that self-enhancement takes place when the individual is subjectively self-aware; it is even reasonable to suggest that without objective self-awareness, an individual would have no self-theory at all. In short, awareness of the self is an important new variable in the psychologist's exploration of implicit self-theory.

In this section, we have noted that self-focused attention typically lowers an individual's self-esteem because personal weaknesses and shortcomings become evident. Self-focused attention also produces a sense of personal responsibility; the objectively self-aware person becomes an observer of his own behavior and thus tends to make internal attributions. The feeling of personal responsibility associated with self-focused attention is conducive to moral behavior.

the implicit psychologist

We have emphasized that the individual's conception of himself is much like a scientific theory. Obviously, a rigorous and sound theory does not just suddenly pop into a scientist's head; rather, it gradually develops from simple common-sense notions by the processes of intention and extension. This is true for the individual's self-theory as well. Important aspects of an individual's self-theory change in many ways as he develops and matures. It is also clear that two scientists examining two different phenomena will often come up with different theories. Similarly, we each experience a self different from others and therefore construct quite different self-theories, each a unique and personal expression of our lives. In this section, we will consider both the development of self-theory, and individual differences in self-theories that arise among different adults.

Developmental Changes

Psychologists and philosophers who have considered the development of the individual's self-theory have traditionally reached the conclusion that the infant has only the rudimentary beginnings of a theory of self. Mead (1934) and Cooley (1902), as we have noted, based their analyses of self-development on the idea that the very young child had no self-theory at all. Only through the appraisals of himself offered by others does the individual begin to consider himself a social object worthy of a theory. This notion has served as the basis for a thorough analysis of self-development conducted by Robert Selman (1976). He has suggested that the child comes to consider himself as an object of thought in a series of stages. Each stage signifies a perspective the child is capable of taking; a child at a particular stage can take the perspectives of earlier stages, but not the perspectives of later ones. This ability comes only with greater maturity and greater experience.

According to Selman, very young children are not capable of differentiating between their own subjective reality and that of another person. This is the *egocentric level* of social perspective taking. The egocentric child does not recognize that other people may interpret events or courses of action differently from the way he does. Although he can differentiate between self and other as entities, he does not consider the possibility that other persons can have other points of view. Slightly older children enter the *subjective level* of social perspective taking. At this stage, the child moves beyond egocentrism and is able to distinguish clearly the subjective perspectives of self and other. The child realizes that, even when two people are in the same situation, their thoughts may differ. At the *self-reflective level,* the child gains the new realization that since both self and other have subjective realities, the other person can view the self as a subject reciprocally. This leads to an awareness that the other's perspective on the self's inner views is an important consideration in interaction with the other and in considering the other's viewpoint. The child realizes that the other person, too, can see himself from the child's point of view.

The last two stages of social perspective taking involve seeing the self from a detached, third-person point of view. Following self-reflection, the child moves into the *third-person dyadic level,* a stage at which the child is able to conceptualize both his own and another person's subjective realities from a third-person point of view; he can "step outside" the dyadic interaction and simultaneously consider the motives and behaviors of another person and himself. The final level is a generalization of this ability to all possible third-person perspectives, the *qualitative systems level.* In essence, the individual at this level is capable of considering the societal view of the self. In addition, this level allows the individual to compare and contrast all sorts of different perspectives on the self. Each of these stages, then, represents a particular point of view on the self; in addition, each represents a new development in the sophistication of the individual's self-theory.

Probably the most intriguing aspect of Selman's research is the finding that levels of social perspective taking are related to levels of intellectual and moral development. He indicates, for example, that a moral concern with being a "good person" cannot be reached until the self-reflective level of perspective taking; why should the child concern himself with conforming and being "good" when he cannot take another's view toward himself? Selman also indicates a relationship between intellectual understanding of physical objects and the ability to conceptualize the self. For example, the child in Piaget's *concrete operations* stage of intellectual development (discussed in Chapter 5) is typically found at the self-reflective level of perspective taking. There appears to be, therefore, a general relationship among many different areas of cognitive development. The ability to consider the self as an object in the world is only one of several capacities that develop with growth, but it seems central to much of social development.

Somewhat ironically, as the child's sources of information about the self expand in number and kind, he has less of a need to rely on them for self-definition. The child who becomes increasingly able to take the perspectives of others on the self becomes increasingly independent of direct social feedback. In part, this growth reflects the individual's cognitive development. Remember that attribution involves fairly complex information processing; thus, relative to the young child, the older child is better able to infer certain characteristics of himself from an observation of his own behavior (Ross, 1976). Self-attribution takes on importance at the expense of social feedback. However, social sources lose some of their hold on the child for another reason as well—over time, the wealth of information to be drawn from others is *internalized,* incorporated into the individual's self-theory. Not only are the evaluative reactions of others learned, but the *basis* of those evaluations is accepted as a standard for self-assessment.

Through taking the perspectives of others, the child comes to monitor and judge for himself the goodness and badness of his own thought and behavior. Without having to be chastised by his parents, for example, the mature child feels guilty when he gives his baby sister a rug burn. Guilt, in this sense, is the self-concept distress that comes from behavior inconsistent with one's self-theory. Since this theory is developed by becoming aware of the perspectives of others, it is an internal representation of the interests and welfare of others. The individual who behaves according to his mature self-theory is both moral and independent.

Individual Differences   There are nearly four billion self-theories at present on this planet. Yet many of the important differences among these theories relate to just a few basic dimensions of personality. In this chapter, we have already discussed some of these dimensions—self-esteem, self-differentiation, and self-integration. Other personality variables discussed earlier in the text—field dependence, internal versus external locus of control, ambivalence, dogmatism, for example—also have clear relevance for self-conception. In this section, we will add to the list two more variables, *self-consciousness* and the *need for approval*, which account for important similarities and differences among self-theories.

Self-consciousness
Earlier we discussed objective self-awareness and the consequences of this state for self-evaluation and self-attribution. At that time, our concern was with the conditions that are likely to cause the typical person to focus attention on himself. It is apparent, however, that individuals differ in their threshold for self-focused attention. Some people seem to have a very high threshold; if confronted with a TV camera in the shower, they might polish the lens or admire the knobs. Other people, meanwhile, behave as though an audience follows them wherever they go; they might wear bathrobes, boots, and helmets in the shower. This characteristic tendency to focus attention on the self, even when the factors that normally produce self-awareness are weak, is referred to as *self-consciousness*. That individuals do differ from one another in self-consciousness has been verified in several studies (for example, Argyle and

Williams, 1969; Fenigstein, Scheier, and Buss, 1975; M. Rosenberg, 1965).

Individual differences in self-consciousness seem to relate to other aspects of self-perception. In large part, these relationships parallel the relationships discussed earlier regarding self-focused attention. Just as objective self-awareness is associated with lowered self-evaluation, for instance, chronically self-conscious people tend to have lower self-esteem than do less self-conscious people (Argyle and Williams, 1969; M. Rosenberg, 1965). But differences in self-esteem also appear to depend on the *kind* of self-consciousness to which the individual is most sensitive. According to Buss and Scheier (1975), it is important to distinguish between public and private self-consciousness. *Public* self-consciousness means that the individual is highly concerned with his public image—how he is perceived and evaluated by others. *Private* self-consciousness, in contrast, is attention to personal motives, fantasies, and other characteristics of the self. Privately self-conscious people are obsessed with their inner life of thoughts and feelings much of the time; publicly self-conscious people are more concerned with evaluations of themselves by others. The public-private distinction is useful for considering the bases of self-evaluation. While the privately self-conscious person evaluates himself against private, personal standards, the self-esteem of the publicly self-conscious person may reflect feedback from, and comparison with, other people.

This distinction implies that the self-esteem of a publicly self-conscious person should correspond to a consensual assessment of his assets and liabilities. If other people have a favorable impression of such a person, he is likely to feel self-satisfied. But if people turn against him, throwing a psychological pie in his face, he may turn against himself. The publicly self-conscious individual, therefore, may be extremely sensitive to social forms of self-information (Fenigstein, 1974). In contrast, the self-esteem of the privately self-conscious person may be remarkably resistant to assessments of the self made by others. No doubt, you have known someone who seemed to have everything in the world going for him—intelligence, good looks, a luxurious veranda, and more—but who nonetheless constantly berated himself. On the other hand, you may also have encountered a person with the objective assets of sour milk, but who persisted in considering himself the cream of the crop. Discrepancies such as these can occur when a person evaluates himself against internal standards. Unlike the publicly self-conscious person, the privately self-conscious individual tends to be more immune to social rewards or punishments.

Need for Approval

Each of us attempts to obtain positive reactions from others. Some people, however, seem to have liking from others as their central goal in life. It is as though they have not overcome the overriding concern with social feedback that characterizes the individual during the early stages of self-theory development. Such individuals are said to be high in *need for approval*. Individuals less motivated by this concern are considered low in need for approval. A test has been developed that discriminates among people in terms of their need for approval (Crowne and Marlowe, 1964). The basic strategy in this test is to determine whether people will admit to their faults. For instance, the person is asked to indicate "true" or "false" to the following items: "I never gossip" and "I can remember playing sick to get out of something." If the person answers "true" to the first item and "false" to the second, he is probably responding in a manner designed to win approval. After all, most people do gossip and most people have played sick to avoid some unpleasant activity. Saying that these faults are not characteristic of himself suggests that the person is doing everything in his power to look good (Hewitt and Goldman, 1974).

You probably have known people like this, and chances are

you don't like them very much. They follow a simple yet almost disgusting set of rules. Always seem sincere, for example, and act interested in what the other person has to say. Be sure to laugh at all jokes, no matter how banal or dumb, and above all, don't antagonize anyone. Always make sure everyone knows that things are just great, and that you have no problems. This seems phony and is unlikely to impress anyone. It is ironic that those people who need approval so much and try so hard to achieve it are typically less successful in the long run than are those who are less concerned (Crowne and Marlowe, 1964). Their persistence in trying to gain approval by being pleasant suggests that they may not be able to obtain self-enhancement in other ways.

Indeed, a number of theorists concerned with approval-seeking have suggested that the person with a strong need for approval is suffering from a chronic lack of self-esteem (Coopersmith, 1967). Such a person may score high on tests of self-esteem, but as a rule, he does so because he is trying to maintain his "faultness" image. According to Crowne and Marlowe (1964), the approval-seeker actually has a low opinion of himself. His concern with appearances, niceties, and graces is a misplaced striving for self-worth. Afraid to test his self-assessment in more stringent and risky ways (through real achievements or close social relationships), the approval-seeker relies on affability and politeness.

Summary The self is the central figure in the individual's phenomenal field. Yet self-construction has much in common with the construction of more peripheral persons. In both cases, information is selected, generated, and organized into a coherent theory. And just as combining new information often poses a threat to one's theories about others, so the incorporation of new data into one's self-theory is often difficult.

Much of the information selected for one's self-theory reflects interpersonal experiences. The person notes how significant others perceive him and how he compares with those similar to himself. Self-attribution is another way of selecting information; attribution provides insight into one's internal states just as it provides insight into the motives of others. On the basis of selected information, the individual generates new information. Extended inferences about oneself follow the same rule as inferences about others—evaluative consistency. In this manner, the individual develops a general evaluation of himself (self-esteem).

The information selected and generated about oneself is organized by means of two principles: differentiation and integration. Through interpersonal experiences, various perspectives on the self are developed; each perspective consists of different pieces of information. The awareness of oneself as a causal agent—an active decision-maker rather than a reactive automaton—allows these differing perspectives to be integrated into a core self. A set of self-values provides this sense of personal causation.

Because most people have a favorable self-theory, negative information—evidence of failure or wrongdoing, negative social feedback, and so forth—is often discounted, distorted, or projected onto others. Somewhat ironically, positive information—successes, glowing feedback—can be distressing to a person with low self-esteem. Though positive information provides self-enhancement for such a person, it also poses a threat to the validity of his self-theory. Thus, only under certain circumstances is positive information accepted by the low-self-esteem person.

To deal effectively with the world, our attention typically is focused on some relevant aspect of the environment. Under some conditions, however, attention is drawn to the self. Self-focused attention (objective self-awareness) has consequences for the individual's thought and behavior: lowered self-esteem, a heightened sense of personal responsibility (self-attribution) for one's actions, and equitable behavior toward others.

Because one's self-theory develops through interpersonal experiences, the very young child's conception of himself is global and diffuse. Intention and extension occur as the child learns to adopt differing perspectives—to see himself from increasingly transcendent vantage points. As these perspectives are internalized, one's self-theory becomes independent of social sources of information.

Everyone has had different interpersonal experiences, so each person has a unique self-theory. One important dimension of difference is self-consciousness. The person who typically experiences public self-consciousness has a self-theory that corresponds to the view of him held by his audience. In contrast, the privately self-conscious person is relatively immune to social information and thus may perceive himself differently from the way other people do. Individuals also differ in their need for approval from others. Chronic approval-seeking represents an attempt to validate an idealized self-theory by obtaining low-risk information. This attempt usually is unsuccessful in the long run; superficial niceness elicits politeness and mild compliments, not respect or intimacy.

chapter seven

How many times have you said something to someone and then realized that he may have taken it the wrong way? Your noble goals and intentions are dashed by a dull look of puzzlement and disbelief in his eyes. Of course, you set about reiterating your meaning, hedging your initial argument, apologizing lamely, or attempting to find some way to explain yourself. In a sense, this chapter has a similar goal. We want to make sure that you, the reader, have not misunderstood this entire book. Because we as authors have both purposely and accidentally left out many things, because we have condensed and presented much material as though it were gospel truth (and not the mere theory that it is), and most important, because we cannot even tell whether you are puzzled or pleased, we have reason to believe that this final chapter may be the most important one in the book.

The first section of this chapter will be a summary of our discussion of implicit psychology. Although we will deal with a number of ideas that recur throughout earlier chapters, we will also introduce a general way of looking at implicit psychology that we have not presented before. In the second section of the chapter, we will bring up the issue of the *accuracy* of the implicit psychologist; here we will reach some tentative conclusions about the relationship between implicit psychology and the explicit science of psychology. In the third section, we will outline some of the other chapters we might have written; the chapters included in this volume are limited, in large part, by the research already conducted and the theory already built. We hope to answer the question "Where do we go from here?" by showing how the implicit psychological approach can be applied to a number of additional areas of social experience. So, while this chapter

overview of implicit psychology

is an overview, it is also an attempt to include things that thus far have been overlooked.

Principles of Implicit Psychology

The assertion that "each person is an implicit psychologist" carries with it a variety of implications. First, the proposition suggests that the individual builds theories about people. We have emphasized this facet of implicit psychology to the exclusion of others because more is now known about the structure and content of these theories than about the processes whereby the theories are applied. Traditionally, psychologists have considered these two areas of inquiry as distinct. The first is a concern with cognitive structure—the organization of thought; the second is a concern with cognitive dynamics—the process of thought. In the next few pages, we will explain some of the general strategies experimental psychologists use to develop an understanding of the structure of implicit psychological theories; then we will turn to a discussion of the processes of implicit psychology.

Cognitive Structure

How is implicit psychological theory organized? If, when you have Thought A, you are also likely to have Thought B, what is the nature of the system that links the thoughts together? Although experimental psychologists have provided a number of different answers to this question, it is possible to identify some major themes. Models of implicit theory usually assume a *categorical, dimensional,* or *relational* structure. The thoughts "A" and "B" may be linked because they belong to the same cognitive category; they may be linked because they have similar values on some cognitive dimension; or they may be linked by a particular relational statement (for example, "A likes B"). In each case, the implicit psychologist is presumed to have a theory in which "A" and "B" are concepts; these concepts are related to each other in the theory in a categorical, dimensional; or relational manner.

The categorical model of social cognition emphasizes the notion that we humans are a symbol-using species. The labels we have for objects, the words we use to signify both physical and social events, the abstractions we create to stand for our experiences, are all categorical in nature. We use an abstract symbol such as *cow* to symbolize a variety of things, all of which have in common certain features that add up to "cowness." The word *cow,* of course, has none of these features. It is totally incapable of reacting to cold hands by kicking over a milk pail. Yet this word stands for an entire set of entities that have this quality. Since there are both superordinate categories (such as *animal*) and subordinate categories (such as *Guernsey*), cognitive structure can be seen as a hierarchical system of categories ranging from the most specific to the most general (see Figure 7.1).

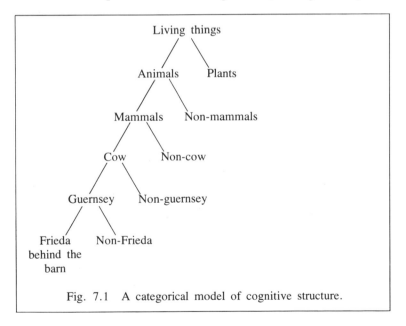

Fig. 7.1   A categorical model of cognitive structure.

In previous chapters, we considered several categorical models without identifying them as such. Attributes (Chapter 3), group stereotypes (Chapters 3 and 4), labels (Chapter 4), and grouping schemas (Chapter 5) are all names for cognitive categories. All these methods of describing implicit theory hold in common the idea that each person categorizes his or her experiences. In addition, these methods suppose that all cognitive organization takes place through perceptions of similarity and difference; we place in the same category those experiences which we see as similar, whereas we sort into different categories those experiences we see as different. Our reactions to various social stimuli—people and groups—depend on how we have categorized them. Although this simplistic view of cognitive structure does have considerable usefulness, it falls short of a full explanation of implicit theory. Individuals are quite capable of perceiving and responding to differences in, say, the brightness of a light, or the relative intelligence of a person. The categorical model is concerned only with "either-or" judgments (since an object either is a member of a category or is not), and therefore cannot represent the *quantitative* judgments people may make.

Dimensional models of cognitive structure are specifically designed to incorporate this "quantitative" aspect of human thought. In our discussions of articulation (Chapter 3) and ordering schemas (Chapter 5), for example, we noted that people frequently do order objects of cognition along certain dimensions. The dimensional model is built on the assumption that the individual perceives gradations of similarity or difference among the objects of thought, and that these gradations are best represented by dimensions of judgment. So, while the categorical model implies that we perceive similarities or differences among objects because of *qualities* of the objects (for example, a rock is hard, while a dumpling is soft), the dimensional model implies that we make such judgments on the basis of underlying dimensions that represent *quantities* of a quality (for example, a rock is harder than a dumpling).

As we have seen in previous chapters, dimensional models of cognitive structure frequently take the form of "maps." Recall, for instance, the maps of attribute inference and personality judgment in Chapter 3, and the maps of perceived interpersonal relations in Chapter 5. These spatial representations of cognitive organization result when we consider multiple dimensions of judgment at the same time. Such maps provide especially appealing portrayals of cognitive structure; we can see the organization of cognition at a glance; we can examine the specific similarities and differences perceived among objects (because objects near each other on the map are psychologically similar); and we can inspect the major dimensions of judgment that are employed (see Figure 7.2). Because of these features, dimensional models are effective ways to represent the structure of thought.

Individuals often think in ways that defy both categorical and dimensional representation. This is because both the categorical and dimensional models can only represent a single kind of relationship—"A is similar to B." Many other kinds of relations might exist in a person's implicit theory. Consider, for example, a thought such as "Horton likes lard." We can stretch a categorical model to fit the thought by suggesting that Horton belongs to the category of lard-likers. To construct a dimensional model of this thought, we would also have to propose that there are different amounts of lard-liking, and that Horton might be assigned a place on a dimension of "very much a lard-liker versus not at all a lard-liker." But all this seems like so much foolishness in light of the simple fact that Horton likes lard. Sometimes it becomes useful to represent thoughts in *relational* models (see Figure 7.3). Cognitive structure, from a relational

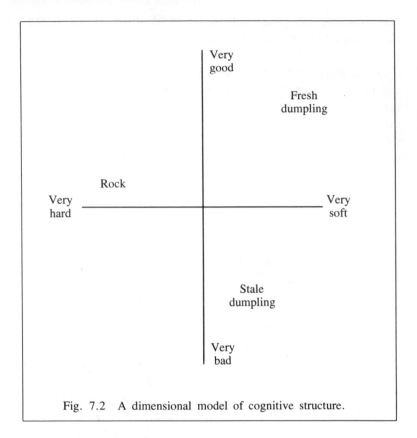

Fig. 7.2   A dimensional model of cognitive structure.

point of view, is the network of relations among cognitions.

Relational models include balance theory and linear ordering (both discussed in Chapter 5), and even include much of attribution theory as discussed in Chapter 2 (since "A causes B" is a relational statement). In a relational model, almost any statement of "subject-verb-object" can be represented as part of a network of relational statements. Thus, the relational model has a very wide-ranging usefulness. Every sentence a person can say can be used to infer a relation between concepts in the person's implicit theory. Models of cognition can be constructed on the basis of an individual's verbal statements about things, or on the basis of the individual's logic and reasoning. Of course, this capacity to represent almost every kind of cognitive organization means that the relational model may be too general. Therefore, most specific relational models are limited to particular kinds of relations; balance theory, for example, deals only with liking and belonging relations. As a rule, relational models of cognitive organization must be limited to specific subsets of relations.

Although it would be nice to have one grand model of the organization of thought, experimental psychologists have found such a model difficult to construct. Considering the nature of the task, this failure is not surprising. And considering the unique usefulness of each of the three models we have discussed, the absence of a grand model is not so distressing. Categorical models describe quite well the "grouping" function of thought;

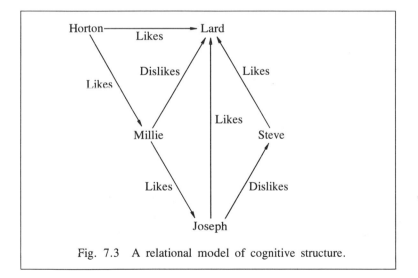

Fig. 7.3   A relational model of cognitive structure.

dimensional models are more than sufficient for representing the "ordering" function of thought; and relational models elucidate the connectedness of thought.

Cognitive Dynamics

Investigations of cognitive structure are much like snapshots. When you take a picture, you realize that the image captured in your camera is merely a "slice" of the action, a caricature of the way things were at one time. In the same way, models of cognitive organization are usually insensitive to the temporal qualities of thought. People change their minds, learn new and different ways to think about things, and most important, engage in actions on the basis of their thoughts. Thus, there is a process of thought as well as a structure. A number of influential philosophers and psychologists have also recognized this important distinction (for example, Kelly, 1955; Neisser, 1976; Piaget, 1950; Schutz, 1932). In general, they have stressed the cyclic nature of the thought process, suggesting that there is a continuous cycle of interaction among our cognitive structures, our actions, and our experiences. The cycle goes like this: Cognitive structure guides action and attention toward certain experiences; these experiences in turn modify cognitive structure; the modified structure then guides action and attention toward further experiences.

This cyclic view of cognitive processes suggests that cognitive structure has two functions. On the one hand, cognitive structure can be viewed as *memory*: it is a storehouse of past experiences. On the other hand, cognitive structure can be viewed as *anticipation*: it is a guide to future experiences. As an example of this twofold function, let us consider a particular moment in your life. Suppose that you glance at your hand one day and note that it is grasping another person's hand. If this single fact were *all* you knew, you might stand there holding the person's hand forever (or until they pried you loose). The philosopher Alfred Schutz (1932) has pointed out that such an event, unaccompanied by a context of past experience or by a context of anticipated future experience, is totally meaningless. Placed in past and future contexts, however, this event becomes an action—you shake the person's hand. You are able to do this because you have a cognitive structural memory of past experience (knowing, for instance, that you have shaken hands in the past, that this person offered his hand to you, and that this person has not met you before), and because you have a cognitive structural anticipation of future experience (expecting, for instance, that you will have shaken hands in a moment, and that such hand-shaking is a necessary prelude to your conversation). Without these contexts, your hand-holding might be interpreted as the beginning of a square dance, a demonstration of grip strength, or preparation for a surgical procedure. Cognitive structure, in light of this analysis, is an effect of past experience (memory), a cause of future experience (anticipation), and a context within which the present becomes meaningful.

We have emphasized in past chapters that the individual behaves on the basis of his or her cognitions. But the individual also engages in *cognitive* acts (for example, paying attention to a particular experience) on the basis of both memory and anticipation. We notice a yellow traffic light, for instance, because we have seen them in the past and therefore anticipate their occurrence. In the same way, we attend to characteristics of people, to people themselves, and to relations among people both because we have had past experiences with them and because we anticipate future experiences with them. Our attention is always a function of past experience (what has happened) and anticipated future experience (what will happen). In this sense, cognition and behavior are not very different; our thoughts about people and our behaviors toward people both qualify as actions.

Both bridge the gap between memory and anticipation. And both result in new memory and new anticipation.

One final note about the cognitive process is in order. We have pointed out that a number of distinguished scientists and philosophers consider the cognitive process to be cyclic in nature. Where do these thinkers believe that cycle starts? How can we construe an event without anticipating it? How can we anticipate an event without a memory of similar events? How can we have memories without first construing events? This kind of "chicken or egg" debate has come up a number of times in philosophical circles, and has generally been resolved by the suggestion that we are born with some kind of cognitive structure (however primitive) for processing information. In essence, philosophers suggest that there must be a form of knowledge with which we are genetically endowed. This necessity was recognized by Immanuel Kant. He proposed that certain very basic forms of knowledge were present in the human organism *a priori*, and that these simple structures (such as "time" and "space") provided the initial knowledge upon which all further knowledge was constructed. This is not to say, of course, that the infant can take apart a clock or measure a room for carpeting. Rather, the infant is capable (like most higher animals) of understanding events that occur in a temporal sequence or in a spatial arrangement. According to this view, cognitive processes are inherent in the nature of human beings.

The principles of implicit psychology, in summary, are the principles of social cognition. Just as implicit psychological theory is analogous to social cognitive structure, so the process of implicit psychology is analogous to the process of social cognition. We have frequently commented on the "theory building" process; this is the process of incorporating social experiences into an implicit psychological theory. In essence, it is cognitive structure functioning as memory. We have also noted the "prediction" process; this is the process of forming expectations about future social experiences. In essence, it is cognitive structure functioning as anticipation. Implicit psychology is the process of constructing theories about people and using the theories to predict people.

The Accuracy of Implicit Psychology

It is possible that this book, at first glance, could be taken as a tremendous insult to all professional psychologists. We have amassed quite a bit of evidence suggesting that people get along quite well without ever reading a psychology book, without ever talking to a psychologist, and without ever even considering their own psychological theories. We have even suggested that, at times, the individual may have more accurate and realistic implicit theories than those developed by the professionals. But there are many instances, too, in which the professional psychologist is right while the individual is totally wrong. We hope that the comparison of implicit and explicit psychology can be of some benefit to both. Some insights adapted from the realm of professional psychology can help us all to be better implicit psychologists; at the same time, the study of implicit psychology may have some benefits for explicit, professional psychology. In this section of the chapter, therefore, we will relate evidence regarding the relative accuracy of implicit and explicit psychology, attending first to the errors made most frequently by implicit psychologists, and then to some misconceptions held by professional psychology that become evident on consideration of the implicit psychologist's approach.

Implicit Errors

Studies of the accuracy of the individual's social judgments were a booming business in psychology throughout the forties and early fifties. A massive amount of research focused on identifying the most accurate individuals. Under the assumption that there was a *trait* of predictive accuracy—such that some individuals were marvelous predictors of people, while others were unable to predict accurately the sex of a person who was giving birth to a child—psychologists set out to measure this trait. They were hoping, of course, that they could find these accurate people and convince them to become psychologists. Unfortunately, in a series of articles criticizing the methods and assumptions of such studies (Cronbach, 1955; Gage and Cronbach, 1955; Campbell, 1955), the hopes cherished by this research tradition were dashed. It was shown that there were an unwieldy number of different kinds of predictive accuracy (for example, accuracy in judging the average of a group, accuracy in judging the variation of behavior in a group, accuracy in judging the deviation of an individual from a group, and so on), that there was no reliable trait of predictive accuracy (because an individual accurate in one kind of prediction might not be accurate in another), and that differences in the extent to which an individual assumed that others were similar to him (and in the amount of real similarity) were largely responsible for the accuracy scores individuals received on tests of their predictive ability. In short, treating accuracy as a trait was not a workable approach.

What are we left with? In recent years, there has been a cautious return to the topic of accuracy—but accuracy of a different kind. Interest has turned to the accuracy of an individual's causal attributions for behavior. Such studies are not concerned with identifying the "best" attributors, but rather with examining the most frequent kinds of attributional errors people make. The accuracy of these causal attributions can be determined in two ways. We can compare an individual's attributions with those made by another person; if the two patterns of attribution differ, then there is some inaccuracy on the part of one or both persons. Or, we can arrange causal factors in a particular situation and determine whether the individual can identify them correctly. Both of these methods have been used to study the accuracy of attributions made by both actors and observers.

Although it seems that the attributions an actor makes to himself should be highly accurate (after all, who knows him better?), actors nevertheless do make mistakes. We have explained some possible sources of such misattributions to self in Chapters 2 and 6. These can be summarized in terms of two major factors: *egotism* and *the illusion of control.* Actors may make incorrect attributions for their own behavior in an attempt to preserve their feelings of self-esteem and self-worth; this is egotistic attribution. The individual takes credit for good outcomes (such as success at a task) by attributing causality internally (to ability or effort), but avoids blame for bad outcomes (such as failure) by attributing causality externally (to luck or task difficulty). The illusion of control tends to bias attributions in another way. Generally, actors tend to believe that they have great freedom to behave as they wish (Kelley, 1967), and that they have great control over the outcomes they receive (Langer, 1975). Thus, actors may often discount or ignore what seem like minor possible causes of their behavior (such as a simple request), and similarly may fail to recognize external causes of their outcomes (such as luck). They attribute "control over events" to themselves. Both of these factors—egotism and the illusion of control—stem from the individual's inclination to see himself in a positive light. Subtle causes are overlooked because the actor is looking for causes where the light is better.

While actors do indeed make inaccurate attributions at times, observers are even more likely to err in attributing causes for an actor's behavior (see Monson and Snyder, 1977). We noted some of the biases present in observers' judgments in Chapters 2 and 3; Kelley (1967, 1971) has noted a number of others. To summarize this parade of observers' attributional errors, here is a list:

1. *The "he did it because he's like that" error.* Observers often fail to attend sufficiently to the actor's situation, and, as a result, attribute too much responsibility to the actor's personal qualities.

2. *The "do what I do and you're OK" error.* Observers frequently judge the appropriateness of an actor's behavior in terms of their own behavior.

3. *The "you really know how to hurt (help) a guy" error.* Observers tend to make especially strong internal attributions to an actor when the actor's behavior has negative or positive consequences for them.

4. *The "if he did it once, he'll do it again" error.* Observers often make snap judgments on the basis of a single occurrence of a behavior; they assume consistency.

5. *The "I've seen this kind of thing before" error.* Observers are influenced by illusory correlations, making confident judgments of relationships between characteristics of persons when such relationships are nonexistent.

This list of attributional errors is by no means complete; future research may well support additions to the list, and even deletions. The present state of our knowledge, however, suggests that observers are often subject to precisely these kinds of errors. Are people, then, not really the scientists we have made them out to be? Why do they interpret the behaviors and characteristics of others incorrectly? The answer, of course, is that people are not "ivory tower" scientists; they cannot afford to spend years in the laboratory perfecting their understanding of others. They must *act* on the basis of their theories. Their motivations to understand and to predict are often overtaken by their motive to control.

Therefore, one major difference between the implicit psychologist and the professional is that the implicit psychologist must regularly act on the basis of his theory. We have emphasized this facet of implicit psychology by frequently concerning ourselves with the *evaluative* aspects of thought and with the *behaviors* that such evaluations imply. So, while the implicit psychologist does generate complex and intricate theories about people, his theorizing is usually cut short when he reaches a decision about how to behave; his concern with implicit theory is the pragmatic concern of an applied scientist, not the simple "thirst for knowledge" of the pure scientist. If you meet a stranger, your search for an understanding of him is predicated on the possibility that you might have to lock him in a closet. If you meet an attractive person of the opposite sex, your search for an understanding of that person is based on the possibility that you might want to lock yourself in the closet as well.

Implicit theories are built because they are needed and used, not because they are nice to have. In our quest for prediction and control of a person, we load him down with traits, judge his behavior on the basis of our own, judge him harshly when his behavior affects us, ignore his history, and make guesses about his future and past. It is unlikely, therefore, that our implicit theories will always be accurate. Is this, then, the end of the story? Are we implicit psychologists doomed to a life of mistakes, shaky predictions, overgeneralizations, and sloppy theories? Not necessarily.

There are many instances in which the implicit psychologist can form a very sophisticated theory about particular other persons. We avoid many of our theoretical errors when, instead of judging strangers or casual acquaintances, we are judging our close friends. When we become close to others, we begin to empathize with them, seeing things more frequently from their perspective. An empathic orientation leads an observer to make attributions similar to those of the actor (Regan and Totten, 1975). Repeated close contact with another person leads an observer to refine his theory, and, in so doing, to avoid many possible errors that he otherwise might make in haste.

Closeness, however, is not the perfect answer. Couples who

have been together for some time still, on occasion, disagree about the causes of each other's behavior (Orvis, Kelley, and Butler, 1976). The female partner, for example, stops on the way home from the office for a drink. Met at the door later by the male, she explains her behavior by saying that the activity is enjoyable, the crowd at work invited her, and that she felt she deserved a drink after a hard day. The male explains her behavior in another way—she is obviously a lush, a barfly, a strumpet, and a floozy. Sometimes, no matter how close a relationship may be, it is still impossible to take the other person's point of view. The male partner was planning to meet the female at the door with a martini, an offer of a backrub, and a series of concentrated efforts to help her relax. His anticipated pattern of behavior was in conflict with hers, and conflicting attributions were the result. Unfortunately, goals held by individuals will always conflict at some time or another because their implicit theories are different; they have slightly different anticipations of the future. Thus, while closeness seems to be one important way in which people can know each other better and thereby make more valid attributions about each other, it is still limited by the pragmatic nature of implicit psychology. What is needed, therefore, is a method of explaining the behaviors of others that is not directed toward immediate action. The explicit science of psychology provides this important path toward understanding. Because the research psychologist is primarily interested in knowledge about others rather than action toward others, he potentially can develop the error-free theories we find beyond the reach of the implicit psychologist.

Explicit Errors

Although we have used explicit psychological theory as a metaphor for the individual's implicit construction of social reality, the true state of affairs is actually the other way around. Psychological theory and research is an extension of concerns held by the average individual. The most elegant theory, the finest research study, and the greatest achievement of the science of psychology are all logical extensions of activities carried on by your paperboy, Rudy, who wants to be a taxidermist. In other words, everyone has the beginnings of a psychological theory; otherwise, what would a professional psychologist have to start with?

It is unfortunate that many psychologists have missed this point entirely. Little (1972) has noted that some of the most deeply entrenched psychological theories (for example, the psychoanalytic theory of Freud and the behaviorist theory of Skinner) hold the unstated assumption that the psychologist is somehow different from the person being studied. The writings of psychologists are typically filled with allusions to their own active intellectual pursuit of knowledge about people. Psychologists clearly see themselves as active agents in their environs. Yet these same theorists persist in characterizing the average individual as a pawn, a puppet, or a robot. This individual is explained in the same way one might explain a light switch— "See, you flip this lever and it turns on." For Freud, the person is the pawn of his own unconscious instincts; for Skinner, the person is the pawn of rewards and punishments in the environment. Clearly, something is awry here. What good is a theory of psychology that ignores the activities of the theorist who penned it?

Psychologists are, after all, in a very peculiar position. They are both the subject and object of their theories, both the theorist and that which is theorized about. To some extent, both Freud and Skinner recognized this and tried to apply their mechanistic theories to themselves. Freud wrote of his own sexual instincts, and Skinner wrote of the impact of the environment on his own behavior. But according to Little (1972), such attempts to reconcile theories of "passive human beings" with the obviously active and constructive behavior of the theorists are inadequate.

A better approach is to *begin* with a theory of "active and constructive human beings." This approach not only reinforces human dignity, it increases the likelihood that psychological theories will be accurate. Scientists studying behavior from mechanistic perspectives are likely to make frequent, unwarranted errors for the simple reason that they fail to understand their own theory-building process.

We have seen in previous chapters that the science of psychology is not without its blunders. Many of these are direct extensions of the errors made by implicit psychologists. Personality theorists (as noted in Chapter 2) spent an inordinate amount of time trying to explain behavior by means of trait theories when the average observer, although biased toward trait explanations, nevertheless recognized the important influence of situations on behavior. Scientific psychology compounded the errors made by observers and multiplied them into tremendous scientific delusions. In recent years, researchers aware of implicit psychology have attempted to include situational factors in the explanation of behavior (see, for example, Endler and Hunt, 1969), and have also begun to study the individual's perception of the situation (see Mischel, 1973). Indeed, there have been recent studies examining the individual's perception of his own behavioral causation. Some individuals see themselves as more influenced by situations, while others see themselves as more directed by their own traits (see, for example, Bem and Allen, 1974; Snyder and Monson, 1975). Psychologists who take the individual's implicit theories into account have had remarkable success in explaining and predicting the individual's behavior.

Just as scientific psychology can benefit from an appreciation of implicit psychology, so also can clinical psychology benefit from such an approach. All too often, the mechanistic avenue toward understanding people has led the clinician to think about people as "objects to be explained," and therefore to *treat* people as objects. The naturalness and empathy that ought to characterize the relationship between the psychologist and the client has been sabotaged by procedures that serve only to expand the distance between them. Psychologists give their clients projective tests, asking them to draw a person, interpret an inkblot, or write an imaginative story, when they could just as well be chatting together over coffee. The psychologist, because of his mechanistic theory, is convinced that people cannot tell him about themselves. He resorts to these projective tests in an attempt to help them reveal the things deep in their psyches. The client, in turn, may be aghast at these strange psychological tools of the trade, confused by all the unlikely things the psychologist asks, and estranged by the entire experience. When the psychologist assumes that he and the client are different, these distance-producing activities naturally follow.

In the past few years, there has been a growing body of evidence indicating that the best way for a psychologist to understand and to predict a person is to observe the person's behavior and ask the person about it (Mischel, 1968). Although the individual's self-report is considered inadmissable evidence by most practitioners of the mechanistic theories, such evidence has proved to be quite valid. Moreover, it is welcomed by psychologists who understand implicit psychology.

New Directions   Implicit psychology is not limited to the topics in this book. It is true that much research has already been conducted on social cognition, attribution, impression formation, evaluation, balance and group organization, and self-perception. But there are many other ways in which the individual's understanding of the social world has consequences for his social behavior. To demonstrate that the door is open, let us take a peek down the hall.

Implicit Social Influence Theory
People seem to spend a reasonably large amount of time trying

to get each other to do things. It is conceivable that they have implicit theories on which to base decisions about social influence tactics. A parent who wants a child to behave must decide whether to offer him a Mr. Goodbar, threaten him, or reason with him. An employee who wants a raise must decide whether to buy his boss a birthday present, offer a good reason why he deserves more, or scratch warnings on the washroom wall. Some of these influence tactics are used frequently, while others are best avoided. The individual has an implicit theory that suggests not only which tactics are permissible, but also which tactics tend to produce results in each particular situation.

Of the variety of different ways in which a person can be influenced by another person (for example, because of reward or punishment, because he likes the influencer, because he has agreed to be influenced, or because the influencer has greater information than he does), only one method of influence has been investigated systematically from an implicit psychological perspective. This is the work of Edward E. Jones (1964) on *ingratiation*. Basically, ingratiation is the attempt to gain influence over another person by becoming attractive to the person. In a recent review of research on this topic, Jones and Wortman (1973) have shown that individuals who are placed in positions of dependency on another person (such as an employee and his boss, or a student and professor) frequently try to gain greater power by ingratiating the powerful person. These ingratiation attempts may take the form of *compliments* ("Gee, Dr. Munchkin, your lecture today got me all excited"), *conformity* ("I find your point of view both lucid and persuasive, Dr. Munchkin, and I can't help but agree"), *favors* ("When will you be home so I can pick up your laundry?"), and *self-presentation* ("I'll drop by right after my Phi Beta Kappa meeting"). The individual attempting to gain influence may use any or all of these tactics, and will also generally be quite talkative, congenial, and "nice."

Jones also speaks of the "ingratiator's dilemma." If an individual uses all of these techniques to their fullest extent, his tactic is very likely to backfire. Indeed, even small indiscretions may result in failure. Just a little too much ingratiation can make the target aware of the attempted manipulation of his affections. When he realizes that all the candy coating is covering up an old tennis shoe, he is not likely to be amused or influenced any more. It seems clear, however, that individuals regularly engage in such influence attempts, and that such tactics are no doubt guided by some implicit theoretical system. In addition, it may also be interesting to consider the possibility that the recipient of an influence attempt has an implicit theory to guide his reaction. The future of research in implicity psychology probably will include social influence as an important new topic.

Implicit Child Psychology
Adults behave and communicate differently with children from the way they do with other adults. The hostess at a dinner party is not likely to say "Hot, hot!" when she places a steaming dish before a guest, but often makes similar remarks to her five-year-old. She does not say "Look both ways, now" when she sends the guests across the street to their cars, but often will repeat this warning to her child. Around adults, her language may be strong at times, but around children she uses mild curses ("Good grief, rats, shucks, heavens!"). Jean Gleason (1973) has noted many examples of adult language to children. Many of these wholesome and insipid expressions would be totally inappropriate in adult conversation. It seems, then, that adults adjust their communication on the basis of the communication target; they have implicit theories about the nature of children.

Adults have implicit theories about what children are like, about the causes of children's behavior, and about the way children should be trained. These theories are different for children of different ages and are quite unlike the theories adults hold about other adults. Consider, for example, a person who pounds a nail into your mahogany piano bench. If he is a young child, you will think he did not really intend to cause harm, and thus will punish him only lightly. If he is older, however, you will hold him responsible for his action and punish him more severely. If he is an adult, you may even try to have him arrested. Buldain and Wegner (1976) have shown that adults do make more extreme judgments of the transgressions committed by older than younger children, and also that adults are more likely to *reward* an older child for *good* actions. The young child who shares his candy is seen as having little intention to do so—he was probably looking in the wrong direction while the other child reached into the bag. The older child sharing the same candy is seen as more competent and responsible, and hence is given greater praise for the same action.

Until recently, both social psychologists and child psychologists have taken little advantage of the idea that adults' views of children change as the child grows older. Instead, they have focused on the *child's* developing conceptions of the social world. This seems to be a mistaken emphasis. It assumes that the social environment is always the same for the child from infancy through adulthood. But since adults see children differently as children grow, the child is actually subject to a *series* of different social environments, each one perpetrated by adults who see their behaviors and communications as appropriate for a child of that specific age.

A detailed examination of implicit child psychology is potentially very useful. After all, adults' conceptions of a child have tremendous impact on the way a child develops and on the kind of adult the child turns out to be. If a parent were *not* to change judgments and standards for the child over time, it is likely that the child would have great difficulty in growing up normally. Imagine, for example, a child who is trying to succeed at a task—washing the family dog. The child fails, and Dad comes out in the yard to take over. What will Dad say? To what does he attribute the child's failure? Wegner, Buldain, and Kerker (1977) have found that adults typically see this as a very difficult task for the young child; they do not blame the child's lack of ability. When Dad takes over, he will probably comment on how hard it is to make Rover hold still (even though this is easy for him). The adult seems to judge the young child against standards for young children, not against the standards of adults. In so doing, the adult prevents the child from making an "I'm just no good" attribution. This, in turn, probably helps the child to achieve greater success later on. His father has cushioned the blow of a "low ability" attribution by judging him in terms of his age. Although this is only one example, there is an important underlying principle. It could well be that many problems individuals have as adults (in achievement settings, social settings, and elsewhere) are traceable to erroneous implicit child psychology theories held by their parents. The examination of implicit child psychology is essential for this reason.

There are, of course, many other implicit psychological theories—one, perhaps, for each form of conscious social experience. Possibilities such as "implicit situation theory" (how the person sees his social and physical environment) and "implicit cognitive psychology" (how the person infers the thoughts and thought processes of others) hold promise for future study. Still other implicit theories have yet to be defined or explored. As Heider (1958) has explained, the crucial task of scientific psychology is to pierce the "veil of obviousness that makes so many insights of intuitive psychology invisible to our scientific eye."

References

Abelson, R. P., and Rosenberg, M. J. Symbolic psycho-logic: A model of attitudinal cognition. *Behavioral Science,* 1958, *3,* 1–13.

Allport, G. W. *Personality.* New York: Holt, Rinehart and Winston, 1937.

Anderson, N. H. Adding versus averaging as a stimulus combination rule in impression formation. *Journal of Experimental Psychology,* 1965, *70,* 394–400.

Argyle, M., and Williams, M. Observer or observed?: A reversible perspective in person perception. *Sociometry,* 1969, *32,* 396–412.

Aronson, E., and Cope, V. My enemy's enemy is my friend. *Journal of Personality and Social Psychology,* 1968, *8,* 8–12.

Asch, S. E. Forming impressions of personality. *Journal of Abnormal and Social Psychology,* 1946, *41,* 258–290.

Atwood, G. A developmental study of cognitive balancing in hypothetical three-person systems. *Child Development,* 1969, *40,* 73–85.

Bateson, G., Jackson, D. D., Haley, J., and Weakland, J. Toward a theory of schizophrenia. *Behavioral Science,* 1956, *1,* 251–264.

Battle, E. S., and Rotter, J. B. Children's feelings of personal control as related to social class and ethnic group. *Journal of Personality,* 1963, *31,* 482–490.

Beckman, L. Effects of students' performance on teachers' and observers' attributions of causality. *Journal of Educational Psychology,* 1970, *61,* 76–82.

Bem, D. J. Self-perception: An alternative interpretation of cognitive dissonance phenomena. *Psychological Review,* 1967, *74,* 183–200.

Bem, D. J. Self-perception theory. In L. Berkowitz (Ed.), *Advances in experimental social psychology,* Vol. 6. New York: Academic Press, 1972.

Bem, D. J., and Allen, A. On predicting some of the people some of the time: The search for cross-situational consistencies in behavior. *Psychological Review,* 1974, *81,* 506–520.

Berscheid, E., and Walster, E. *Interpersonal attraction.* Reading, Mass.: Addison-Wesley, 1969.

Bieri, J., Atkins, A. L., Briar, S., Leaman, R. L., Miller, H., and Tripodi, T. *Clinical and social judgment.* New York: Wiley, 1966.

Bigner, J. J. A Wernerian developmental analysis of children's descriptions of siblings. *Child Development,* 1974, *45,* 317–323.

Biskin, D., and Crano, W. D. Structural organization of impressions derived from inconsistent information: A developmental study. Unpublished manuscript, Michigan State University, 1973.

Bowers, K. J. Situationism in psychology: An analysis and a critique. *Psychological Review,* 1973, *80,* 307–336.

Bramel, D. A. A dissonance theory approach to defensive projection. *Journal of Abnormal and Social Psychology*, 1962, *69*, 121–129.

Brickman, P., Ryan, K., and Wortman, C. B. Causal chains: Attribution of responsibility as a function of immediate and prior causes. *Journal of Personality and Social Psychology*, 1975, *32*, 1060–1067.

Brown, J. S. Gradients of approach and avoidance responses and their relation to motivation. *Journal of Comparative and Physiological Psychology*, 1948, *41*, 450–465.

Bruner, J. S., and Tagiuri, R. The perception of people. In G. Lindzey (Ed.), *Handbook of social psychology*. Cambridge, Mass.: Addison-Wesley, 1954.

Buldain, R. W., and Wegner, D. M. Adult perception of moral responsibility in children. Paper presented at the meeting of the Midwestern Psychological Association, Chicago, May, 1976.

Buss, A. H., and Scheier, M. Self-consciousness: Private and public. Unpublished manuscript, University of Texas, May, 1975.

Byrne, D. *The attraction paradigm*. New York: Academic Press, 1971.

Campbell, D. T. An error in some demonstrations of the superior social perceptiveness of leaders. *Journal of Abnormal and Social Psychology*, 1955, *51*, 694–695.

Campbell, D. T. Stereotypes and the perception of group differences. *American Psychologist*, 1967, *22*, 817–829.

Campus, N. Transituational consistency as a dimension of personality. *Journal of Personality and Social Psychology*, 1974, *29*, 593–600.

Cantril, H. Perception and interpersonal relations. *American Journal of Psychiatry*, 1957, *114*, 119–127.

Carlsmith, J. M., and Aronson, E. Some hedonic consequences of the confirmation and disconfirmation of expectancies. *Journal of Abnormal and Social Psychology*, 1965, *66*, 151–156.

Carr, J. E. Differentiation as a function of source characteristics and judge's conceptual structure. *Journal of Personality*, 1969, *37*, 378–386.

Chaikin, A. L., and Darley, J. M. Victim or perpetrator?: Defensive attribution of responsibility and the need for order and justice. *Journal of Personality and Social Psychology*, 1973, *25*, 268–275.

Chapman, L. J., and Chapman, J. P. Illusory correlations as an obstacle to the use of valid psychodiagnostic signs. *Journal of Abnormal Psychology*, 1969, *74*, 271–280.

Cialdini, R. B., and Mirels, H. L. Sense of personal control and attributions about yielding and resisting persuasion targets. *Journal of Personality and Social Psychology*, 1976, *33*, 395–402.

Cohen, A. R. Some implications of self-esteem for social influence. In C. I. Hovland and I. L. Janis (Eds.), *Personality and persuasibility*. New Haven: Yale University Press, 1959.

Cooley, C. H. *Human nature and the social order.* New York: Scribner, 1902.
Coopersmith, S. *The antecedents of self-esteem.* San Francisco: Freeman, 1967.
Crano, W. D., and Cooper. R. E. Examination of Newcomb's extension of structural balance theory. *Journal of Personality and Social Psychology,* 1973, *27,* 344–353.
Crockett, W. H. Structural analysis of the organization of written impressions. Unpublished manuscript, University of Kansas, 1970.
Cronbach, L. J. Processes affecting scores on "understanding of others" and "assumed similarity." *Psychological Bulletin,* 1955, *52,* 177–193.
Crowne, D. P., and Marlowe, D. *The approval motive: Studies in evaluative dependence.* New York: Wiley, 1964.
Deaux, K., and Emswiller, T. Explanation of successful performance on sex-linked tasks: What is skill for the male is luck for the female. *Journal of Personality and Social Psychology,* 1974, *29,* 80–85.
deCharms, R. *Personal causation.* New York: Academic Press, 1968.
Deci, E. L. *Intrinsic motivation.* New York: Plenum, 1975.
De Soto, C. Learning a social structure. *Journal of Abnormal and Social Psychology,* 1960, *60,* 417–421.
De Soto, C., and Albrecht, F. Conceptual good figures. In R. P. Abelson et al. (Eds.), *Theories of cognitive consistency: A sourcebook.* Chicago: Rand-McNally, 1968.
Dion, K. K. Physical attractiveness and evaluations of children's transgressions. *Journal of Personality and Social Psychology,* 1972, *24,* 207–213.
Dion, K. K., Berscheid, E., and Walster, E. What is beautiful is good. *Journal of Personality and Social Psychology,* 1972, *24,* 285–290.
Dornbusch, S. M., Hastorf, A. H., Richardson, S. A., Muzzy, R. E., and Vreeland, R. S. The perceiver and the perceived: Their relative influence on the categories of interpersonal perception. *Journal of Personality and Social Psychology,* 1965, *1,* 434–440.
Duval, S., and Hensley, V. Extensions of objective self awareness theory: The focus of attention—causal attribution hypothesis. In J. H. Harvey, W. J. Ickes, and R. F. Kidd (Eds.), *New directions in attribution research,* Vol. 1. Hillsdale, N.J.: Erlbaum, 1976.
Duval, S., and Wicklund, R. A. *A theory of objective self-awareness.* New York: Academic Press, 1972.
Duval, S., and Wicklund, R. A. Effects of objective self-awareness on attribution of causality. *Journal of Experimental Social Psychology,* 1973, *9,* 17–31.
Elkind, D. Egocentrism in adolescence. *Child Development,* 1967, *38,* 1025–1034.
Endler, N. S., and Hunt, J. McV. Generalizability of contributions from

sources of variance in the S-R inventories of anxiousness. *Journal of Personality*, 1969, *37*, 1–24.

Epstein, S. The self-concept revisited: Or a theory of a theory. *American Psychologist*, 1973, *28*, 404–416.

Feldman-Summers, S., and Kiesler, S. B. Those who are number two try harder: The effect of sex on attribution of causality. *Journal of Personality and Social Psychology*, 1974, *30*, 846–855.

Fenigstein, A. Self-consciousness, self-awareness, and rejection. Unpublished doctoral dissertation, University of Texas, 1974.

Fenigstein, A., Scheier, M. F., and Buss, A. H. Public and private self-consciousness: Assessment and theory. *Journal of Consulting and Clinical Psychology*, 1975, *43*, 522–527.

Feshbach, S., and Feshbach, N. Influence of the stimulus object upon the complementary and supplementary projection of fear. *Journal of Abnormal and Social Psychology*, 1963, *66*, 498–502.

Festinger, L. A theory of social comparison processes. *Human Relations*, 1954, *7*, 117–140.

Festinger, L. *A theory of cognitive dissonance.* New York: Row, Peterson, 1957.

Festinger, L., and Carlsmith, J. Cognitive consequences of forced compliance. *Journal of Abnormal and Social Psychology*, 1959, *58*, 203–210.

Fitch, G. Effects of self-esteem, perceived performance, and choice on causal attributions. *Journal of Personality and Social Psychology*, 1970, *16*, 311–315.

Flavell, J. H., Botkin, P. T., Fry, C. L., Wright, J. W., and Jarvis, P. E. *The development of role-taking and communication skills in children.* New York: Wiley, 1968.

Ford, J. G., Cramer, R., and Knight, M. The perception of interpersonal distance. Paper presented at the meeting of the Southwestern Psychological Association, Fort Worth, Texas, April, 1977.

Gage, N. L., and Cronbach, L. J. Conceptual and methodological problems in interpersonal perception. *Psychological Review*, 1955, *62*, 411–422.

Gergen, K. J. *The concept of self.* New York: Holt, Rinehart and Winston, 1971.

Gifford, R. K. Information properties of descriptive words. *Journal of Personality and Social Psychology*, 1975, *31*, 727–734.

Glass, D. C., Singer, J. E. and Friedman, L. N. Psychic cost of adaptation to an environmental stressor. *Journal of Personality and Social Psychology*, 1969, *12*, 200–210.

Gleason, J. B. Code switching in children's language. In T. E. Moore (Ed.) *Cognitive development and the acquisition of language.* New York: Academic Press, 1973.

Goldberg, L. R., and Werts, C. E. The reliability of clinicians' judgments: A multitrait-multimethod approach. *Journal of Consulting Psychology*, 1966, *30*, 199–206.

Goldberg, P. A., Gottesdiener, M., and Abramson, P. R. Another put-down of women? Perceived attractiveness as a function of support for the feminist movement. *Journal of Personality and Social Psychology*, 1975, *32*, 113–115.

Gollin, E. S. Forming impressions of personality. *Journal of Personality*, 1954, *23*, 65–76.

Gollin, E. S. Organizational characteristics of social judgment: A developmental investigation. *Journal of Personality*, 1958, *26*, 139–154.

Gollob, H. F. Some tests of a social inference model. *Journal of Personality and Social Psychology*, 1974, *29*, 157–172.

Gutman, G. M., and Knox, R. E. Balance, agreement, and attraction in pleasantness, tension, and consistency ratings of hypothetical social situations. *Journal of Personality and Social Psychology*, 1972, *24*, 351–357.

Hall, E. T. *The silent language*. New York: Doubleday, 1959.

Hamilton, D. L., and Gifford, R. K. Illusory correlation in interpersonal perception: A cognitive basis of stereotypic judgments. *Journal of Experimental Social Psychology*, 1976, *12*, 392–407.

Harvey, J. H., Harris, B., and Barnes, R. D. Actor-observer differences in the perceptions of responsibility and freedom. *Journal of Personality and Social Psychology*, 1975, *32*, 22–28.

Harvey, O. J. Personality factors in the resolution of conceptual incongruities. *Sociometry*, 1962, *25*, 336–352.

Harvey, O. J., Hunt, D. E., and Schroder, H. M. *Conceptual systems and personality organization*. New York: Wiley, 1961.

Harvey, O. J., Kelley, H. H., and Shapiro, M. M. Reactions to unfavorable evaluations of the self made by other persons. *Journal of Personality*, 1957, *25*, 393–411.

Heider, F. *The psychology of interpersonal relations*. New York: Wiley, 1958.

Hewitt, J., and Goldman, M. Self-esteem, need for approval, and reaction to personal evaluations. *Journal of Experimental Social Psychology*, 1974, *10*, 201–210.

Holmes, D. S. Dimensions of projection. *Psychological Bulletin*, 1968, *4*, 248–268.

Hovland, C., Janis, I., and Kelley, H. H. *Communication and persuasion*. New Haven, Conn.: Yale University Press, 1953.

Ickes, W. J., Wicklund, R. A., and Ferris, C. B. Objective self awareness and self-esteem. *Journal of Experimental Social Psychology*, 1973, *9*, 202–219.

Irwin, M., Tripodi, T., and Bieri, J. Affective stimulus value and cognitive complexity. *Journal of Personality and Social Psychology*, 1967, *5*, 444–448.

Jacobs, L., Berscheid, E., and Walster, E. Self-esteem and attraction. *Journal of Personality and Social Psychology*, 1971, *17*, 84–91.

James, W. *The principles of psychology*. New York: Dover, 1950 (original, 1890).

Johnson, T. J., Feigenbaum, R., and Weiby, M. Some determinants and consequences of the teacher's perception of causality. *Journal of Educational Psychology*, 1964, *55*, 237–246.

Jones, C., and Aronson, E. Attribution of fault to a rape victim as a function of respectability of the victim. *Journal of Personality and Social Psychology*, 1973, *26*, 415–419.

Jones, E. E. *Ingratiation*. New York: Appleton-Century, 1964.

Jones, E. E., and Davis, K. E. From acts to dispositions: The attribution process in person perception. In L. Berkowitz (Ed.) *Advances in experimental social psychology*, Vol. 2. New York: Academic Press, 1965.

Jones, E. E., Davis, K. E., and Gergen, K. J. Role playing variations and their informational value for person perception. *Journal of Abnormal and Social Psychology*, 1961, *3*, 302–310.

Jones, E. E., and Nisbett, R. E. The actor and observer: Divergent perceptions of the causes of behavior. In E. E. Jones, D. E. Kanouse, H. H. Kelley, R. E. Nisbett, S. Valins, and B. Weiner (Eds.), *Attribution: Perceiving the causes of behavior*. Morristown, N.J.: General Learning Press, 1971.

Jones, E. E., Rock, L., Shaver, K. G., Goethals, G. R., and Ward, L. M. Pattern of performance and ability attribution: An unexpected primacy effect. *Journal of Personality and Social Psychology*, 1968, *10*, 317–341.

Jones, E. E., and Wortman, C. *Ingratiation: An attributional approach*. Morristown, N.J.: General Learning Press, 1973.

Jones, L. E., and Young, F. W. Structure of a social environment: Longitudinal individual differences scaling of an intact group. *Journal of Personality and Social Psychology*, 1972, *24*, 108–121.

Jones, S. C. Self and interpersonal evaluations: Esteem theories versus consistency theories. *Psychological Bulletin*, 1973, *79*, 185–189.

Kanouse, D. E. *Language, labeling and attribution*. Morristown, N. J.: General Learning Press, 1971.

Kanouse, D. E., and Hanson, L. R. *Negativity in evaluations*. Morristown, N.J.: General Learning Press, 1971.

Kaplan, A. *The conduct of inquiry*. San Francisco: Chandler, 1964.

Kaplan, B., and Crockett, W. H. Developmental analysis of modes of resolution. In R. P. Abelson et al. (Eds.), *Theories of cognitive consistency: A sourcebook*. Chicago: Rand-McNally, 1968.

Karabenick, S. A., and Wilson, W. Dogmatism among war hawks and peace doves. *Psychological Reports*, 1969, *25*, 419–422.

Kelley, H. H. Attribution in social psychology. *Nebraska Symposium on Motivation*, 1967, *15*, 192–238.

Kelley, H. H. *Attribution in social interaction*. Morristown, N.J.: General Learning Press, 1971.

Kelly, G. A. *The psychology of personal constructs.* New York: Norton, 1955.

Kemp, C. G. Perception of authority in relation to open and closed belief systems. *Science Education,* 1963, *47,* 482–484.

Kendler, H. H., and Kendler, T. S. Effect of verbalization on reversal shifts in children. *Science,* 1961, *134,* 1619–1620.

Knox, R. E., and Inkster, J. A. Postdecision dissonance at post time. *Journal of Personality and Social Psychology,* 1968, *8,* 319–323.

Koltuv, B. B. Some characteristics of intrajudge trait intercorrelations. *Psychological Monographs,* 1962, *76,* No. 33 (Whole No. 552).

Kruglanski, A. W. The endogeous-exogenous partition in attribution theory. *Psychological Review,* 1975, *82,* 387–406.

Kuethe, J. L. Pervasive influence of social schemata. *Journal of Abnormal and Social Psychology,* 1964, *68,* 248–254.

Kuethe, J. L. Social schemas. *Journal of Abnormal and Social Psychology,* 1962, *65,* 31–38.

Kuusinen, J. Affective and denotative structures of personality ratings. *Journal of Personality and Social Psychology,* 1969, *12,* 181–188.

Langer, E. The illusion of control. *Journal of Personality and Social Psychology,* 1975, *32,* 311–321.

Leonard, R. R. Self-concept and attraction for similar and dissimilar others. *Journal of Personality and Social Psychology,* 1975, *31,* 926–929.

Lepper, M. R., Greene, D., and Nisbett, R. E. Undermining children's intrinsic interest with extrinsic reward. *Journal of Personality and Social Psychology,* 1973, *28,* 129–137.

Lerner, M. J., Miller, D. T., and Holmes, J. G. Deserving and the emergence of forms of justice. In L. Berkowitz and E. Walster (Eds.), *Advances in experimental social psychology,* Vol. 9. New York: Academic Press, 1976.

Lerner, M. J., and Simmons, C. Observer's reaction to the "innocent victim": Compassion or rejection? *Journal of Personality and Social Psychology,* 1966, *4,* 203–210.

Lewin, K. *A dynamic theory of personality.* New York: McGraw-Hill, 1935.

Little, B. R. Psychological man as scientist, humanist, and specialist. *Journal of Experimental Research in Personality,* 1972, *6,* 95–118.

Little, K. B. Personal space. *Journal of Experimental Social Psychology,* 1965, *1,* 237–247.

Luchins, A. S. Primacy-recency in impression formation. In C. Hovland (Ed.), *The order of presentation in persuasion.* New Haven, Conn.: Yale University Press, 1957.

McArthur, L. Z., and Post, D. L. Figural emphasis and person perception. *Journal of Experimental Social Psychology,* 1977, (in press).

McCormick, L. H. *Characterology: An exact science.* Chicago: Rand-McNally, 1920.

McCulloch, R. A., Wegner, D. M., Heil, J. J., and Vallacher, R. R. An operational definition of double bind communication. Paper presented at the meeting of the Western Psychological Association, Los Angeles, April, 1976.

McKeachie, W. J. Lipstick as a determiner of first impressions of personality. *Journal of Social Psychology*, 1952, *36*, 241–244.

Maracek, J., and Mettee, D. R. Avoidance of continued success as a function of self-esteem, level of esteem certainty and responsibility for success. *Journal of Personality and Social Psychology*, 1972, *22*, 98–107.

Maslow, A. *Motivation and personality*. New York: Harper and Row, 1954.

Mead, G. H. *Mind, self, and society*. Chicago: University of Chicago Press, 1934.

Miller, D. T. Ego involvement and attributions for failure. *Journal of Personality and Social Psychology*, 1976, *34*, 901–906.

Miller, D. T., and Ross, M. Self-serving biases in the attribution of causality: Fact or fiction? *Psychological Bulletin*, 1975, *82*, 213–225.

Miller, N. E. Experimental studies of conflict. In J. M. Hunt (Ed.), *Personality and the behavior disorders*. New York: Ronald, 1944.

Mischel, W. *Personality and assessment*. New York: Wiley, 1968.

Mischel, W. Toward a cognitive social learning reconceptualization of personality. *Psychological Review*, 1973, *80*, 252–283.

Monson, T. C., and Snyder, M. Actors, observers, and the attribution process: Toward a reconceptualization. *Journal of Experimental Social Psychology*, 1977, *13*, 89–111.

Morse, S., and Gergen, K. J. Social comparison, self-consistency, and the concept of self. *Journal of Personality and Social Psychology*, 1970, *16*, 148–156.

Neisser, U. *Cognition and reality*. San Francisco: Freeman, 1976.

Newcomb, T. M. *The acquaintance process*. New York: Holt, Rinehart and Winston, 1961.

Newcomb, T. M. Interpersonal balance. In R. P. Abelson et al. (Eds.) *Theories of cognitive consistency: A sourcebook*. Chicago: Rand-McNally, 1968.

Nisbett, R. E., Caputo, C., Legant, P., and Maracek, J. Behavior as seen by the actor and as seen by the observer. *Journal of Personality and Social Psychology*, 1973, *27*, 154–165.

Novak, D., and Lerner, M. J. Rejection as a consequence of perceived similarity. *Journal of Personality and Social Psychology*, 1968, *9*, 147–152.

Olshan, K. M. The multidimensional structure of person perception in children. Unpublished Ph.D. dissertation, Rutgers University, 1974.

Orvis, B. R., Kelley, H. H., and Butler, D. Attributional conflict in young couples. In J. H. Harvey, W. J. Ickes, and R. F. Kidd (Eds.), *New directions in attribution research*, Vol. 1. Hillsdale, N.J.: Erlbaum, 1976.

Peevers, B., and Secord, P. F. Developmental changes in attribution of descriptive concepts to persons. *Journal of Personality and Social Psychology*, 1973, *27*, 120–128.

Piaget, J. *The moral judgment of the child*. London: Kegan Paul, 1932.

Piaget, J. *The psychology of intelligence*. New York: Harcourt-Brace, 1963.

Reed, T. R. Connotative meaning of social interaction concepts: An investigation of factor structure and the effects of imagined contexts. *Journal of Personality and Social Psychology*, 1972, *24*, 306–312.

Regan, D. T., and Totten, J. Empathy and attribution: Turning observers into actors. *Journal of Personality and Social Psychology*, 1975, *32*, 850–856.

Rogers, C. R. *Client-centered therapy*. New York: Houghton-Mifflin, 1951.

Rokeach, M. *Beliefs, attitudes, and values*. San Francisco: Jossey-Bass, 1968.

Rokeach, M. *The open and closed mind: Investigations into the nature of belief systems and personality systems*. New York: Basic Books, 1960.

Rosch, E. H. On the internal structure of perceptual and semantic categories. In T. E. Moore (Ed.), *Cognitive development and the acquisition of language*. New York: Academic Press, 1973.

Rosenberg, M. *Society and the adolescent self-image*. Princeton: Princeton University Press, 1965.

Rosenberg, M. J. When dissonance fails: On eliminating evaluation apprehension from attitude measurement. *Journal of Personality and Social Psychology*, 1965, *1*, 28–42.

Rosenberg, S., and Jones, R. A. A method for investigating a person's implicit theory of personality: Theodore Dreiser's view of people. *Journal of Personality and Social Psychology*, 1972, *22*, 372–386.

Rosenberg, S., Nelson, C., and Vivekananthan, P. S. A multidimensional approach to the structure of personality impressions. *Journal of Personality and Social Psychology*, 1968, *9*, 293–294.

Rosenfeld, H. M. Effect of an approval-seeking induction on interpersonal proximity. *Psychological Reports*, 1965, *17*, 120–122.

Rosenhan, D. L. On being sane in insane places. *Science*, 1973, *179*, 250–258.

Rosenthal, P., and Jacobson, L. *Pygmalion in the classroom: Teacher expectation and pupils' intellectual development*. New York: Holt, Rinehart and Winston, 1968.

Ross, M. The self-perception of intrinsic motivation. In J. H. Harvey, W. J. Ickes, and R. F. Kidd (Eds.), *New directions in attribution research*, Vol. 1. Hillsdale, N.J.: Erlbaum, 1976.

Rotter, J. Generalized expectancies for internal versus external control of reinforcement. *Psychological Monographs*, 1966, *80*, No. 1, (Whole No. 609).

Scarlett, H. H., Press, A. N., and Crockett, W. H. Children's descriptions of peers: A Wernerian developmental analysis. *Child Development*, 1971, *42*, 439–453.

Schachter, S. *The psychology of affiliation*. Palo Alto: Stanford University Press, 1959.
Schroder, H., Driver, M. J., and Streufert, S. *Human information processing*. New York: Holt, Rinehart and Winston, 1968.
Schutz, A. *The phenomenology of the social world*. Evanston, Ill.: Northwestern University Press, 1967 (Original, 1932).
Scott, W. A. Structure of natural cognitions. *Journal of Personality and Social Psychology*, 1969, *12*, 261–278.
Scott, W. A. Varieties of cognitive integration. *Journal of Personality and Social Psychology*, 1974, *30*, 563–578.
Segal, M. W. Alphabet and attraction: An unobtrusive measure of the effect of propinquity in a field setting. *Journal of Personality and Social Psychology*, 1974, *30*, 654–657.
Seligman, M. E. P. *Helplessness: On depression, development, and death*. San Francisco: W. H. Freeman, 1975.
Selman, R. L. Toward a structural analysis of developing interpersonal relations concepts. In A. D. Pick (Ed.), *Minnesota Symposium on Child Psychology*, Vol. 10. Minneapolis: University of Minnesota Press, 1976.
Sherif, M. *The psychology of social norms*. New York: Harper, 1936.
Shrauger, J. S. Self-esteem and reactions to being observed by others. *Journal of Personality and Social Psychology*, 1972, *23*, 192–200.
Shrauger, J. S. Responses to evaluation as a function of initial self-perceptions. *Psychological Bulletin*, 1975, *82*, 581–596.
Signell, K. A. Cognitive complexity in person perception and nation perception: A developmental approach. *Journal of Personality*, 1966, *34*, 517–537.
Skinner, B. F. *Beyond freedom and dignity*. New York: Knopf, 1971.
Snyder, M., and Monson, T. C. Persons, situations, and the control of social behavior. *Journal of Personality and Social Psychology*, 1975, *32*, 637–644.
Snyder, M. L., Stephan, W. G., and Rosenfield, D. Egotism and attribution. *Journal of Personality and Social Psychology*, 1976, *33*, 435–441.
Sommer, R. *Personal space: The behavioral basis of design*. Englewood Cliffs, N.J.: Prentice-Hall, 1969.
Steiner, I. D. Perceived freedom. In L. Berkowitz (Ed.), *Advances in experimental social psychology*, Vol. 5. New York: Academic Press, 1970.
Storms, M. D. Videotape and the attribution process: Reversing actors' and observers' points of view. *Journal of Personality and Social Psychology*, 1973, *27*, 165–175.
Taylor, S. E., and Mettee, D. R. When similarity breeds contempt. *Journal of Personality and Social Psychology*, 1971, *20*, 75–81.
Thibaut, J. W., and Riecken, H. W. Some determinants and consequences of the perception of social causality. *Journal of Personality*, 1955, *24*, 113–133.
Thompson, E., and Phillips, J. The effects of asymmetric liking on the attribu-

tion of dominance in dyads. *Bulletin of the Psychonomic Society*, 1977 (in press).

Thorndike, E. L. A constant error in psychological ratings. *Journal of Applied Psychology*, 1920, *4*, 25–29.

Vallacher, R. R. Dimensions of the self and the perception of others. Paper presented at the meeting of the Midwestern Psychological Association, Chicago, May, 1975.

Vallacher, R. R. Public self-awareness and person perception. Paper presented at the meeting of the Western Psychological Association, Los Angeles, April, 1976.

Walster, E. Assignment of responsibility for an accident. *Journal of Personality and Social Psychology*, 1966, *3*, 73–80.

Walster, E., Berscheid, E., and Walster, G. W. New directions in equity research. *Journal of Personality and Social Psychology*, 1973, *25*, 151–176.

Wegner, D. M. Attribute generality: The development and articulation of attributes in person perception. *Journal of Research in Personality*, 1977, (in press).

Wegner, D. M., Benel, D. C., and Riley, E. N. Changes in perceived intertrait correlations as a function of experience with persons. Paper presented at the meeting of the Southwestern Psychological Association, Albuquerque, April, 1976.

Wegner, D. M., Buldain, R. W., and Kerker, R. M. Adult judgment of achievement in children. Paper presented at the meeting of the Southwestern Psychological Association, Fort Worth, April, 1977.

Wegner, D. M., and Finstuen, K. Observers' focus of attention in the simulation of self-perception. *Journal of Personality and Social Psychology*, 1977, *35*, 56–62.

Wegner, D. M., and Vallacher, R. R. Sense of separate identity: Witkin's hypothesis revisited. Unpublished manuscript, 1975.

Weiner, B. (Ed.) *Achievement motivation and attribution theory*. Morristown, N.J.: General Learning Press, 1974.

Weiner, B., and Peter, N. A cognitive-developmental analysis of achievement and moral judgments. *Developmental Psychology*, 1973, *9*, 290–309.

Weingarten, E. M. A study of selective perception in clinical judgments. *Journal of Personality*, 1949, *17*, 369–406.

Werner, H. *Comparative psychology of mental development*. (Rev. ed.) Chicago: Follett, 1948.

West, S. B., Gunn, S. P., and Chernicky, P. Ubiquitous Watergate: An attributional analysis. *Journal of Personality and Social Psychology*, 1975, *32*, 55–65.

White, R. W. Motivation reconsidered: The concept of competence. *Psychological Review*, 1959, *66*, 297–333.

Wicklund, R. A. Objective self awareness. In L. Berkowitz (Ed.), *Advances in experimental social psychology,* Vol. 8, New York: Academic Press, 1975.

Wish, M., Deutsch, M., and Kaplan, S. J. Perceived dimensions of interpersonal relations. *Journal of Personality and Social Psychology,* 1976, *33,* 409–420.

Witkin, H. A., Dyk, R. B., Faterson, H. B., Goodenough, D. R. and Karp, S. A. *Psychological differentiation.* New York: Wiley, 1962.

Wyer, R. S., Jr. *Cognitive organization and change: An information processing approach.* Potomac, Md.: Erlbaum, 1974.

Wylie, R. *The self concept: A critical survey of pertinent research literature.* Lincoln: University of Nebraska Press, 1961.

Zajonc, R. B. Cognitive theories in social psychology. In G. Lindsey and E. Aronson (Eds.), *Handbook of social psychology.* Vol. 1. (2nd ed.) Reading, Mass.: Addison-Wesley, 1968.

Zimbardo, P. The human choice: Individuation, reason, and order versus deindividuation, impulse, and chaos. In W. Arnold and D. Levine (Eds.), *Nebraska Symposium on Motivation,* 1969, *17,* 237–307.

index

Abelson, R. P., 190, 306, 311
Ability attributions, 54–57
  self-consistency and, 265
Abnormal psychology, 167–77
Abramson, P. R., 99, 310
Accuracy of implicit psychology, 293–
  301
  attributional errors and, 294–96
  actors', 295
  observers', 295–96
Achievement attributions
  ability, 54–55
  for children, 305
  effort, 56
  luck, 57
  sex differences in, 85–86
  task difficulty, 56–57
Activity dimension, 119
Actor-observer differences, 59–67
  in accuracy of attributions, 295–96
  empathy and, 64
  focus of attention and, 64, 65
  situational vs. personal attributions as,
    62–63
  summary of, 60
  in trait attribution, 67
Adding model of impression formation,
  123. See also Weighted average
  model of impression formation
Affective balance, 228
Aggregation, 125–26, 137
Agreement bias, 212–13
Albrecht, F., 220, 308
Allen, A., 72, 300, 306
Allport, G., 68, 306
Ambivalence, 113–35
  and affective balance, 228
  causes of, 135
  consequences of, 133–34
  definition of, 133
Analysis of variance, 46
Anderson, N. H., 123, 143, 306

Anticipation, cognitive structure as, 9,
  290–91
Anxiety
  effect on information selection, 97
  personal and situational determinants
    of, 69–71
Approval, need for, 278–79
Argyle, M., 276–77, 306
Aristotle, 221
Arnold, W., 317
Aronson, E., 9, 160–61, 208, 306, 307,
  311, 317
Articulation
  definition of, 93
  developmental increases in, 130–31
  of personality judgments, 96, 115
  and self-consciousness, 97
Asch, S. E., 101, 306
Atkins, A. L., 306
Attention
  focus of. See Focus of attention
  states of. See Objective self-awareness
Attitude, 25
  definition of, 26. See also Evaluation
Attitude similarity, 23, 152–54
  effect on attraction of, 152–54
  dogmatism and, 183–84
  self-esteem and, 182–83
  prejudice and, 23
Attractiveness, physical, 150–52
Attribute generality, 93–94, 130, 235
  and attribute articulation, 94
  definition of, 93
Attribute inferences
  evaluative dimensions in, 113
  models of, 109–14
    multidimensional scaling in, 109.
    See also Inferences
Attribute maps, 109, 191–94
Attribution
  accuracy in, 294–96
  actor-observer differences in, 59–67

definition of, 41
egotistic, 244, 295
expectancies and biases in, 47–51
focus of attention and, 51–52
of internal-external causes, 43–51
to self, 238–43
cognitive dissonance vs., 239–41
objective self-awareness and, 270–71
self-interest in, 57–59
sex differences in, 84
sources of information for, 44–47
for success and failure, 53–59
Atwood, G., 224, 306
Authority, obedience to, 184
Autokinetic effect, 10
Averaging model of impression formation, 123. See also Weighted average model of impression formation

Balance theory, 204–10
alternatives to, 210–14
imbalanced triads in, 204–7
predicting liking relations through, 207–10. See also Social relations
Barnes, R. D., 262, 310
Bateson, G., 134, 306
Battle, E. S., 82, 306
Beckman, L., 59, 306
Behaviorism, 299
Belief congruence. See Attitude similarity
Belonging relations, 194, 196–203
exclusive, 215
schemas of, 196–203
causality in, 197–98
liking and, 201–3
proximity in, 198–201
similarity in, 197
static nature of, 202
symmetry of, 203
Bem, D. J., 72, 239, 240–41, 300, 306
Benel, D. C., 105, 316
Berkowitz, L., 311, 312, 315, 317
Berscheid, E., 150, 152, 248, 271, 306, 308, 311, 315
Biases in attribution, 47–51
Bieri, J., 93, 147, 306, 310
Bigner, J. J., 129, 306
Biskin, D., 131, 306

Botkin, P. T., 309
Bowers, K. J., 72, 306
Bramel, D. A., 262–63, 307
Briar, S., 306
Brickman, P., 173, 307
Brown, J. S., 141, 307
Bruner, J. S., 89, 100, 307
Buldain, R. W., 304, 305, 307, 316
Buss, A. H., 277, 307, 309
Butler, D., 298, 313
Byrne, D., 153, 307

Campbell, D. T., 104, 294, 307
Campus, N., 169, 307
Cantril, H., 1, 2, 3, 307
Caputo, C., 67, 313
Carlsmith, J. M., 9, 239, 240, 307, 309
Carr, J. E., 148, 307
Categorical model of cognitive structure, 285–86
Cattell, R. B., 68
Causal attribution. See Attribution
Causal chains, 172–73
Causality in belonging schemas, 197–98
Central traits, 101–4, 114
negativity effect and, 143
Centration, 30
Chaiken A. L., 307
Chapman, J. P., 106, 174, 307
Chapman, L. J., 106, 174, 307
Chernicky, P., 61, 316
Cialdini, R. B., 84, 307
Clinical judgment, 169–76
causal chains in, 172–73
psychological testing and, 174
Clinical psychology, 167–77, 300–301
Cognitive clarity, 11
Cognitive complexity, 29
articulation as a measure of, 120
dimensionality as a measure of, 120. See also Differentiation; Integration
Cognitive consistency, 28, 120–28
evaluative. See Evaluative consistency
of self-theory, 264–66
Cognitive development, 5
concrete-abstract thought in, 178–79
egocentric thinking in, 179
and moral judgment, 78–80, 177–78.

See also Intellectual development;
    Moral development; Role-taking,
    developmental levels of
Cognitive dissonance, 28, 239–41
Cognitive dynamics, 290–93
Cognitive structure, 4–16
    as anticipation, 9, 290–91
    evaluative component of, 26
    and information selection, 91–94
    as memory, 290–91
    models of
        categorical, 285–86
        dimensional, 286–87
        qualitative and quantative aspects of,
            286–87
        relational, 287–91
    origin of, 292
Cohen, A. R., 263, 307
Concrete operational stage, 224–25, 275
Conformity, 10, 302
Consensus information, 45, 51, 54, 168
    definition of, 45
Consistency information, 45, 54, 168
    and actor-observer differences, 65
    definition of, 45. *See also* Stable-
        variable attributions
Control, personal. *See* Locus of control;
    Personal causation
Cooley, C. H., 232, 234, 273, 308
Cooper, R. E., 211, 214, 308
Coopersmith, S., 248, 279, 307
Cope, V., 208, 306
Cramer, R., 199, 309
Crano, W. D., 131, 211, 214, 306, 308
Crockett, W. H., 125, 131, 179, 308,
    311, 314
Cronbach, L. J., 294, 308, 309
Crowne, D. P., 278, 279, 308

Darley, J. M., 307
Darwin, C., 221
Davis, K. E., 43, 44, 48, 50, 51, 145,
    311
Deaux, K., 85, 308
de Charms, R., 258, 308
Deci, E. L., 242, 308
Defense mechanism, 260
    denial as, 263
    projection as, 262
Deindividuation, 271

Descriptive inconsistency, 121
DeSoto, C., 217, 218, 219, 220, 308
Deutsch, M., 191, 317
Differentiation, 29–31
    and affective balance, 228
    articulation as, 93, 115, 119. *See also*
        Articulation
    definition of, 29
    as developmental change in evaluation,
        180
    dimensionality as, 115, 119. *See also*
        Dimensionality
    for liked vs. disliked persons, 146–48
    perceptual, 33
    of self-theory, 249–54
Dimensionality
    definition of, 115
    independence of dimensions and,
        117–18
    in personality judgments, 115
Dimensional model of cognitive structure,
    286–87
Dion, K. K., 150, 151, 308
Distinctiveness information, 45, 51, 168
    and actor-observer differences, 65
    definition of, 45
Dogmatism, 183–85
Dominance relations, 193, 217–23
    asymmetry of, 217
    schemas of, 217–23
    liking in, 221–23
    ordering in, 218–21
Dornbusch, S. M., 91, 152, 308
Double-bind communication, 134–35
Dreiser, T., 109, 112, 113 .
Driver, M. J., 254, 255, 258, 315
Duval, S., 52, 267, 269, 270, 308
Dyk, R. B., 317

Effort attributions, 54, 56, 85
Egocentric thought, 170
Egotistic attribution, 244, 295
Elkind, D., 37, 308
Empathy, 64, 297
Emswiller, I., 85, 308
Endler, N. S., 300, 308
Envy in social relations, 216–17
Epstein, S., 232, 309

Evaluation
and approach-avoidance responses,
141–43
by clinical psychologists, 167–77
and cognitive organization, 26
effect of dogmatism on, 183–85
effect of self-esteem on, 181–83
intellectual good-bad dimension of,
113–14, 180
negativity effect in, 143–48
definition of, 143
in personality judgments, 102, 119
social good-bad dimension of, 113–14,
180
source of information for, 148–67
just-world assumption as, 157–61
labels as, 161–67
personal characteristics as, 149–52
similarity-difference of others as,
152–57. See also Evaluative consistency; Halo effect
Evaluative consistency, 26, 121, 126
of inferences about others, 102
of inferences about self, 244
vs. self-enhancement, 264–65
Exclusive belonging relations, 215–17
Expectancies in attribution, 47–51. See
also Labels; Self-fulfilling prophecy
Extension, theory-building through, 18,
19, 22, 272

Factor analysis, 118
Faterson, H. B., 317
Fear arousal, effect on information selec-
tion of, 95–96
Feigenbaum, R., 58, 311
Feldman-Summers, S., 85, 308
Fenigstein, A., 277, 309
Ferris, C. B., 269, 310
Feshbach, N., 95, 309
Feshbach, S., 95, 309
Festinger, L., 28, 154, 239, 240, 309
Field dependence-independence, 33–36
Figure-ground hypothesis, 144–45
Finstuen, K., 272, 316
Fitch, G., 261, 309
Flavell, J. H., 13, 309
Focus of attention, 52
on self, 267–72. See also Objective
self-awareness

Ford, J. G., 199, 309
Formal operational stage, 225–26
Freud, S., 68, 299
Friedman, L. N., 259, 309
Fry, C. L., 309

Gage, N. L., 294, 309
Gambler's fallacy, 82
General attributes. See Attribute
generality
Gergen, K. J., 48, 236, 237, 238, 253,
309, 311, 312
Gestalt psychology, 196
Gifford, R. K., 103, 106, 107, 309, 310
Glass, D. C., 259, 309
Gleason, J. B., 303, 309
Global evaluative dimension, 180. See
also Evaluation
Global self-evaluation. See Self-esteem
Goethals, G. R., 261, 311
Goldberg, L. R., 169, 310
Goldberg, P. A., 99, 310
Goldman, M., 279, 310
Gollin, E. J., 125, 131, 310
Gollob, H. F., 190, 310
Good-bad dimension. See Evaluation
Goodenough, D. R., 317
Gottesdiener, M., 99, 310
Grain-of-truth hypothesis, 105
Greene, D., 241, 312
Grouping schemas, 218
Gunn, S. P., 61, 316
Gutman, G. M., 211, 310

Haley, J., 134, 306
Halo effect, 102, 113
definition of, 102. See also Evaluation;
Inferences
Hall, E. T., 199, 310
Hamilton, D. L., 106, 107, 310
Hanson, L. R., 143, 311
Harris, B., 262
Harvey, J. H., 262, 310, 313, 314
Harvey, O. J., 235, 254, 310
Hastorf, A. H., 308
Hedonic relevance, 51, 149
Heider, F., 43, 189, 190, 191, 196,
197, 202, 203, 204, 210, 211, 213,
214, 215, 229, 258, 305, 310

Heil, J. J., 135, 313
Hensley, V., 52, 308
Hewitt, J., 278, 310
Holmes, D. S., 262, 310
Holmes, J. G., 157, 312
Hovland, C., 26, 310, 312
Hunt, D. E., 254, 310
Hunt, J. McV., 300, 308, 313
Hypothesis, 19

Ickes, W. J., 269, 310, 313, 314
Illusion of control, 258–59, 295
Illusory correlation, 106–7
Imaginary audience, 32
Implicit child psychology, 303–5
    achievement attributions in, 304
    responsibility attributions in, 305
Implicit personality theory, definition of, 89
Implicit social influence theory, 301–3
    ingratiation in, 302–3
Impression formation, 122–28
    models of, 123–24
    primacy-recency in, 126–28
    resolving inconsistency in, 125–28
Inferences, 98–100
    development of, 131
    origin of, 104–8
    role of evaluation in, 102
    about self, 243–48
    for strangers vs. familiar persons, 100.
    See also Attribute inferences
Information selection
    about others, 90–98
        role of cognitive structure in, 91–94
        role of perceiver in, 92
        situational influences on, 94–98
    about self, 233–43
        through self-attribution, 238–43
        through social comparison, 235–38
        through social feedback, 234–35
Ingratiation, 302–3
Inkster, J. A., 27, 28, 312
Integration, 29–31, 125–26
    in the development of cognitive structure, 29–31
    definition of, 29
    as a mode of inconsistency resolution, 125–26, 131

definition of, 125
    of self-theory. See Self-integration
Intellectual development, stages of
    concrete operational, 224–25, 275
    formal operational, 225–26
    preoperational, 224–25
Intention
    theory building through, 18, 19, 22, 272
    in moral judgment, 79, 181
Internal-external causation, 43–51. See also Attribution
Internal-external locus of control. See Locus of control
Irwin, M., 147, 310

Jackson, D. D., 134, 306
Jacobs, L., 248, 311
Jacobson, L., 163, 314
James, W., 232, 267, 311
Janis, I., 310
Jarvis, P. E., 309
Jealousy in social relations, 214–17
Johnson, T. J., 58, 311
Jones, C., 160, 161, 311
Jones, E. E., 43, 44, 48, 50, 51, 55, 60, 63, 145, 261, 302, 303, 311
Jones, L. E., 119, 311
Jones, R. A., 109, 314
Jones, S. C., 264, 311
Jung, C. G., 68
Just-world hypothesis, 157–61

Kanouse, D. E., 143, 144, 311
Kant, I., 292
Kaplan, A., 18, 311
Kaplan, B., 125, 311
Kaplan, S. J., 191, 317
Karabenick, S. A., 184, 311
Karp, S. A., 317
Kelley, H. H., 43, 44, 51, 54, 65, 69, 76, 235, 295, 298, 310, 311, 313
Kelly, G. A., 9, 129, 133, 253, 290, 312
Kemp, C. G., 184, 312
Kendler, H. H., 6, 312
Kendler, T. S., 6, 312
Kerker, R. M., 305, 316
Kidd, R. F., 313, 314

Kiesler, S. B., 85, 309
Knight, M., 199, 309
Knox, R. E., 27, 28, 211, 310, 312
Koltuv, B. B., 100, 312
Kruglanski, A. W., 242, 312
Kuethe, J. L., 198, 312
Kuusinen, J., 119, 312

Labels
    approach-avoidance based on, 162–63
    clinical psychology and, 170–71
    evaluative information in, 161–76
    expectancies generated through,
        164–65
Langer, E., 258, 295, 312
Leamon, R. L., 306
Legant, P., 67, 313
Leonard, R. R., 183, 312
Lepper, M. R., 241, 312
Lerner, M. J., 157, 158, 159, 161, 166,
    312, 313
Levine, D., 317
Lewin, K., 30, 312
Liking relations, 193, 203–17
    and approach-avoidance reactions,
        140, 202
    and belonging, 201–3
    and dominance, 221–23
    dynamic nature of, 202
    schemas of, 203–17
        alternatives to balance theory and,
            210–14
        balance theory and, 204–10.
        See also Evaluation
Lindsey, G., 317
Linear ordering, 218–21
Little, B. R., 299, 312
Little, K. B., 199, 312
Locus of control, 81–84
Luchins, A. S., 127, 312
Luck attributions, 54, 85–86
    self-consistency and, 265

McArthur, L. Z., 52, 312
McCormick, L. H., 89, 312
McCulloch, R. A., 135, 313
McKeachie, W. J., 99, 313
Maracek, J., 67, 265, 266, 313
Marlowe, D., 278, 279, 308
Marx, K., 221
Maslow, A., 182, 313

Mead, G. H., 232, 234, 235, 267, 273,
    313
Mechanistic theories of psychology,
    299–301
Memory, cognitive structure as, 290–91
Mettee, D. R., 155, 265, 266, 313, 315
Miller, D. T., 59, 157, 244, 261, 312,
    313
Miller, H., 306
Miller, N. E., 141, 143, 313
Mirels, H. L., 84, 307
Mischel, W., 72, 300, 301, 313
Monson, T. C., 169, 295, 300, 313, 315
Moore, T. E., 314
Moral development, 274–75
Moral judgment, 78–80
    intentions-consequences distinction in,
        79
Morse, S., 236, 237, 238, 313
Multidimensional scaling, 109, 191–94
Murray, H. A., 68
Muzzy, R. E., 308

Need for approval, 278–79
Neisser U., 290, 313
Negativity effect, 143–46
    definition of, 143
    figure-ground explanation for, 144–45
    in self-evaluation, 269
    vigilance explanation for, 145–46
Nelson, C., 314
Newcomb, T. M., 152, 213, 229, 313
Nisbett, R. E., 60, 63, 67, 241, 311, 312,
    313
Nonbalanced relations, 213
Novak, D., 166, 313

Object constancy, 6
Objective self-awareness
    conditions producing, 268
    consequence of, 268–72
        attribution to self as, 270–71
        change in self-esteem as, 269
        moral behavior as, 271
        definition of, 267. See also Self-
            consciousness
Olshan, K. M., 132, 180, 313
Ordering schemas, 218–19
    end-anchored, 219

group size and, 220-21
linear, 219-21
single, 219
Orvis, B. R., 298, 313

Peevers, B., 129, 313
Perceived control. *See* Locus of control;
Personal causation
Perceived similarity
in choosing others for social comparison, 154-55
effect on evaluation of, 152-57. *See also* Attitude similarity
Peripheral traits. *See* Central traits
Personal causation, 258-59, 295
Personalism, 51
Personality judgment
factor analysis of, 118
models of, 114-20
Personality similarity. *See* Perceived similarity
Personality traits, 68-69. *See also* Implicit personality theory; Trait attribution
Person *x* situation interaction, 69-71
Perspective-taking. *See* Role-taking
Peter, N., 79, 80, 316
Phenomenology, 4
Phillips, J., 222, 315
Physical attractiveness, 150-52
Piaget, J., 5, 30, 78, 79, 177, 224, 275, 290, 314
Pick, A. D., 315
Positivity bias, 211-12
Post, D. L. 52, 312
Potency dimension, 119
Predictive accuracy, trait of, 294
Prejudice, 21-24
Preoperational stage, 224-25
Press, A. N., 179, 314
Primacy effect, 127-28
Projection, 262
Proximity, 198-201
Psychoanalytic theory, 299
Psychological testing, 174

Recency effect, 127-28
Reed, T. R., 119, 314
Regan, D. T., 64, 297, 314

Relational model of cognitive structure, 287-91
Reversal shift, 6
Reverse-incentive effect, 240
Richardson, S. A., 308
Riecken, H. W., 50, 315
Riley, E. N., 105, 315
Rock, L., 261, 311
Rogers, C. R., 182, 263, 314
Rokeach, M., 23, 24, 183, 256, 314
Role-taking, 13-14
developmental levels of, 273-74
egocentric, 273
qualitative systems, 274
self-reflective, 274
subjective, 273-74
third-person dyadic, 274. *See also* Objective self-awareness; Social feedback
Rosch, E. H., 218, 219, 314
Rosenberg, M., 277, 314
Rosenberg, '1. J., 190, 240, 306, 314
Rosenberg, S., 109, 113, 132, 314
Rosenfeld, H. M., 200, 314
Rosenfield, D., 244, 261, 315
Rosenhan, D. L., 170, 314
Rosenthal, P., 163, 314
Ross, M., 244, 261, 275, 313, 314
Rotter, J. B., 81, 82, 306, 314
Ryan, K., 173, 307

Scarlett, H. H., 179, 314
Schachter, S., 11, 315
Scheier, M. F., 277, 307, 309
Schizophrenia, 134-35
Schroder, H. M., 254, 255, 258, 310, 315
Schutz, A., 232, 267, 290, 291, 315
Scott, W. A., 119, 133, 228, 249, 315
Secord, P. F., 129, 313
Segal, M., W., 201, 315
Self-attribution, 238-43
cognitive dissonance and, 233
definition of, 233
and objective self-awareness, 270-71
simulation by observers of, 241
Self-concept distress, 271
Self-consciousness, 6
in adolescence, 32
effect on information selection of, 97
effect on self-evaluation of, 246-47

as a personality trait, 276–78
  public-private, 277. *See also*
    Objective self-awareness
Self-consistency, 264–66
Self-definition, social, 14–15
Self-differentiation, 249–54
  conflicts resulting from, 253–59
  perspective-taking in, 249–52
Self-enhancement, 264–66
  certainty of self-theory and, 266
  luck and skill attributions in, 265
Self-esteem, 181–83, 244–48
  differentiated self-concept and, 251–52
  effect of self-focused attention on,
    269–70
  effect of social comparison on, 236–38
  and evaluation of others, 182–83
  need for approval and, 278–79
  performance evaluation based on,
    245–48
  predictions of competence based on,
    244–45
  public-private self-consciousness and,
    277–78
Self-fulfilling prophecy, 163
Self-integration, 254–59
  decision rules in, 254–55
  personal causation in, 254, 258–59
Self-perception
  consistency vs. self-enhancement in,
    264–66
  development of, 273–76
    role-taking in, 273–74
  focus of attention in, 268–72
    consequences for self-evalution of,
      269
  individual differences in, 276–79
    need for approval leading to, 278–79
    self-consciousness leading to,
      276–78
  inferred motivation in, 241–42
  information source in, 234–43
    self-attribution as, 238–43
    social comparison as, 235–38
    social feedback as, 234–35
  negative information in, 260–63
  organization of information in, 249–59
    differentiation as, 249–54
    integration as, 254–59
  positive information in, 263–66
  self-esteem in, 244–48

Self-report data, 301
Self-values, 256–57
Seligman, M.E.P., 259, 315
Selman, R. L., 273, 274, 315
Sex differences
  in achievement attributions, 85–86
  in social relations, 227
Shapiro, M. M., 235, 310
Shaver, K. G., 261, 311
Sherif, M., 315
Shrauger, J. S., 246, 264, 265, 315
Signell, K. A., 130, 315
Similarity in belonging schemas, 197
Simmons, C., 158, 159, 312
Singer, J. E., 259, 309
Situational demands, 48
Skinner, B. F., 77, 259, 299, 315
Snyder, M., 169, 295, 300, 313, 315
Snyder, M. L., 244, 261, 315
Social comparison, 154
  information about self through, 235–38
Social control, 77
Social feedback, 234–35
  definition of, 233
Social influence. *See* Implicit social
    influence theory
Social reality, 10
Social relations
  balance theory of, 204–10
  basic, 191–95
    belonging in, 194, 196–203
    dominance in, 193, 217–23
    liking in, 193, 201–3
    multidimensional scaling of,
      191–94
  definition of, 190
  development of, 223–26
  social schemas of, 195–96
Social schemas, 195–96
Sommer, R., 199, 200, 315
Spatial contiguity, 52
Spatial relations. *See* Spatial schemas
Spatial representations of cognitive struc-
    ture, 110, 111, 116, 118, 192–93, 285
    290–91
Spatial schemas, 198–201
Specific attributes. *See* Attribute
    generality
Stable-variable attributions, 53
  and central traits, 103. *See also* Consis-
    tency information

Steiner, I. D., 258, 315
Stephan, W. G., 244, 261, 315
Stereotypes, 104–5
  as categories, 285–86
  grain of truth in, 105
  illusory correlation in formation of, 106
Storms, M. D., 64, 315
Streufert, S., 254, 255, 258, 315
Subjective self-awareness. See Objective
  self-awareness
Success-failure attributions. See
  Achievement attributions
Symmetry-asymmetry of social relations,
  203, 217, 222–23

Tagiuri, R., 89, 100, 307
Task difficulty attribution, 54
Taylor, S. E., 155, 315
Temporal contiguity, 52
Theory construction
  extension in, 18–19, 22
  formal, 17
  implicit, 21
  intention in, 18–19, 22
Theory, formal
  definition of, 17
  hypotheses in, 19
Thibaut, J. W., 50, 315
Thompson, E., 222, 315
Thorndike, E. L., 102, 316
Totten, J., 64, 297, 314
Trait attribution, 43–51, 68–77. See also
  Attribution; Labels
Tripodi, T., 147, 306, 310

Univalence, 125, 126, 131

Valins, S., 311

Vallacher, R. R., 35, 96, 135, 245, 268,
  313, 316
Vigilance, 145–46, 147
  self-esteem and, 184
Vivekananthan, P. S., 314
Vreeland, R. S., 308

Walster, E., 150, 152, 248, 262, 271,
  306, 308, 311, 312, 316
Walster, G. W., 262, 271, 316
Ward, L. M., 261, 311
Warm-cold variable in first impressions,
  101–2, 114
Weakland, J., 134, 306
Wegner, D. M., 35, 93, 105, 130, 135,
  272, 304, 305, 307, 313, 316
Weiby, M., 58, 311
Weighted average model of impression
  information, 123–24, 128, 143
Weiner, B., 53, 79, 80, 311, 316
Weingarten, E. M., 169, 316
Werner, H., 30, 316
Werts, C. E., 169, 310
West, S. B., 61, 316
White, R. W., 258, 316
Wicklund, R. A., 267, 269, 270, 308,
  310, 317
Williams, M., 277, 306
Wilson, W., 184, 311
Wish, M., 191, 220, 227, 317
Witkin, H. A., 33, 317
Wortman, C. B., 173, 302, 307, 311
Wright, J. W., 309
Wyer, R. S., 203, 212, 317
Wylie, R., 269, 317

Young, F. W., 119, 311

Zajonc, R. B., 203, 212, 317
Zimbardo, P., 271, 317

/301.11W412I>C1/